Agricultural Science Policy

 **Other Books Published in Cooperation with the International Food Policy Research Institute**

IFPRI

Intrahousehold Resource Allocation in Developing Countries: Models, Methods, and Policy
Edited by Lawrence Haddad, John Hoddinott, and Harold Alderman

Sustainability, Growth, and Poverty Alleviation: A Policy and Agroecological Perspective
Edited by Stephen A. Vosti and Thomas Reardon

Famine in Africa: Causes, Responses, and Prevention
By Joachim von Braun, Tesfaye Teklu, and Patrick Webb

Paying for Agricultural Productivity
Edited by Juliam M. Alston, Philip G. Pardey, and Vincent H. Smith

Out of the Shadow of Famine: Evolving Food Markets and Food Policy in Bangladesh
Edited by Raisuddin Ahmed, Steven Haggblade, and Tawfiq-e-Elahi Chowdhury

Agricultural Science Policy

Changing Global Agendas

EDITED BY JULIAN M. ALSTON, PHILIP G. PARDEY, AND
MICHAEL J. TAYLOR

Published for the International Food Policy Research Institute

The Johns Hopkins University Press
Baltimore and London

The Johns Hopkins University Press
2715 North Charles Street
Baltimore, Maryland 21218-4363
www.press.jhu.edu

International Food Policy Research Institute
2033 K Street, NW
Washington, D.C. 20006
(202) 862-5600
www.ifpri.org

Library of Congress Cataloging-in-Publication Data will be found
at the end of this book.
A catalog record for this book is available from the British Library.

ISBN 0-8018-6603-0
ISBN 0-8018-6604-9 (pbk.)

Contents

vii

Figures

Tables

Foreword

Policies governing the agricultural sciences are undergoing a sea change. National governments are scaling back their support for agricultural research and development (R&D)—the support that led to enormous gains for farmers and consumers in the twentieth century. Agricultural R&D has also dropped off the agendas of many donor agencies. Instead, private support for agricultural R&D is on the rise, especially in the developed world. Changes in policies and technologies mean that the gap between developing and developed countries in access to and performance of new agricultural technologies is widening.

At the same time agriculture is being asked to produce ever greater amounts of food and other products to satisfy growing populations on a finite and fragile resource base. IFPRI, for example, estimates that the world will require a 40 percent increase in cereal production in the next 20 years. Such an increase can come about only through intensification of agriculture—that is, greater production on the same amount of land—and the key to intensified agriculture is R&D.

Agricultural Science Policy addresses these issues and helps define the agenda for agricultural science policy for the coming years. Based on a 1996 conference on global agricultural science policy, the book brings together experts who have looked at the changing environment for agricultural science from varying perspectives. Extending previous scholarly work in this area, such as *Resource Allocation in Agricultural Research,* edited by Walter L. Fishel (1971), and *Resource Allocation and Productivity in National and International Agricultural Research,* edited by Thomas M. Arndt, Dana G. Dalrymple, and Vernon W. Ruttan (1977), this volume goes beyond the earlier work to consider new issues, such as intellectual property rights over agricultural material and the interaction of agriculture and the environment.

This book will be of great interest to those who work in the field of agricultural R&D or who make policies that affect this important work.

Per Pinstrup-Andersen
Director General, International Food Policy Research Institute

Preface

In August 1996, an international conference was held in Melbourne, Australia. Entitled "Global Agricultural Science Policy for the Twenty-First Century," it brought together leaders in agricultural science and agricultural science policy and agricultural economists from around the world for five days of meetings. A primary motivation for the conference was the perception of a global pattern of declining growth in support for agricultural research overall and a shift away from traditional pursuits toward newer agendas, changing institutional structures for financing and managing agricultural research, increasing pressures on public agricultural research institutions to achieve more with less resources, increasing privatization of agricultural research and development, and a shift in the scientific basis for agricultural research incorporating modern biotechnology.

That such changes in policy have arisen despite the enormous contributions of agricultural research toward staving off mass starvation, promoting economic development, and lifting the shackles of poverty during the past 50 years suggests that those achievements have been misunderstood or that it is being taken for granted that the future will look after itself. The purpose of the conference was to allow agricultural economists to share, with others interested in agricultural science policy, what they had learned about the economics of agricultural research and development and agricultural research policy in the hope that policymakers may make use of this work to define and address better the new agendas for agricultural research and development policy.

The conference "Global Agricultural Science Policy" attracted 250 participants from 30 countries. A total of 48 papers were presented, and these were included in a two-volume set of conference proceedings of 1,352 pages. Those papers provided the genesis for this volume. After the conference, we selected 11 papers that addressed important issues, made significant contributions to our understanding of those issues, and highlighted elements of the changing policy agendas in a way that could be useful to all readers who are interested, regardless of their backgrounds. The authors revised the conference papers in response to comments and suggestions from conference participants and reviewers (which included merging two papers into one chapter), and this book is the end result.

Agricultural Science Policy

PART I

Changing Global Contexts and Agendas for Agricultural Research and Development

1 Changing Contexts for Agricultural Research and Development

JULIAN M. ALSTON, PHILIP G. PARDEY, AND
MICHAEL J. TAYLOR

Agricultural research and development (R&D), which has generated astounding increases in food production in the twentieth century, is vital to assuring food security for the burgeoning global population in the coming decades. But recent years have seen important changes in the financing, management, and organization of agricultural R&D. After decades of rapid expansion, the rate of growth of spending on public agricultural research has slowed in most countries since the early 1980s, and in some countries annual spending has even declined. Moreover, the private sector is now paying for and conducting an ever larger share of agricultural research, while governments are reducing their agricultural R&D spending. These and other changes are pushing the agricultural research agenda in new directions, raising a range of important questions.

For many, the primary questions still concern food security—whether agricultural R&D will be able to play its appropriate part in helping meet the food needs of the poor and hungry beyond 2000. World food security beyond 2000 depends on continued global investments in agricultural R&D. The basic facts are well known. World population is expected to increase by about 2.3 billion people by 2020, the amount of new land that can be brought under cultivation is limited, and other natural renewable resources used in agriculture, like water, are becoming increasingly scarce. Ensuring the future security of adequate food supplies is not a question of simply maintaining agricultural productivity; global agricultural productivity must continue to improve, particularly through research and innovation.

Along with the ever present concern for food security, the agenda for agricultural R&D now includes a greater and growing emphasis on issues such as the environment, genetic diversity, food safety, poverty, human health, the structure of agriculture, and animal rights. These issues compete for funds against the more traditional agenda of productivity enhancement, economic growth, farm incomes, and food security and modify the research agenda within the traditional areas as well. Agricultural R&D has come to be seen by many as an instrument of broad social policy.

An important part of the story is the changing context in which agricultural R&D is conducted. Changes in the economy more broadly, as well as in agriculture and in science more generally, have important implications for the funding, organization, and management of R&D. In particular, the emergence of modern biotechnology combined with new intellectual property regimes implies important changes in the public-sector–private-sector nexus in R&D. These changes are intertwined with others arising from a changing perception of the role of government and the social value of science—and even of economic growth.

The chapters in this book address this changing agenda. Several relate to new methods and measures of agricultural productivity growth that address input and output quality change, aggregation theory, and the special features of markets for open-access resources. Another group of chapters deals with R&D related to natural resources and the environment, an area for research policy that has been subjected to comparatively little economic analysis to date, even though a substantial shift of R&D funds in that direction has already taken place. The final section of the book comprises three chapters on issues arising in genetic improvement R&D, an area that includes many of the newest and most contentious issues in agricultural R&D policy. As an introduction to the chapters that follow, this chapter documents the recent evolution of agricultural R&D investments around the world, the changing public- and private-sector roles in funding and performing agricultural R&D, and the evolving institutional setting, which both reflects and shapes the policy setting.

Changing Investment Patterns

As we enter the twenty-first century, notable and seemingly accelerating changes are taking place in the amount and sources of support for agricultural R&D, national and international roles in research, and the respective roles of the private and public sectors.

Global Investment Trends in Public Agricultural Research

Worldwide, investments by national governments in public agricultural research almost doubled in real terms, from $7.3 billion (1985 international dollars) in 1971 to nearly $15 billion in 1991 (Table 1.1). Expenditures on publicly performed agricultural research in developing countries grew by 5.1 percent per year, from $3 billion (1985 international dollars) in 1971 to $8 billion in 1991. Across the developed countries, public agricultural spending grew by 2.3 percent per year, from $4.3 billion (1985 international dollars) in 1971 to $6.9 billion in 1991 and $7.1 billion by 1993.

For all regions of the world, however, real agricultural R&D spending grew at a much slower pace during the 1980s than in the 1970s. In 1971, as a group, developing countries accounted for 41 percent of the spending. By 1991

TABLE 1.1 Public agricultural research expenditures in developed and developing countries, 1971–1991

	1971	1981	1991
	(millions of 1985 international dollars)[a]		
Expenditures			
Developing countries (131)[b]	2,984	5,503	8,009
Sub-Saharan Africa (44)	699	927	968
China	457	939	1,494
Asia and Pacific (excluding China) (28)	861	1,922	3,502
Latin America and Caribbean (38)	507	981	944
West Asia and North Africa (20)	459	733	1,100
Developed countries (22)	4,320	5,744	6,956
Global total (153)	7,304	11,247	14,966
	1971–81	1981–91	1971–91
	(percentages)		
Average annual growth rates			
Developing countries	6.4	3.9	5.1
Sub-Saharan Africa	2.5	0.8	1.6
China	7.7	4.7	6.3
Asia and Pacific (excluding China)	8.7	6.2	7.3
Latin America and Caribbean	7.0	−0.5	2.7
West Asia and North Africa	4.3	4.1	4.8
Developed countries	2.7	1.7	2.3
Global total	4.3	2.9	3.6

SOURCE: Pardey, Roseboom, and Craig (1999).

[a]Research expenditures denominated in current units are first deflated to 1985 prices using local implicit GDP deflators taken from the World Bank (1995) and then converted to international dollars (where one international dollar is set equal to one U.S. dollar) using the purchasing power parities taken from Heston et al. (1995).

[b]Figures in parentheses indicate the number of countries in the respective totals.

the situation had changed markedly. The developing-country share had grown to more than half (about 54 percent) of public-sector agricultural R&D spending worldwide. In 1991, Asian countries accounted for 62 percent of the developing world's publicly performed agricultural research expenditures (19 percent for China alone), with 12 percent spent by both the Latin American and Caribbean region and the Sub-Saharan African region (including South Africa) and 14 percent in West Asia and North Africa.

An alternative perspective on agricultural R&D spending is provided by the agricultural research intensity ratios (ARIs) presented in Table 1.2. The most commonly constructed ARIs express agricultural research expenditures

TABLE 1.2 Agricultural research intensity ratios (ARIs), 1971–1991

	1971–75	1976–80	1981–85	1986–90	1991
	(percentages)				
Developing countries	0.38	0.47	0.50	0.49	0.50
Sub-Saharan Africa	0.78	0.84	0.86	0.74	0.70
China	0.40	0.48	0.41	0.38	0.36
Asia and Pacific	0.26	0.36	0.44	0.50	0.55
Latin America	0.43	0.51	0.57	0.49	0.54
West Asia and North Africa	0.50	0.49	0.52	0.52[a]	0.52[a]
Developed countries	1.38	1.60	1.98	2.18	2.39
Global total	0.67	0.76	0.81	0.79	0.81

SOURCE: Pardey, Roseboom, and Craig (1999).

[a]Extrapolated data.

as percentages of agricultural gross domestic product (GDP) (gross value of output minus the value of purchased inputs). In 1991, as a group, developed countries spent $2.39 on public agricultural R&D for every $100 of agricultural GDP, a sizable increase over the $1.38 they spent per $100 of output two decades earlier. Developing countries, as a group, have much lower ARIs. In the early 1970s their ARI averaged 38 cents per $100 of output, growing to only 50 cents by 1991.

Investments in Private Agricultural Research

A common perception is that agricultural research is primarily the domain of the public sector whereas research in many other sectors of the economy is the province of the private sector. But the data presented in Table 1.3 reveal that privately performed R&D is now a prominent feature of contemporary agricultural R&D in rich countries. Indeed, the private share has trended up significantly since 1981, and now almost half the agricultural R&D in the Organization for Economic Cooperation and Development (OECD) countries is performed by the business sector. Privately performed agricultural R&D totaled $7 billion in 1993, compared with $4 billion in 1981, an annual rate of growth of 5.1 percent, compared with 1.8 percent for publicly performed agricultural R&D and 4.3 percent for private research in all (agricultural and nonagricultural) sectors in the OECD.

Investments in International Agricultural Research

Internationally conceived and funded agricultural R&D is a relatively recent institutional innovation. The Consultative Group on International Agricultural Research (CGIAR) was established in 1971. During its first decade, expansion of the total number of centers, and of the amount of funding per center, led to a

TABLE 1.3 Privately performed agricultural R&D in OECD countries, 1981–1993

	1981	1986	1991	1993	Annual Rate of Growth (1981–93)
	(millions of 1985 international dollars)				
Expenditures					
United States	1,417	1,964	2,256	2,381[a]	4.3
Japan	791	1,146	1,577	1,660	6.7
United Kingdom	404	474	593	614	5.0
France	256	390	504	565	7.2
Germany	426	492	520	459	1.3
Other OECD	701	955	1,199	1,351	5.7
OECD total[b]	3,995	5,420	6,649	7,030	5.1
	(percentages)				
Private share of total national agricultural R&D					
United States	46.6	52.1	52.7	53.7[a]	—
Japan	39.4	47.5	51.4	51.4	—
United Kingdom	52.1	55.8	62.0	62.4	—
France	38.4	47.4	52.5	52.9	—
Germany	58.7	61.8	61.6	58.0	—
Other OECD	28.1	31.0	34.4	37.0	—
OECD total[b]	41.1	46.2	48.9	49.6	—

SOURCE: Pardey, Roseboom, and Craig (1999).

[a]1992 figure.

[b]Includes 22 OECD countries.

tenfold increase in the organization's nominal funding, to $142 million in 1980. During the 1980s, funding continued to grow, more than doubling in nominal terms to reach $288 million in 1990. The rate of growth had slowed but was still impressive. In the 1990s, however, although the number of centers continued to grow—from 13 to 18 at one point (there are now 16)—funding did not keep pace to maintain the level of funding per center, let alone the growth rate. In 1999, 55 donors provided a total of $328.1 million to the CGIAR.

At the same time, the organization's mandate broadened. From an initial focus on productivity improvements in staple food crops—such as maize, rice, wheat, and cassava (principally through breeding higher-yielding varieties)—the CGIAR now conducts research on a range of other crops, as well as agroforestry, natural resource management, aquatic live resources, irrigation management, institutional strengthening, and food policy. Although the CGIAR system has captured the attention of the international agricultural R&D and aid communities, through the impact of its scientific achievements and through its pivotal role in the Green Revolution, it has spent only a small— and now shrinking—fraction of the global agricultural R&D investment. In 1991, the CGIAR was responsible for only 1.8 percent of the nearly $15 billion spent on public-sector agricultural R&D.

Some of these policy and institutional changes in public agricultural R&D have arisen from changes outside agriculture and outside research. Some are directly related to changes in private-sector roles in agricultural R&D.

The Private Sector

In many developed and some developing countries, the private sector has become a much more substantial provider of agricultural research. Spending on private agricultural research rose by just over 5 percent per year for the developed countries since 1981 and by 1993 amounted to almost half of their total agricultural R&D expenditures. This rapid increase was partly a result of expanded intellectual property rights over biological innovations and, in some countries, a movement away from public funding for highly applied, near-market research that previously may have "crowded out" private research. The emerging modern biotechnologies are an important element in this expansion as well.

The private sector has a different agricultural research focus than the public sector. In five countries that collectively account for more than 40 percent of developed-country agricultural R&D investments (Australia, the Netherlands, New Zealand, the United Kingdom, and the United States), more than 80 percent of public research, but only 12 percent of private research, is devoted to farm-level technologies, such as improved crop and livestock production practices.

Moreover, in different countries, private agricultural R&D tends to be specialized in different areas and then exported elsewhere, reflecting the increasing international flow of R&D goods and services. Post-harvest research generally accounts for between 30 and 90 percent of private agricultural research. In countries such as Australia, Japan, and New Zealand, it is the dominant concern of privately funded agricultural R&D. In contrast, whereas agricultural chemical research on fertilizers, herbicides, and pesticides is of minor importance in some countries, it accounts for more than 40 percent of private agricultural research in the United Kingdom and the United States and more than 75 percent of private research in Germany. Clearly, private firms are making strategic investment decisions with a close eye on the potential R&D spillover benefits to be reaped from a global approach to agricultural R&D, notwithstanding the significantly site-specific nature of many primary agricultural production technologies.

Interestingly, however, the composition of private R&D has been changing over time. In the United States, for example, agricultural machinery and post-harvest research accounted for more than 80 percent of private agricultural R&D in 1960, but by 1992 its share had fallen to only 42 percent. Private investments in plant breeding, veterinary, and pharmaceutical research increased substantially in the United States during the same period.

A number of the recent policy developments can be seen as a reflection of the evolving private participation in agricultural R&D and public policy responses to deal with that evolution.

Key Policy Developments

Priorities

The public research agenda has broadened. Public funding has shifted toward research on post-harvest handling, food processing and food safety, and environmental issues such as soil erosion and groundwater pollution; it has shifted away from research dealing with production agriculture. These adjustments reflect the increasing influence of nontraditional interest groups—environmentalists, food processors, and consumer lobbies—in the formulation of agricultural science policy, as well as the expanded research role of the private sector. In addition, some governments have tried to push public funds toward more basic research (the benefits from which are more difficult for the private sector to appropriate) and away from applied research of more immediate consequence for industry. Donor funds directed toward both international and national agricultural R&D agencies (especially those in Africa) have generally shrunk and increasingly reflected developed-country concerns with the environment and agricultural issues beyond the farm. In addition, donors increasingly seem to view agricultural R&D as a means of directly and rapidly tackling poverty problems rather than as an activity best suited to stimulating productivity and growth over the longer term, with poverty reduction brought about as a consequence of that growth.

Privatizing Public R&D

In the developed countries (for which the most comprehensive and up-to-date data are available), many previously public roles have become privatized, and the line between private and public research has become blurred. Private R&D firms have increasingly been able to bid for publicly funded projects, some public research and technology transfer institutions have been explicitly privatized, and others are now able to sell their research services to private firms. In addition, public agricultural research facilities are being phased out in many countries, and management and employment structures have been altered. Changes include the introduction and expansion of contestable funding arrangements or competitive grant processes, a shift away from long-term contracts toward shorter, fixed-term contracts for researchers, and expanded accountability and oversight procedures.

Similar changes have taken place in some developing countries, although the timing and specifics of the changes differ, and the private sector has generally played a smaller role as both a funder and performer of R&D. Some countries (especially in Africa but also in Asia and Latin America) have seen a contraction in real public support for agricultural R&D. During the late 1980s and early 1990s, some of this shrinkage in domestic support was partly supplanted by an increase in donor funding for research, but in more recent years overall donor funding has declined, and public spending priorities have shifted away from agricultural R&D.

Property Protection

The pace and focus of biological innovation in agriculture and related industries—who pays for R&D and how much—and the distribution of the costs and benefits of the research among different groups in society all depend on the form of intellectual property protection afforded the results of specific R&D projects. Many countries are enacting or revising laws to protect biological material and the innovations and research processes surrounding that material. These national efforts are increasingly being shaped and circumscribed by international laws and conventions. Domestic and international changes in intellectual property protection are modifying the roles of the public and private sectors with regard to the funding, performance, and dissemination of results from agricultural R&D, but much else is changing too, so the specific effects of evolving property rights are not clear. Moreover, many of the details of the intellectual property policies remain unresolved, and it is therefore difficult to be certain about their ultimate impact on the nature and rate of technical progress in agriculture.

Overview of the Book

Many of the issues raised here have involved changes so rapid or so recent that it is not possible to make a clear determination of their long-run implications for the world's agriculture and agricultural research systems. Nevertheless, policy is being made—often without the benefit of a clear economic understanding of the consequences or without the benefit of any economic analysis, even though the central questions are essentially economic ones.

One of our purposes has been to extend the margins covered by the analytical and empirical literature on agricultural R&D policy: to encompass rich and poor countries alike and together; to address issues up and down the food-marketing chain, and not just on the farm; to consider natural resource and environmental issues as well as other, newer issues, such as food safety, along with traditional agricultural ones, via integrated rather than adversarial means; and to consider the links between national and international research and research policies. Many of these areas have been either neglected or dealt with piecemeal, often without a solid analytical foundation. In this book, a unifying theme among the chapters is the use of rigorous economic methods to address important elements of the new agenda where previous work has provided neither the analysis nor the evidence needed for sound policy development.

The book is organized into four sections. To complete Part I, the introduction, Ismail Serageldin provides an overview of the changing agendas for agricultural research, emphasizing the issues in international agricultural development. In Part II, "Productivity Measures and Measurement," first Zvi Griliches discusses a range of issues in agricultural productivity measurement—some new, some longstanding, but all important if the policy aspects of productivity are to be inferred correctly. Next, Barbara Craig and Philip Pardey present some new perspectives on U.S. agricultural productivity based on state-level data with input- and output-quality adjustment. To complete that section, Prabhu Pingali and Paul Heisey provide a narrative review of the empirical evidence on past productivity growth in developing-country agriculture (specifically principal crops) and then an assessment of the prospects for future productivity growth.

Part III, "Research, Productivity, and Natural Resources," comprises three chapters. Wilfred Beckerman challenges conventional views on sustainability. He makes the case that the pursuit of conventionally defined sustainability notions flies in the face of intergenerational equity and, in the process, could compromise the standards of living of future generations. James Wilen and Frances Homans ask and answer a new question: how to measure and understand productivity in the context of an open-access resource, where "improved" technology might simply mean more serious overfishing. Last in this section, Peter Lindert presents some new, extensive, and surprising long-run evidence on what has been happening to the stock of soil in China and Indonesia.

The next part, "Research for Genetic Improvement," includes three chapters. First, Derek Byerlee and Greg Traxler discuss the role of technology spillovers and the importance of economies of size in the design of efficient agricultural research systems, presenting examples from wheat breeding. Next, Robert Evenson and Brian Wright appraise the present state of knowledge on valuation methods and measures for agricultural genetic resources as a basis for better informed policies related to intellectual property rights for commercial seeds. In the final chapter, Richard Gray and Stavroula Malla report the results from an evaluation of the benefits from R&D undertaken to develop canola, taking into account for the first time the health benefits (and externalities) from the development, adoption, and consumption of a genetically altered agricultural product. In conclusion, Walter Armbruster and Peter Barry pinpoint the key findings of the various chapters and highlight the policy findings contained therein.

This book is based on selections of papers from the international conference "Global Agricultural Science Policy for the Twenty-First Century," held in 1996 in Melbourne, Australia. Another five papers from the same conference were published in the September 1997 issue of the *Australian Journal of Agricultural and Resource Economics,* and others went on to other outlets. These papers span a range of issues in agricultural science and technology impacts and policies that extend beyond the coverage of this book. Here we have focused on less technical treatments of what appeared in 1996 to be the newer and larger emerging issues. In the years between the conference and the publication of this volume, we have seen a confirmation of the importance of the issues raised at the conference and treated here, as well as the emergence of issues demanding further attention—especially in the areas of biotechnology, intellectual property, and the implications of agricultural science and related policy for the environment, food safety, food security, and the world's poor. Even if we have succeeded in clarifying the agenda, much of the real work remains to be done.

2 Changing Agendas for Agricultural Research

ISMAIL SERAGELDIN

The world is facing a crisis. We must promote sustainable agriculture for food security in the developing world and rise to the triple challenge of poverty reduction, food security, and sound natural resource management. These challenges must be met in a political environment that dangerously mixes complacency, fiscal constraints, aid fatigue, and fundamental disagreements about the magnitude of the problem and appropriate paths to its solution.

The Basic Proposition

The world's basic objectives of poverty reduction, food security, and sustainable natural resource management cannot be met unless rural well-being in general, and a prosperous private agriculture for smallholders in particular, are nurtured and improved. Central to improving the productivity and profitability of agriculture are improved technology, appropriate policies, and supportive institutions. At the core of technological improvement is agricultural research.

The Fundamental Challenges

Poverty and Hunger

The Green Revolution that took hold in the 1970s staved off the Malthusian shadow of famine in South Asia. Concurrent increases in agricultural productivity also resulted in a sustained decline in the real prices of food. But despite these achievements, rising populations and unequal participation in growth have left 1.3 billion people in the world struggling to survive on less than a dollar a day. About 800 million of them are hungry, undernourished, or malnourished. More than 500 million children under the age of five are not receiving the nutrition they need to develop fully mentally and physically.

Ironically, nearly three-quarters of the poor and hungry live in the rural areas where food is produced. These are concentrated in poor, slow-growing

13

countries, often in regions with poor agricultural potential. Despite rapid urban growth, the bulk of poverty in the developing world is rural and will remain so for the next generation. Addressing this problem requires concentrated attention to agricultural and rural development throughout the world, but especially in slow-growing and food-deficit countries.

Food Security

The world's population is expected to exceed 8 billion people by 2025, an increase of 2.5 billion in the 30 years beginning 1995. Much, but not all, of the increase will occur in developing-country cities where urban populations will more than double. Hence, given moderate income growth, food needs in developing countries are expected to more than double, and global food demand could nearly double. The challenge to world agriculture is enormous.

Future increases in food supplies must come primarily from rising biological yields, rather than from area expansion and more irrigation, because land and water are becoming increasingly scarce. Most new lands brought under cultivation are marginal and ecologically fragile and cannot make up for the land being removed from cultivation by urbanization and land degradation each year. The sources of water that can be developed cost-effectively for irrigation are nearly exhausted, and irrigation water will increasingly need to be reallocated for municipal and industrial use. Therefore, yields on existing land will need to more than double.

Sustainable Natural Resource Management

Unsustainable agricultural practices are promoted by bad institutional frameworks and policies that severely undervalue natural resources. If yields are to double in the next 30 years, the policy and institutional failures that cause or contribute to the negative environmental impacts of agriculture must be reversed and sustainable production systems developed, encouraged, and applied. The challenges described in this chapter all require action on a broad and complex rural-development front. It is a matter not only of agricultural production but of widely shared and sustainable rural growth and development.

The Challenge to Agricultural Science

The challenge ahead can be stated directly and relatively simply, but its accomplishment will chart new territory for agricultural science. The task is to intensify complex agricultural production systems, especially of smallholder farmers, in a sustained manner while contributing to the improved welfare of farmers. Doubling the yields of complex farming systems in an environmentally positive way is an enormous and difficult challenge.

Agricultural science has done a far better job of increasing individual commodity yields, in input-intensive monocultures, than it has in improving the productivity of complex farming systems. The use of modern reductionist science has tended to focus on commodity yield rather than on the long-run sustainability of production systems. Yet for many in the developing world, even that approach bypassed them. Where it has been applied—for example, semidwarf rices and wheats—it has been in favorable, well-watered areas. In many intensive monoculture systems, negative externalities such as poor water quality, loss of biodiversity, chemical pollution, and soil degradation threaten their long-run sustainability. What is required is a systems and interdisciplinary approach to the sustainable improvement of complex systems. Developed-country science has lessons to offer developing-country colleagues in commodity improvement. It is less clear that they are role models for the sustainable intensification of complex systems for smallholders.

Defining the Scope of Agricultural Research

In this chapter, discussion is limited to research that is clearly an international public good. Private goods research should be left to the private sector. While private-sector leaders determine the priorities of the research investments they make, clearly, policy research to identify and remove the price and market distortions that affect their decisions would be a legitimate and important area of public goods research. National agricultural research priorities should also focus on public goods but must be set by each country, in the light of its own unique circumstances. Agricultural research, defined here, is intended to include agriculture, forestry, fisheries, livestock, and the like. The focus is basic food crops, assuming that cash crops per se—for instance, cotton and rubber— are definitely the domain of the private sector. Research on public goods for agriculture—as I have broadly defined it—is also intended to include policy research, post-harvest technologies, and the natural resource management aspects of the production process.

Parameters for Setting Research Priorities

In order to examine the priorities for agricultural research, some basic questions on the parameters of the issues first need to be settled.

GETTING THE FACTS RIGHT.   Debate on interpretations and theories or postulates is sound, but we should agree on the basic facts, such as the amount of land under cultivation in China or the deforestation rate in a particular country. Indeed, it is inconceivable that protagonists in the recent public debate on Chinese food production use figures for acreage under cultivation that differ by 30 percent.

Clearly, new breakthroughs in geographic information systems (GIS) and computing make it possible to reach more accurate figures on these kinds of questions and to map site-specific ecological and socioeconomic data at the local and supranational levels. This, in turn, should make it possible to maintain and make available proper relational databases, a major contribution that scientists could make to better the understanding of the issues and (more important) to monitor and evaluate trends put forward by countless researchers and groups.

CORRECTLY STATING THE PROBLEM.   Although food security is a topic of great importance, it is still surprising how unidimensional much of the debate is. We need to remind the world that the issues are more complex. It's not just production but also access; not just technology but also policy; not just the global level but also the national; not just the national level but also the household; not just rural but also urban; and not just amount of food but also nutritional content.

All these dimensions make the issues of food security part of a bigger whole in which many policies come together to confront the nexus of problems relating population growth, environmental sustainability, poverty reduction, and agricultural production, distribution, and marketing. It cannot easily be reduced to a single set of equations, nor is economic efficiency sufficient to provide guidance for the allocation of the exact shares of research resources if we are—for ethical, normative reasons—focusing on the needs of the destitute, the marginalized, and the hungry. Many of these people are not active participants in the marketplace.

IDENTIFICATION OF NEW TECHNOLOGIES.   The primary responsibility of research is to help provide new technologies that will enable significant and sustainable intensification of agriculture. These will undoubtedly include the better management of natural resources and the use of integrated pest-management techniques. Clearly, biotechnology is also a key area for attention. Yet its promise has remained elusive, and it raises a high level of discomfort among many.

DEGREES OF UNCERTAINTY AND RISK.   Decisionmakers and the public are ignorant of the degrees of uncertainty and risk associated with the research itself, as well as the application of the technologies. This continues to encourage Luddite, antiscientific public sentiment and timidity among the decisionmakers. We need clearer statements by the science community on these issues.

Macro Questions

Assuming that we have agreement on the broad parameters of this discussion, we could proceed to state some macrolevel questions. The first is how much the public purse should fund in terms of agricultural research, compared with such competing claims as, say, health research. If we get beyond that—for instance, with a relatively broad statement, such as 1–2.5 percent of agricultural gross domestic product (GDP), depending on the country—then we get into another set of questions, including how resources should be distributed among local, national, and international research. Should every country have a full-blown research system? How much should donors invest in the Consultative Group on International Agricultural Research (CGIAR) versus national programs that may need strengthening? What role should multinational firms play in the global research systems, including making some contributions to the public part of that research? Although we are trying at the outset to set some conceptual definitions to distinguish between national and international and public and private research, in real life the boundaries are never sharp. Many questions occur precisely in these gray areas. What are truly public research goods—nationally and internationally?

Coming from the perspective that the returns to international agricultural research are very high, and because such research is given a very small percentage of Official Development Assistance (ODA) budgets, it would be wonderful to recommend that the donor community increase its contribution to the CGIAR from the current 0.3–0.4 percent share to something like 0.8 percent of the total budget. That is unlikely to happen, however, given the reality of political attitudes toward research constrained budgets.

So another set of macro issues emerges—competing shares of a finite set of resources for agricultural research, underscoring that it is not an either-or choice but a question of how much for each. What should the balance be between the various subsectors of agriculture, forestry, fisheries, livestock, and so on? How much should be focused on research for new technologies of production, as opposed to research on removing the impediments to applying the known technologies? This is not a trivial question. Paul Waggoner (1995) has estimated that if the average Iowa farmer were to produce at the level of the best Iowa farmer and the average world farmer were to produce at the level of the average Iowa farmer, the world could feed 10 billion people on the lands currently under production.

How much research should focus on the production process, compared with post-harvest technologies? Today, as much as 15 to 30 percent of the produced crops are lost between the farmgate and the consumer. This issue will likely gain importance as the large increase in urban consumers causes a greater need for food storage and transportation.

Should there be significant effort to establish the global environmental effects of agricultural practices? Agriculture has a huge effect on the global environment in terms of land and water use. But is it also affecting climate change, biodiversity loss, and pollution of international waters? Should there be an effort to identify the likely long-term impact of a small but cumulative effect over many years?

Geographic resource allocation is a recurrent theme. Should one look to the possibility of transferring results across a spectrum of agroecological zones or assume a specificity that implies some a priori definable shares? Should the criteria for the geographic focus of research efforts include the ability of countries within a region to do their own research, versus the value of spillover effects from that research?

Specific Issues of Research-Strategy Priorities

Beyond these questions, there are a number of key considerations that highlight the problems of trying to set priorities for global action on agricultural research.

FAVORED VERSUS LESS-FAVORED AREAS.   This debate has gone on forever. We are past treating this as an either-or choice. But then the question moves to what the proportion should be in a period of finite resources. How do you weigh poverty reduction for subsistence farmers against low food prices for the urban poor? How do you determine resource allocation between traded food grains and subsistence roots and tubers? And how do you target groups in most need—the poorest, the women, and those who cultivate fragile environments?

TRADITIONAL VERSUS EXOTIC CROPS.   The Sahel is one of the most difficult environments in the world. How can we improve the productivity and income potential of these poor farmers? Should we invest in improving the yields of indigenous crops—millet and sorghum—or try to improve the stress resistance of higher-yielding, nontraditional maize? Should we invest in developing "tropical" wheat or potatoes or improving yams, sweet potatoes, and cassava?

TIME HORIZON CHOICES.   What should the time frame of expected impact be? Often, improved agronomic practices, such as spacing, seeding time, weed control, and planting depth, can have short-term yield impacts, whereas genetic improvement, particularly involving complex characteristics, takes much longer but has higher long-run yield potential. What is the appropriate discount rate for high-risk, high-impact research? How much should the international system invest in small incremental improvements (including removing impediments to the application of known technologies) versus the development of radical new technologies such as transgenic techniques for apomixis and plant resistance to pests?

ENVIRONMENTAL IMPROVEMENT VERSUS YIELD MAXIMIZATION. Frequently this is posed as a major trade-off in priority choices, but it cannot persist as such. Clearly, a major challenge to agricultural science is to turn this apparent win-lose situation into one that is win-win. This is a nontrivial, scientific task that is long run and interdisciplinary. How much should be invested in fundamental research as opposed to applied systems improvement?

INTEGRATING TRADITIONAL KNOWLEDGE WITH NEW SCIENCE. The documentation of traditional knowledge, including the identification of wild races, should be undertaken before it is lost. It must be integrated in a two-way commerce of ideas between modern science and farmers—and the poor farmers who are the custodians of this knowledge should benefit from these efforts. How much of the available resources should be directed toward this kind of effort?

INTEGRATED FARMING TECHNOLOGIES VERSUS BROADLY APPLIC-ABLE NEW TECHNOLOGIES. Integrated farming practices that reflect local specificities would reduce the vulnerability of small-holder farmers and increase their incomes. Such farming practices would require international research with local adaptation, such as the introduction of multipurpose leguminous trees like *Leucaena* or *Sesbania* or the introduction of fish ponds for super *Tilapia,* which turn out to help with on-farm water management in addition to producing fish. How much attention should be given to these types of activities as opposed to cutting-edge technologies such as transgenic biotechnology to attack the problems of the developing world?

The Challenge of Priority Setting and Optimal Investment

Many more examples in this vein could be raised, but those given provide insight into the difficult choices decisionmakers face. Ex ante and ex post impact assessment, priority setting, and the devising of optimal investment patterns are therefore critical to informing those choices. The increasing complexity of the problem and tight fiscal resources make these choices all the more difficult and complex.

Two Broad Concerns

Closing Up the International Regime

The international regime in which the next generation of agricultural science will take place is unlikely to allow the same free flow of information and germplasm that has been known to date. Paradoxically, despite the Internet and collaborative mapping of plant genomes, we risk the future becoming more constrained if patenting of process, as well as of product, increases markedly—especially in the area of biotechnology and transgenic plants. Obstacles to the movement of germplasm also increase as national governments assert control over their genetic resources. All of this could lead to a scientific apartheid whereby the 80 percent of humanity in the developing world is increasingly locked out of the most recent advances of modern science. These risks may be offset by a greater flow of scientific output. Prudence, however, requires special efforts to make the international agricultural research system more open and integrated and to reach special arrangements with the private sector on the use of new technology for the poorest parts of the world.

Beyond Agricultural Science

Meeting the agricultural science challenge is only a necessary condition; it is not sufficient. Much more is required. Doubling agricultural output while preserving the natural resources on which production is based will require several approaches. It will require rapid technological change in both the developed and the developing world. The private sector will have to undertake an increasing share of the necessary research and its diffusion. Public-sector financing will be needed for areas of limited interest to the private sector, such as genetic resource conservation, common-property resource management, integrated pest management, research on subsistence crops, and other public-good areas. Massive increases in the efficiency of irrigation water use will be needed, requiring changes in water policies, water rights, and institutions for allocating water and technical improvements in water conveyance and use. Other requirements include dramatic improvements in the management of soils, watersheds, forests, and biodiversity by local and community-based institutions; accelerated private investment in the rural economies of the developing world; and enhanced support by the international community to the agricultural and rural development programs of poor countries. Last, special attention should be focused on the needs of the poor, especially women.

Even if world food supplies grow dramatically over the next 30 years, fast-growing countries such as China and India could become major food importers. If such countries are to pursue economically optimal food strategies, they must have stable, long-term access to world markets. They, and other countries, may then focus on producing only those goods that they can produce efficiently—including food products. Only with stable, long-term access to world markets can countries comfortably refrain from costly food self-sufficiency.

Ensuring household, national, and world food security poses enormous challenges, both technological and political. They cannot be tackled by economic analysis alone, essential as such analysis remains. They require dramatic improvements in national and international policies, institutions, and public expenditures, but the role of research remains fundamental.

PART II

Productivity Measures and Measurement

3 Issues in Agricultural Productivity Measurement

ZVI GRILICHES

Current work on the role of public and private research in productivity growth has deep roots in the early work of agricultural economists. The first micro-production function estimates (Tintner 1944), the first detailed total-factor productivity (TFP) calculations (Barton and Cooper 1948), the first estimates of returns to public research and development (R&D) expenditures (Griliches 1958; Schultz 1953), and the first production function estimates with an added R&D variable (Griliches 1964) all originated in agricultural studies. Other original contributions to applied econometrics by agricultural economists include Waugh (1929) on hedonics, Nerlove (1958) on distributed lags, and Hoch (1955) and Mundlak (1961) on panel data econometrics.[1]

The specific subfield for discussion here, the impact of R&D on productivity, has expanded enormously from its modest beginnings (Griliches 1995). One of the best surveys—Australian Industry Commission (1995: vol. 3, app. QA)—lists 27 studies estimating the returns to R&D at the firm level, 28 at the industry level, 10 at the country level, and 20 studies for agriculture alone.[2]

Major progress was made in the past 30 years in this field: new databases were developed at the firm, business unit, and project levels, and other measures of innovation were added, especially observations on patents. Still, in the light of this progress, it became clearer how much we do not know and how thin our data are.

Recent Results and Puzzles

The major framework for the analysis of the relationship between R&D and productivity has been the "R&D capital in the production function model":

---

1. See Berndt (1991: chap. 4), Griliches (1996), Griliches and Mairesse (1995), and Heady and Dillon (1961) for historical surveys of some of these topics.

2. Additional surveys can be found in Alston and Pardey (1996: chap. 6), Hall (1996), Huffman and Evenson (1993: chap. 7), Mairesse and Mohnen (1995), Mairesse and Sassenou (1991), and Nadiri (1993).

$$Q = AX^{\beta}K^{\gamma}, \tag{3.1}$$

where Q is output, X is an index of conventional inputs including physical capital, K is the "stock of knowledge" (or R&D), A is the level of disembodied technology, and β and γ are the parameters of interest (Griliches 1973). The focus in such analysis is on estimating γ, the elasticity of output with respect to R&D capital. Recent studies using 1980s data have raised the possibility that γ may have declined over time. The issue is important substantively and needs further investigation. Is it a temporary phenomenon? Has it been reversed recently? Is it a drop in private returns rather than social returns (Hall 1993)? In addition, a change in γ is not the same as a change in the net rate of return to R&D:

$$\rho = \gamma\frac{Q}{K} - \delta, \tag{3.2}$$

where δ is the depreciation rate of such capital. The rate of return to R&D may decline if K grows faster than Q or if δ rises, or both, without this implying necessarily a change in γ.

There are three more pieces of unfinished business in the results area:

1. Often the productivity growth equation is estimated with the R&D intensity rather than the growth in R&D capital as the relevant variable. Sometimes this version gives "better" results. An argument can be made for it (Griliches and Lichtenberg 1984), but a convincing reconciliation of the results of these two versions of the same model, in my opinion, has yet to be seen. An encompassing test is in order here.
2. There is parallel literature on estimating the valuation of R&D capital (or investment) in the framework of market value equations (Griliches 1981; Hall and Hall 1993; Pakes 1985). This literature should be connected to the production function estimation literature.
3. Work has been done at both the firm and industry levels. One might expect higher estimates of the rate of return to R&D (ρ) at the industry level owing to the internalization of spillover effects, but the bulk of the results do not go in this direction, and no convincing exploration of the aggregation problem has, to my knowledge, yet been done in this context. One possibility is a higher δ at the individual firm (private) level because of obsolescence and the creative destruction of rents as against a larger component of more slowly depreciating social returns at the more aggregate levels.

The "Central" Model and Its Discontents

The central model treats R&D as another investment stream, parallel to physical investment, and constructs an analogous knowledge capital stock using the perpetual inventory method and an assumed (fixed) depreciation rate δ. But knowledge is not like refrigerators, and each of the steps in the construction of such a capital concept is problematic. The list of problems is long. The standard approach aggregates R into a K concept linearly, ignoring the possibility that knowledge production depends nonlinearly not only on current R&D efforts but also on previously accumulated results. Moreover, R as a producer of additions to K may be subject to short-run decreasing returns to the intensity of research and to longer-run diminishing returns owing to the fishing-out of technological opportunities, unless they are recharged by science or other sources of new discoveries. This is not a new concern. It is alluded to in Griliches (1979), was raised in a number of papers by Evenson (for example, 1984), and has been revived in a number of recent papers.

Formal properties of models where $\dot{K} = f(R,K)$ have been considered by Bachrach (1990), Hall and Hayashi (1989), Jones (1995), Klette (1994), and Lach (1994), among others. A reasonable version of such a model is:

$$\dot{K}_i = R^\gamma K_i^\varphi K_A^h \tag{3.3}$$

where the φ parameter associated with the firm's own stock of knowledge reflects the within-firm spillovers and time interdependencies in the research process, while the h parameter, associated with the aggregate state of knowledge, reflects both positive external spillovers and negative crowding-out effects. Having started with such a model, there is no clear role left for a separate depreciation effect, though some of the authors add a linear depreciation component to such models.

In estimation, such models lead to the solving-out of the unobservable K stock and to the estimation of productivity growth as a function of R and lagged levels of output, TFP, or patent stocks. The current results along these lines are interesting but not fully convincing, both because of econometric problems associated with the use of lagged dependent variables and because of the likely endogeneity of R, discussed further later in this chapter.

Other conceptual problems are associated with the whole notion of depreciation of knowledge and with the question of how knowledge should be incorporated into the production function. Much of what we think of as depreciation is not physical forgetting but rather the dissipation of rents as the result of obsolescence. It is a valid private cost component of innovation but not necessarily a social one. Its implications for measurement depend on the state of price-index measurement technology and on the market structure of the relevant industries. In computers, an area in which the incumbents have little market power, prices and revenues fall, but quantities need not. If it is correctly deflated, there is little depreciation to knowledge capital in a "true" quality-constant production function. In pharmaceuticals, where incumbents choose to depreciate their patent monopolies optimally and the appearance of new substitutes does not cause incumbent prices to decline, deflated revenues will fall, and we would interpret it as the depreciation of private R&D capital and a decline in productivity (since the same set of resources are still used in the industry producing essentially the same quantities as before). All that has happened is that the previously accumulated R&D capital is now available to others in the industry and hence cannot collect much rent. But it is still contributing to the productivity (technology) of the industry. From a social perspective the loss of patent protection does not result in a decline in such capital but rather a rise in its utilization. The fact that in most cases our microproduction functions are closer to revenue functions than to true quantities makes the second case more prevalent than the first. But often the data are a mixture of the two, leading to great difficulties in the interpretation of the empirical results.

It is obvious that such capital does not depreciate just with the efflux of time or mechanical wear and tear. The obsolescence of privately generated R&D-based knowledge is clearly a function of the activity of others and is unlikely to occur at a constant rate. A major challenge before us is to model this process convincingly. A start has been made by Caballero and Jaffe (1993), but this has yet to be transferred to the work on microproduction functions.

The previous discussion does not imply that there is no obsolescence in social knowledge. There has surely been loss in the social value of the knowledge stocks associated with making carbon copies of documents and shipbuilding technology, both in the sense that existing stocks are applied to much smaller industries and hence the implicit social returns, the consumer surpluses attributable to the original invention of these products, become smaller as demand falls, and in the sense that they become much harder to retrieve because of the lack of use, the retirement and death of associated human capital, and just plain forgetting. Such depreciation need not have the usual declining-balance (geometric) form, except possibly in the aggregate, where the population renewal theorem (Jorgenson 1973) comes into play.

The final set of problems is associated with the nonrival nature of knowledge (Arrow 1962; Romer 1990). If $\check{K}$ is to be measured by the outputs of the knowledge-producing processes, it becomes an index of the level of productivity along the lines of quality ladders or variety models of Grossman and Helpman (1991) and not a parallel capital input within the list of standard inputs. If $\check{K}$ is measured by R&D input rather than output, the question is still: "Should the resulting production function be interpreted as having constant returns including the R&D input?" The usual solution to this internal versus external economies-of-scale question was to treat the firm's own R&D effects as subject to decreasing returns and include them in the standard list of inputs, while treating the spillovers from the R&D of others as externalities (Griliches 1979, 1991), assuring perfect competition within the relevant sectors. But the nonrival nature of R&D results makes perfect competition solutions unlikely, leading to the patent system and other appropriability mechanisms and a divergence between price and marginal costs of production. The recent revival in monopolistic competition theory and its application in this context make it clear that knowledge-producing firms will have non-negligible markups whose magnitude will depend on the conditions of competition in their industries and the strengths of their appropriability positions. What we have, then, in our data are revenue functions with nonzero markups and downward-sloping demand functions "solving" the increasing returns "problem" (it is only a problem for our models, not necessarily for the real world). In particular, as elaborated below, if one assumes that R&D affects only demand, one would interpret estimates of γ as a measure of $-\varphi/\eta$, where φ is the demand elasticity with respect to R&D, and η is the price elasticity of demand. This is equivalent to the Dorfman and Steiner (1954) result for advertising. Even if only partially true, this has serious implications for estimation—the next topic.

Econometric Issues

There are a number of sources of misspecification that afflict the "standard" production function estimates of the elasticity of output with respect to R&D capital (γ). The major ones are:

1. The simultaneity of the R&D decision.
2. Heterogeneity and endogeneity of individual product prices.
3. Heterogeneity of the underlying production functions.
4. The role of spillovers.

Simultaneity

The more general topic of the simultaneity of input decisions was discussed recently in Griliches and Mairesse (1995). If R&D is chosen on the basis of economic incentives, it is unlikely to be fully independent of the shocks and errors that affect the production relations being estimated. This is the simultaneity problem. If all firms face the same production function and the same factor prices, it is not clear why different firms would choose different R&D levels. If they all do the same thing, we may not be able to estimate anything. If they do not, then we need to understand why not. That is the identification problem.

The simultaneity problem refers to the possible confusion in causality: future output and its profitability depend on past R&D, while R&D, in turn, depends on both past output and the expectation about its future. With long time series and detailed lag assumptions one might be able to analyze a recursive equations system with current output depending on past R&D, and past R&D depending on past rather than current output. In cross-sectional data with only a few observations per firm, it is much harder to make such distinctions, particularly since current expectations about the future are based on current and past data.

There are several "solutions" to the simultaneity problem. First, if one has good series on the real factor costs of the various inputs, one could use them as instrumental variables for the estimation of the production function. Unfortunately, in the R&D context one is unlikely to have good factor price series.[3] Even if one had the prices, they are likely to be highly collinear over time. There is one possible exception to this pessimistic view. With good data one could construct different "tax prices" of R&D facing different firms, which would provide us with some relevant cross-sectional variation. But, to my knowledge, that has not been implemented yet in this context. In addition, the implicit assumption of certainty about the future underlying such static models makes little sense in the R&D context. What is maximized here is the present value of all future profits, and the relevant output price concept is an expected one and not the current one, especially if current output (and demand) is subject to special and transitory circumstances.

Second, if both time-series and cross-sectional data are available and one is willing to assume a simple, permanent-transitory model:

$$u = \alpha + e, \tag{3.4}$$

where α is the permanent component that affects input demand choice while e, the transitory component, does not, then consistent parameter estimates can be had from the within-firm covariances. This is equivalent to allowing a separate constant term (dummy variable) for each firm, which would absorb the offending term in it. Unfortunately, such data sets are rare. Moreover, the covariance approach may exacerbate other problems, such as errors in the variables, which also afflict these kinds of data.

Third, one may be able to find other indicator variables of interest, and they may help to solve the identification problem in such models. I discuss one such approach later in the chapter.

The question of whether the R&D stock measure is contaminated by simultaneity depends on what is in the production-function disturbance and to what extent it is anticipated by the decisionmakers. The usual construction of $K_t = \Sigma (1 - \delta)^j / R_{t-1-j}$, with j going from zero to infinity, puts only lagged values of R&D into the equation. But to the extent that there are more or less permanent firm effects, reflecting market positions, differences in quality of the labor force, and other misspecifications, they would be correlated also with past R&D decisions. Going "within" (that is, using only the time-series variation within a firm, not among firms, for empirical work) or using growth rates eliminates such fixed effects but may still leave other specification errors, such

---

3. First, there are no published R&D deflators at the detailed industry level; second, if they were available, they would still be very highly correlated with the cost of labor and cost of capital indexes, which are likely to be major ingredients of such indexes. What we will not have are changes in "real" R&D costs, in the productivity of such expenditures, in a field or industry, caused by various technological and scientific breakthroughs.

TABLE 3.1a Alternative estimates of production function parameters: U.S. R&D-performing firms, 1973, 1978, 1983, and 1988

	Balanced Panel		Full Sample[a]			
	Total	Within	Total OLS		Nonparametric *F*	
Variables[b]	(1)	(2)	(3)	(4)	(5)	(6)
Labor	.496	.685	.578	.551	.591	
	(.022)	(.030)	(.013)	(.013)	(.013)	
Physical capital	.460	.180	.372	.298	.321	.320
	(.014)	(.027)	(.009)	(.012)	(.016)	(.017)
R&D capital	.034	.099	.038	.027	.081	.077
	(.015)	(.027)	(.007)	(.007)	(.016)	(.019)
Investment	—	—	—	.110	—	
				(.011)		
Other variables[c]	—	—	—	—	Powers of *h*	Polynomial in *P* and *h*
Number of observations[d]	856		2,971		1,571	

SOURCE: Adapted from Griliches and Mairesse (1995).

NOTE: Standard errors are shown in parentheses.

[a]See Griliches and Mairesse (1995) for details of the estimation algorithm leading to columns 5 and 6.

[b]The dependent variable in columns 1 to 4 is the log of sales, while in column 5 and 6 the dependent variable is the log(value added) $- \beta \times$ log(labor).

[c]Other variables in the equations are Year, and Year $\times$ Industry 357 (i.e., computers) dummy variables.

[d]The number of observations in the balanced panel for regressions in columns 1 and 2 consists of the observations for those firms that have continuous data over the period. Similarly, the 2,971 observations in columns 3 and 4 are all the observations in the full sample. (Only 6 observations had to be discarded because of zero investment.) The number of observations in the last two columns decreases to 1,571 because lagged values of some of the independent variables are needed in the estimation.

as changing utilization rates and demand conditions. These may still influence current R&D decisions.

An example of current approaches to such problems can be seen in Table 3.1a, which is adapted from Griliches and Mairesse (1995). The first part, columns 1 and 2, presents "standard," ordinary least-squares (OLS) production-function estimates for a heavily selected panel of 214 R&D firms in U.S. manufacturing. As usual, the capital coefficient declines as one moves to within-firm data, but the estimated R&D coefficient actually increases. Table 3.1b, which is new, applies the more general Chamberlain (1984) Π-matrix approach to the estimation of such a model to ask whether the R&D coefficients have declined over time. As can be seen from comparing the estimated γ's in columns 3 and 5 or 4 and 6, they did not. The allowance for correlated effects

TABLE 3.1b Alternative estimates of production function parameters: U.S. R&D-performing firms, 1973, 1978, 1983, and 1988, balanced panel

Variables[a]	Uncorrelated Random Effects		Correlated Effects			
	SUR[b] (1)	MD[c] (2)	SUR (3)	MD (4)	SUR (5)	MD (6)
Labor	.594	.686	.664	.805	.671	.818
	(.037)	(.020)	(.020)	(.029)	(.044)	(.030)
Physical capital	.334	.260	.163	.062	.164	.062
	(.031)	(.014)	(.033)	(.022)	(.033)	(.022)
R&D capital	.067	.065	.092	.080	—	—
combined	(.022)	(.015)	(.035)	(.022)		
1973	—	—	—	—	.086	.065
					(.036)	(.024)
1978	—	—	—	—	.087	.072
					(.035)	(.023)
1983	—	—	—	—	.073	.059
					(.036)	(.024)
1988	—	—	—	—	.094	.076
					(.035)	(.023)
χ^2	—	366	—	121	—	110
		(45)		(33)		(30)

SOURCE: Author's calculations.

NOTE: Sandard errors are shown in parentheses. The number of observations is 856 (214 firms × 4).

[a]Variable: log deflated sales; other variables: year dummy variables, computer (357), industry dummy variable, and computer year interaction variable; χ^2: degrees of freedom.

[b]SUR represents seemingly unrelated (multivariate) regression estimates.

[c]MD represents minimum distance (individual heteroskedasticity weighted).

hits the physical-capital coefficient primarily, and the allowance for individual firm heteroskedasticity introduces an additional puzzling instability in the estimated coefficients—compare the estimates in the seemingly unrelated (multivariate) regression estimates (SUR) versus minimum distance (MD) columns—but leaves the R&D coefficients largely unchanged. Neither of these estimates takes care, however, of the simultaneity of the employment decision, if the latter is affected by current shocks in production or correlated with unmeasured changes in capacity utilization.

An interesting new approach to the simultaneity problem is presented by Olley and Pakes (1996). This paper deals jointly with two topics—selectivity and simultaneity. The sample selectivity problem may be quite serious for panel data. If observations (and data) are not missing at random, estimates that are based on "clean" and balanced subsamples could be badly biased. For example, a bad draw of u may force a firm or plant to exit from the industry. Such a negative correlation between estimated productivity shocks and future probabilities of exit was observed by Griliches and Regev (1995) in their analysis of Israeli industrial firms. They called it "the shadow of death." If the impact of negative us on exit is stronger for smaller firms (the larger ones having more resources to survive a shock), then this will induce a negative correlation between u and the stock of capital among the surviving firms and bias the estimated capital coefficient downward in such samples. (See Griliches and Mairesse [1995] for a more detailed exposition.)

The major innovation of Olley and Pakes is to bring in a new equation, the investment equation, as a proxy for α, the unobserved transmitted component of u.[4] Trying to proxy for the unobserved α (if it can be done right) has several advantages over the usual within estimators: it does not assume that α reduces to a fixed (over time) firm effect; it leaves more identifying variance in the "independent" variables and is therefore a less costly solution to the omitted variable and/or simultaneity problem; and it should also be substantially more informative.

Olley and Pakes's argument goes roughly as follows: the investment demand of the firm at time t can be written as a function of the predetermined capital-stock variables and that part of the shock in the production function u, the α, which is transmitted to both the employment and the investment decision. Inverting this relationship and solving for α as a function of investment and capital stock, one can approximate it now semiparametrically and estimate the production function in two steps (three, if one also deals with selectivity at the same time). First, one gets a consistent estimate of the coefficient of the labor variable; then, one retrieves the capital coefficient by using the estimated labor coefficient to move the endogenous labor variable to the left-hand side of the equation.

An application of their approach to our data is presented in columns 3 through 6 of Table 3.1b. Because exit (being taken over) is often a success rather than a failure for our R&D firms, the selection problem is not particularly severe in our data (compare the results in columns 1 and 3). Once one shifts to the more complete unbalanced samples, the remaining selectivity (mainly attrition) does not appear to be too important (compare columns 5 and 6).

As far as the simultaneity problem is concerned, either it is of no great import in these data or the introduction of investment, and the associated Olley and Pakes procedure, does not fully adjust for it. Investment is highly significant when added to the production function (see column 4), but at the end of the procedure (having allowed for selectivity and unbalance), the coefficients

---

4. In their notation α is ω, and they refer to it simply as "productivity."

change little (compare columns 1 and 3 with 6) except that, once again, we get a higher R&D coefficient.

The Olley and Pakes solution to the simultaneity problem is a clever way to exploit the fact that the unobserved productivity shocks are transmitted to more than just one equation and should be estimated within a system of behavioral equations. The solution does rest, however, on two very strong assumptions: (1) that there is only a *single* component unobservable in the system, the α_{it}, which follows a first-order Markov process and is fully transmitted to the investment equation, and (2) that no other variables or errors are present. Investment also depends, however, on other individual factors such as interest-rate expectations, tax treatments, and changes in future demand prospects not fully captured in the initial state variables (the capital stocks). In principle, there may be additional instrumental variables and other indicators of α, such as R&D, which could help solve the errors in the investment equation problem, except for the extreme nonlinearities introduced by their semiparametric approach.[5]

Other approaches lean more heavily on assumptions about lags in the transmission of the disturbances to the other decision variables and use lagged values as instrumental variables in estimating such models (see Blundell and Bond 1995; Mairesse and Hall 1996). One can write a simple model of the production function as:

$$y_{it} = \beta x_{it} + \gamma k_{it} + \alpha_i + u_{it}, \quad u_{it} = \rho u_{it-1} + e_{it}, \tag{3.5}$$

where small letters represent the logarithms of the variables, x is a composite of conventional inputs including physical capital, k is a measure of the R&D stock, α_i is an unobserved permanent firm effect, and u is a randomly changing "technical" disturbance. The innovation in u, the e_{it}, is unpredictable, but whether x and k are independent of it depends on the assumed lag structure of the decisions affecting their evolution. (Of course, u could be modeled as a higher-order autoregression.) In such a world, we could solve out u_{it} and rewrite the equation as:

$$y = \beta(x - \rho x_{-1}) + \gamma(k - \rho k_{-1}) + \rho y_{-1} + e + (1 - \rho)\alpha_i, \tag{3.6}$$

and use past differences in x, k, and y, which should be independent of the α_i and e_i, as instruments.[6]

In Table 3.2, a larger sample (including also non-R&D firms) is analyzed in this framework using the generalized method of moments (GMM) approach (see Mairesse and Hall [1996] for a recent exposition in a similar context).

---

5. The current state of estimating nonlinear errors-in-variables models is not completely hopeless, but it is not easy either.

6. This assumption is right for "stationary" αs, where their effect on y is unchanged over time.

TABLE 3.2 Alternative estimates of production function parameters: U.S. R&D and non-R&D manufacturing firms, 1982–1987

Variable	Levels					First Differences		
	OLS		Instrumented by Differences			Instrumented by Levels		OLS
	(1)	(2)	(3)[a]	(4)[a]	(5)[b]	(6)[c]	(7)[d]	(8)
Labor	0.567	0.616	0.665	0.750	0.652	0.705	0.611	0.613
	(0.008)	(0.013)	(0.048)	(0.027)	(0.046)	(0.024)	(0.062)	(0.013)
Capital	0.402	0.122	0.277	0.289	0.314	0.084	0.110	0.114
	(0.007)	(0.012)	(0.036)	(0.027)	(0.031)	(0.019)	(0.037)	(0.012)
R&D stock	0.016	0.041	0.033	0.025	0.030	0.046	0.059	0.030
	(0.004)	(0.012)	(0.017)	(0.017)	(0.010)	(0.017)	(0.022)	(0.013)
Lagged output	0	0.981	0	0.573	0.654	1	1	1
		(0.004)		(0.023)	(0.031)			

SOURCE: Griliches (1996).

NOTE: Standard errors are shown in parentheses. The number of observations is 676. Estimates in columns 2, 4, and 5 (equation 3.6) are constrained to the same ρ coefficient in $(x - \rho_{x-1})$ and ρ_{y-1}. Additional variables in the equations include no-R&D dummy variable, year dummies, computer industry dummy, and interaction with year.

[a]Instrument sets: all differences as of $t-2$ and earlier, for l, c, k, and y_{-1}.

[b]Instrument sets: c and k treated as predetermined. Only l and y_{-1} instrumented.

[c]Instrument sets: levels of l, c, and k as of $t-2$ and earlier.

[d]Instrument sets: only l instrumented.

Columns 1 and 8 present the OLS estimates for levels and first differences, respectively. Column 2 allows for serial correlation, which is very high (as could be expected). Columns 3 and 4 repeat these level computations allowing for the endogeneity of all the input (and lagged output) variables, using past differences in these variables as instrumental variables. Column 5 is similar, but only instruments the labor and lagged output variables, treating the two capital stocks as predetermined.[7] Columns 6 and 7 present the corresponding estimates of this equation in first differences, instrumented by past levels. The first differences transformation is optimal if $\rho = 1$, or if $\rho = 0$ and the "not so fixed effect" is a random walk, that is, $\alpha = \alpha_{-1} + e$. Column 6 uses past levels as instruments for all three variables, which is appropriate if there are random measurement errors in them or some remaining contemporaneous simultaneity, while column 7 only instruments the labor variable.

The preferred specification, column 5, indicates a statistically significant R&D coefficient of about .03. It also finds that the individual firm effects are not entirely "fixed" but include a component that does depreciate, albeit slowly. If one approaches the limit of $\rho = 1$ (first differences), there is hardly any identifying variance left in the annual changes in our measures of physical and R&D capital. Measurement and timing errors now predominate, while the remaining information content in the instruments is too small to allow one to extract whatever signal is still left in these variables. In the end, what is clear is that there seems to be a significant R&D coefficient, but its magnitude is uncertain, varying from about .03 to .08, based on estimates from reasonably robust specifications (Table 3.1a, column 6; Table 3.1b, column 4; and Table 3.2, column 5).

The GMM approach uses past values of the inputs and outputs as instruments. What is their identifying content? Inputs today depend on past demand and supply shocks because, presumably, there are lags in adjustment and also erroneous decisions. But without specifying nontrivial, real factor demand and supply equations with measurable exogenous shifters of such functions, we have no interesting variables for use to interpret (identify) their behavior. There are no measures of shifts in the potential demands for a firm's products or of changes in technological opportunities, market structure, or individual firm cost of capital. Without such shifters it is hard to tell whether the lagged values represent an interesting "experiment" that would allow us to identify something.

Heterogeneity of Prices among Firms

Another major specification problem revolves around the unlikely assumption that all firms within an industry charge the same price. If product prices are

---

7. Using instruments from $t - 3$ rather than $t - 2$ increases the standard errors but has little effect on the reported results.

both different and endogenous, then what is estimated is a revenue function, not a production function, with left-out product prices in the residual. This problem is considered by Klette and Griliches (1996), who, reinventing an argument already made by Marschak and Andrews (1944), start with a model of firms facing symmetric, logarithmic, market-share (demand) functions:

$$y_i - y_I = \eta(p_i - p_I) + e, \tag{3.7}$$

where y_i and y_I respectively are the real output of the firm and the industry, p_i is the firm's own price (or price index), η is demand elasticity with respect to the relative price of the firm's own products, p_I is the aggregate industry price index (relative to the overall economy price level), and e represents all other demand shifters for the products of this firm. If the variable that we observe is not *real* output y but deflated revenue (sales):

$$r_i = (y_i + p_i) - p_I, \tag{3.8}$$

then the "revenue production" function is:

$$r = \beta x + \gamma k + u + (p_i - p_I). \tag{3.9}$$

There would be no problem here if the p_is were random and exogenous. But if firms have a modicum of market power, at least in the short run, p_i will be set by them and will be correlated with u, x, and k. Setting price equal to marginal revenue and solving out for p_i yields the pseudo production function:

$$r = (\beta x + \gamma k + u)/m - (y_I)/\eta - e/\eta, \tag{3.10}$$

where the markup coefficient $m = \eta/(1 + \eta)$ is likely to be larger than one. Since y_I and p_I are aggregates, they can be controlled for by the introduction of period dummy variables. It is clear now that the estimates of α and β will be biased *downward* on the order of $1/m$, implying diminishing returns to scale in contexts in which there actually may be increasing returns.

This model can be extended by adding R&D capital to the demand function, with φ as its elasticity.[8] The coefficient of k in the "deflated" sales equation is then $(\gamma/m - \varphi/\eta)$, a combination of its effects on both productivity and demand, attenuated by the price elasticity of demand. This coefficient can also be rewritten as $\gamma + (\gamma - \varphi)/\eta$, showing that the pure productivity effect of R&D will be underestimated as long as it is smaller than its demand effect (φ). Klette and Griliches show that if one has a measure of the demand shifter (they use aggregate industry sales y_I for that) one can identify η and β, but one cannot separate φ from γ, unless one assumes $\varphi = 0$. Without actual individual

---

8. In this form, R&D capital is a separable demand shifter, leaving the price elasticity of demand unaffected. (See Griliches and Mairesse [1984] for an early formulation of this model.) A more complex model might also include an interaction term, making the price elasticity itself a function of K.

firm prices, there may be little that we can do here except be more careful in our interpretation of such results.

Heterogeneity of Production Functions

All of this discussion has focused on estimating the effects of R&D, but what makes different firms choose to undertake different amounts of R&D? I have already noted the lack of good "external" causal variables. To the extent that differences in R&D reflect technological opportunities, they could be modeled as differences in γ, firms facing (or possessing) different knowledge-producing technologies (though keeping the conventional input component the same within an industry). But unless one brings in some substantive variables that would explain this heterogeneity, such apparent generality adds very little content. (See Mairesse and Griliches [1990] for a parallel discussion of heterogeneity in the physical capital elasticity.) The open modeling question is how to use the observed differences in R&D intensity to infer something interesting about the underlying sources of the heterogeneity in γ.

Spillover

The final estimation-cum-specification problem for discussion here is the estimation of spillover effects. The standard approach (for which I must take some responsibility [Griliches 1979]) introduces a distance-weighted measure of the research efforts of other firms within the same and/or neighboring industries or technological areas. It is clearly a first step in the right direction, but it is also subject to a serious identification problem: Does it work because a firm benefits from the efforts of others, or is it just a reflection of spatially correlated technological opportunities? It could be a response to common differences across fishing grounds, or in more technical terms, the individual firm effects α_i may not be independent of each other but subject to some local clustering that will be picked up by the spillover measures. This issue is discussed in a more general context by Manski (1991), under the title "the reflection problem." It would be nice if someone could come up with an approach that could distinguish between these two interpretations, but that is unlikely because the basic model is not identified without much more explicit restrictions and priors on the possible channels of communication.

I have concentrated today on the unfinished business not to emphasize the "glass half-empty" aspect but rather to indicate the rich research opportunities ahead. "Our song is not finished, it's only beginning!"

4 Inputs, Output, and Productivity Developments in U.S. Agriculture

BARBARA J. CRAIG AND PHILIP G. PARDEY

What accounts for the major increases in agricultural output in the United States and elsewhere in the post–World War II period? Professional and policy interest in the nature and sources of such economic growth has resurfaced in recent years, but as Griliches (1992) correctly points out, some of the ideas in this "new growth theory" are not new. The growth and productivity consequences of nonconventional factors such as education, research and development (R&D), and publicly provided infrastructure are being given renewed emphasis. To assess the economic significance of these sources of growth requires dealing with the persistent problems of obtaining meaningful measures of productivity. Moreover, deriving policy prescriptions from productivity analysis presupposes a clear understanding of the construction and interpretation of productivity measures.

Whether one is studying the productivity of an entire economy or a specific sector such as agriculture, the underlying measurement problems are the same. To *quantify* the behavior of output, it is necessary to aggregate over a heterogeneous group of products. This typically involves deflating the total value of output or constructing an explicit output index. To *explain* the behavior of aggregate output, analysts turn to measures of aggregate input. Unfortunately, these input measures are never comprehensive. Inputs to production that pass through a market are relatively easy to value, and hence to aggregate, using total value or some index number procedure. Less conventional inputs, however, are less amenable to conventional aggregation techniques.

Productivity measures are simple ratios of aggregate input and output quantities. These ratios are often treated as measures of technological change, but not without obvious pitfalls. The residual productivity measure is always made up of unmeasured, perhaps unmeasurable, inputs. For agriculture, these are such things as environmental inputs, research and extension services, unobserved managerial characteristics of farm operators, or unmeasured changes in the quality of specific inputs.

A positivist approach to productivity measurement would seek to measure all inputs and "explain away" the residual, thereby accounting for all output

37

growth. In an idea attributed to Griliches, Schultz (1956) characterized the ideal input-output formula as one in which output over inputs—that is, a productivity index—stayed at or close to one. "The closer we come to a one-to-one relationship in our formulation, the more complete would be our (economic) explanation" (758). The reality of data and measurement techniques makes this Schultzian productivity index unobtainable, but it is nevertheless a useful idea. The basic premise is that the productivity measure itself is a measure of what we are unable to account for. Its use and interpretation should be informed by a consideration of the data that it does and does not include.

In this chapter, we report new productivity measurements for agriculture for the United States and for 48 individual states for the 1949–91 period. We highlight the construction of the input aggregates because we made a concerted effort to account for quality change in inputs in an attempt to "whittle away" measured productivity gains in post–World War II agriculture. In U.S. agriculture, labor is now more educated and experienced, farm machinery has become more powerful, new crop varieties are available, and there have been significant changes in the composition of chemicals used on-farm. To capture changes in the quality of agricultural inputs we use disaggregated data that distinguish 58 categories of inputs, each further differentiated by the state in which the inputs were used. Defining inputs this narrowly has three distinct advantages. First, the sheer number of state-specific input categories helps to ensure comparability over time of individual inputs. Second, this definition enables us to capture changes in the mix of inputs *within* broad input classes such as land, labor, and capital. Finally, this definition reveals economically significant differences across states in the pattern of agricultural development.

The next section briefly describes the aggregation procedures used to construct input and output quantity measures for U.S. agriculture and their use in estimating multifactor productivity (MFP). Data construction methods are also briefly reviewed. The main body of this chapter is devoted to presenting our new state series, drawing on these data to throw new light on input, output, and productivity developments in U.S. agriculture.[1] We also provide quantitative indications of the extent of changes in the quality of agricultural land and labor in the post–World War II period.

Aggregation Methods

Conventional productivity measures are based on a ratio of the quantity of outputs to the quantity of inputs. If outputs or inputs consist of heterogeneous

---

1. Alternative estimates of aggregate input, output, and MFP for U.S. agriculture are found in Ball (1985), Ball et al. (1996, 1999), Capalbo and Vo (1988), and Jorgenson and Gallop (1992). Huffman and Evenson (1993) report the state-level estimates constructed by Evenson, Landau, and Ballou (1987).

components, an aggregation procedure must be used. To keep bias from aggregation to a minimum, at least three important problems need to be solved: choosing the appropriate index type; carefully selecting representative value weights for all inputs and outputs; and disaggregating outputs and inputs as finely as possible.

The importance of the choice of the index number type for time-series analysis has been discussed widely in economics literature. When index numbers are chosen to be consistent with behavioral assumptions (see, for example, Richter [1966] and Diewert [1976]), the consensus is that a chained index—specifically an approximation of the Divisia index—is to be preferred. Chained indexes allow for changes in relative prices in a way that minimizes the misrepresentation of substitution effects because they use rolling price weights; price-induced change in the input or output mix is less likely to be misinterpreted as a change in the scale of the respective quantity aggregate.

The importance of appropriate or representative value weights has received much less attention (see the discussions in Drechsler [1973] or Craig and Pardey [1990]). If economic behavior is the rationale for the use of a particular indexing procedure, it would be inconsistent to evaluate the consequences of economic behavior using any prices other than those on which production decisions were based. Therefore, every effort should be made to use the most representative prices available for the production unit being studied.

When making productivity comparisons, there is a need to start with finely disaggregated data in order to account for possible changes in the quality of outputs or inputs over time. Hulten (1992), Jorgenson and Griliches (1967), and Star (1974) all demonstrate the empirical consequences of disaggregation when calculating MFPs for total U.S. output and U.S. manufacturing. The message of these articles, stated formally in Star, is that one is safe in using preaggregated inputs—that is, in taking all labor to be a single class of input—only if all inputs in the class are growing at the same rate or are perfect substitutes for one another. If rates of change in higher-priced inputs exceed rates of change in lower-priced inputs, the rate of growth of the group is biased downward in any index that fails to treat high- and low-priced items as separate components. Under the behavioral assumption that market prices of inputs are consistent with farmers' evaluations of their productive quality, growth rates of agricultural productivity will be overstated if we fail to disaggregate when the faster-growing inputs are higher-quality inputs.

Here we report state and national price and quantity indexes that were constructed using the Törnqvist-Theil approximation of the Divisia index. The formula for this index is given by

$$I(t) = I(t-1) \prod_{i=1}^{N} \left[\frac{Q_i(t)}{Q_i(t-1)} \right]^{w_i(t)}$$

where $w_i(t) = \dfrac{1}{2} \left[\dfrac{P_i(t)Q_i(t)}{\displaystyle\sum_{j=1}^{N} P_j(t)Q_j(t)} + \dfrac{P_i(t-1)Q_i(t-1)}{\displaystyle\sum_{j=1}^{N} P_j(t-1)Q_j(t-1)} \right]$ (4.1)

For our state output indexes, $Q_i(t)$ represents the quantity of commodity i produced in the state at time t, and $P_i(t)$ is the price received by farmers in that state for the corresponding commodity and time period. For state input indexes, $Q_i(t)$ represents the quantity of input i employed in the state at time t, and $P_i(t)$ is the price or rent paid for the corresponding input and time period. The national output and input indexes are true Divisia indexes in the sense that each aggregate index is constructed using all relevant state-level quantities and state-level prices for commodities produced or inputs used. The state and national MFP indexes we report are simple ratios of the respective output and input quantity aggregates.

Data

The input, output, and productivity measures presented here for U.S. agriculture span the 48 contiguous states and are annual observations from 1949 to 1991.[2] For each state's output index, there are 54 commodities, including 9 livestock commodities, 14 field crops, and 26 fruits and vegetables. The remaining 5 "commodities" include 3 tree nuts, implicit quantities of machines rented out by farmers, and implicit quantities of nursery and greenhouse products. The prices used in the output index calculation are state-specific prices received by farmers for all commodities except machine hire and nursery and greenhouse products. For each of these composite commodities, a price index based on national prices for its subcomponents was constructed to deflate reported current dollar income.

In the construction of the U.S. output aggregate, each of the 54 commodities was further differentiated by the state in which it was produced. Consequently, for the U.S. output aggregate we have 2,592 commodities.

---

2. Craig and Pardey (1996a, 1996b) provide a more complete description of these data and sources. Preliminary versions of these data were reported and used by Craig and Pardey (1990), Deininger (1993), and Pardey, Craig, and Deininger (1994). These latest measures are based on updated and, for many variables, completely revised data; they supersede the figures reported earlier.

Treating different states' commodities as distinct is our method of handling quality differences on the output side. Total rice produced in California is of different average quality than rice produced in Arkansas because the two states produce a different mix of rice varieties.

For each state's input index there are 58 types of inputs. For the national input index the inputs are again differentiated by the state in which each was used. We developed time series on 32 distinct types of labor in agriculture to account for quality change in the labor input. We differentiate between hours worked by hired workers, family members, and 30 classes of farm operators with different age and education profiles. We also factor in data on days worked off-farm by farm operators, to account for the substantial but uneven shift toward part-time farming. Wages, explicit and implicit, are taken to represent the relative quality of these different labor inputs. Hired-labor wages inclusive of perquisites and taxes are based on state-level data. Family workers are assumed to have the same wage as hired workers in the same state. Implicit operator wages were developed using the national income earned by farm operators categorized by age and educational attainment.

The land input is the service flow from land of three basic types: pasture or rangeland, nonirrigated cropland, and irrigated cropland. The quantity measure used here differs from the more traditional land-in-farms figure in that it excludes nongrazed forest and woodlands, which are land in farms but not in agriculture, and includes tracts of federally owned land that was rented or leased for rangeland grazing purposes. Our cropland measures include acres made idle for whatever reason. The price weights used in aggregation are annual, state-level, cash rents for each of the three land types.

The capital input includes seven classes of physical capital (trucks, automobiles, tractors, combines, pickup balers, mower conditioners, and buildings) and five classes of biological capital (dairy cows, beef cows, ewes, chickens, and sows). Assuming that market values reflect the expected, discounted value of real capital services over the lifetime of the capital, the rents were taken to be different particular fractions of unit value for specific types of capital. The fraction used to construct rents from unit values depended on the parameterization of life span, depreciation, and age for each capital class. For each class of physical capital, the rent was based on the national value of a representative machine. State-level rents were derived from state-level value per head for all types of biological capital. In all capital rent calculations we used the same constant real interest rate (4 percent per year) for discounting service flows.

Besides identifying as many separate capital classes as possible, we adjusted inventories of the physical capital classes to reflect quality change over time. The method used depended on the nature of the data available and the service flow profile of each capital type. For all farm machinery, automobiles, and trucks, inventories on-farm were converted to numbers of new-machine equivalents by incorporating information on the average age of machines. For tractors and combines, additional information on the productive characteristics of machines on-farm was used to adjust for quality as well, leaving us with inventories measured in numbers of a new, numeraire tractor or combine. For only one capital class—buildings—the quantities were implicit quantities derived by deflating the inferred total rental value of buildings on farm.

Eleven types of purchased inputs were also used in the aggregate input indexes. We included fertilizers broken down into three distinct elements (nitrogen, phosphorus, and potash) and implicit quantities of purchased seed, purchased feed, a preaggregated pesticides, herbicides, and fungicides category, fuels and oils, electricity, repairs, and machine hire. We also included a miscellaneous input category—a preaggregation of a long list of disparate inputs such as fencing, irrigation fees, hand tools, veterinary services, insurance costs, and so on. State-specific prices for purchased inputs were available only for electricity; all other prices were national prices or price indexes based on national prices paid by farmers. Except for fertilizer, our input quantities were derived from state-level expenditure totals.

Input, Output, and Productivity Measures

In aggregate terms, U.S. agriculture produced more than twice the quantity of output in 1991 that it did in 1949. It did this with marginally less aggregate inputs, causing our index of MFP to grow faster than the rate of growth in output. In annual rate-of-change terms we estimate that output increased by 1.58 percent over the 1949–91 period and inputs used in agriculture declined by 0.19 percent, so that measured MFP grew by 1.76 percent per year (Table 4.1).

Figure 4.1 presents the trends in the national input, output, and MFP indexes. Measured input use at the national level deviates little from its long-run trend. There is, however, considerable volatility in the underlying state series, which cancels out in an aggregate measure of input use for U.S. agriculture. The relative stability of the input aggregate contrasts with the sizable drop in the quantity of aggregate output and, correspondingly, MFP in 1983 and 1988 reflecting a major drought.[3] The drought-induced decline in 1983 was exacerbated by the output effect of the payment-in-kind program, introduced in the 1981 U.S. Farm Bill.

The comparatively small drop in aggregate input use hides a good deal of variation across different categories of inputs, even for a national index. The quantity of labor used in U.S. agriculture in 1991 was only 40 percent of the labor used in 1949, an average annual rate of decline of 2.2 percent per year. Land in agriculture also declined, while there was a slow overall growth in the

---

3. National average corn yields in 1983 were 22 percent lower than the average for the previous three years; in 1988, yields of feed grains were 30 percent lower than in the previous year.

TABLE 4.1 Annual average growth rates in U.S. agriculture, 1949–1991

	National Growth Rates	State Growth Rates			Standard Deviation of State Growth Rates	States with Annual Average Growth Rates		
		Minimum	Maximum	Range		Above U.S. Average	More than 1.5% Above	More than 1.5% Below
		(percent per year)				(number)		
MFP	1.76	1.06	4.11	3.06	0.70	35	7	0
Output	1.58	-0.63	3.89	4.52	1.16	28	5	5
Input	-0.19	-2.21	1.38	3.59	0.91	23	1	7
Land	-0.30	-3.34	0.47	3.81	0.94	20	0	9
Labor	-2.21	-4.14	-0.13	4.02	0.96	22	6	2
Capital	0.05	-1.60	2.45	4.05	0.82	27	1	1
Intermediate inputs	1.97	-1.29	4.13	5.42	1.30	27	2	8

SOURCE: Authors' calculations.

FIGURE 4.1 National input, output, and productivity trends, 1949–1991

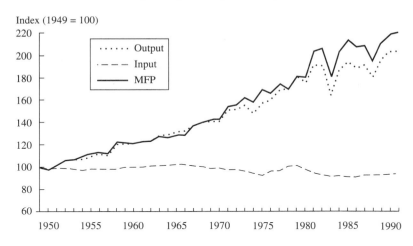

Index (1949 = 100)

SOURCE: Authors' calculations.

capital services used by agriculture. Purchased inputs represent the only rapidly growing category of inputs; U.S. farmers have more than doubled the quantity of such inputs used since 1949.

These national trends are broadly consistent with developments at the state level, but there are some significant differences across states. Productivity growth in 35 states was faster than the national average, ranging from a low of 1.06 percent per year in Nevada to 4.11 percent in North Dakota. Even greater variation occurred across states in the growth of inputs and still larger cross-sectional variation in the growth of outputs. Table 4.1 provides summary statistics related to the variation across states in inputs, output, and MFP growth. State-specific measures of productivity growth for the 1949–91 period and selected subperiods are given in Table 4.2.

To gain an alternative perspective on the spatial differences regarding input, output, and productivity developments in the United States, Table 4.3 reports the correlation between state and national indexes. While productivity trended up in all states, the year-to-year changes for Montana, New Hampshire, Wyoming, and New Jersey did not closely conform with national developments over our sample period. And, while agricultural output grew in the aggregate for most regions of the country, it declined in the New England states of Connecticut, Massachusetts, New Hampshire, and Rhode Island as well as New Jersey and West Virginia. Figure 4.2a presents some of these state-specific developments pictorially and contrasts them with the aggregate output

TABLE 4.2 Annual average growth rates in multifactor productivity, 1949–1991

	1949–59	1960–69	1970–79	1980–91	1949–91
	(percent per year)				
Alabama	3.86	2.51	2.74	4.83	3.52
Arizona	1.57	1.21	3.55	1.93	2.05
Arkansas	2.94	4.03	3.07	3.57	3.40
California	1.55	2.30	2.79	0.58	1.77
Colorado	1.90	2.01	1.56	2.12	1.90
Connecticut	1.94	1.77	0.99	1.39	1.53
Delaware	4.03	2.83	1.06	2.77	2.71
Florida	1.65	3.22	4.25	0.22	2.27
Georgia	4.52	3.08	2.32	4.38	3.62
Idaho	1.75	3.26	2.34	2.48	2.44
Illinois	1.21	0.29	3.48	4.06	2.27
Indiana	1.14	0.71	3.28	2.50	1.90
Iowa	1.10	0.90	2.89	1.71	1.64
Kansas	5.13	0.54	1.52	2.35	2.45
Kentucky	1.11	1.88	1.99	4.29	2.33
Louisiana	1.77	4.52	2.40	2.74	2.83
Maine	3.15	4.33	0.04	1.02	2.13
Maryland	2.52	2.44	1.25	2.71	2.25
Massachusetts	2.48	2.73	2.17	−0.26	1.75
Michigan	0.60	2.17	4.02	2.67	2.33
Minnesota	1.82	1.62	3.01	2.19	2.15
Mississippi	4.21	3.95	1.95	3.93	3.54
Missouri	1.48	0.76	2.42	1.63	1.57
Montana	1.83	2.52	1.35	4.17	2.49
Nebraska	3.15	1.27	2.08	3.78	2.62
Nevada	−0.09	2.29	1.85	0.37	1.06
New Hampshire	3.08	2.95	0.20	0.36	1.65
New Jersey	2.51	0.61	0.54	1.88	1.42
New Mexico	1.24	2.42	1.70	2.25	1.90
New York	1.78	1.89	2.06	1.37	1.77
North Carolina	2.84	2.53	3.25	5.18	3.48
North Dakota	2.96	3.29	0.50	9.30	4.11
Ohio	0.79	0.81	3.92	1.32	1.68
Oklahoma	2.68	0.46	3.07	1.26	1.87
Oregon	1.28	1.94	2.67	0.47	1.56
Pennsylvania	2.04	2.03	2.22	1.67	1.98
Rhode Island	2.69	2.67	0.73	3.49	2.43
South Carolina	2.42	3.27	3.26	4.98	3.49
South Dakota	3.85	1.67	2.09	3.80	2.90
Tennessee	1.33	1.13	3.13	2.48	2.01
Texas	0.79	1.33	2.08	3.13	1.84

(continued)

TABLE 4.2 *Continued*

	1949–59	1960–69	1970–79	1980–91	1949–91
Utah	1.13	2.42	0.68	2.21	1.62
Vermont	1.86	2.51	0.16	0.91	1.36
Virginia	1.43	1.48	1.79	4.05	2.21
Washington	0.62	2.84	3.86	1.05	2.03
West Virginia	2.03	1.41	2.62	2.80	2.23
Wisconsin	1.80	1.39	1.97	1.21	1.59
Wyoming	1.77	1.50	0.97	1.59	1.47
United States	1.91	1.50	2.33	1.38	1.76

SOURCE: Authors' calculations.

growth at the national level. Figure 4.2b shows trends in selected aggregate input indexes.

Figures 4.3a to 4.3d help characterize the temporal and spatial diversity of developments regarding the use of specific input groups. Although land input qualities have generally declined, they have increased in quality-adjusted terms in some of the drier western and southern states, reflecting a more rapid increase in the quality of higher-quality irrigated cropland in those states (Figure 4.3a). For example, the total agricultural acreage of states in the Northern Plains states of North Dakota, South Dakota, Nebraska, and Kansas declined at an annual average rate of 0.12 percent. However, with a Divisia index of land, which allows for differential rates of change in land of different quality, we measure an annual average increase of 0.26 percent in land use in those states.

Disaggregation of the labor inputs reveals that the temporal pattern of change was not the same in every part of the United States. The reduction in total hours worked was more dramatic in the southern states than in the rest of the 48 states. But for Arizona, California, Florida, New Mexico, and Washington, the quantity of labor used in agriculture has actually been increasing over the past two decades against a national trend of decreasing labor use (Figure 4.3b). Given their emphasis on specialty horticultural crops and the nature of production of those crops, Florida and California may have been less able to substitute other factors for labor, but in fact they have some of the highest measured growth rates in capital and intermediate inputs.

The comparative smoothness in the national labor and land indexes contrasts with a good deal of variability over time in the use of capital services and purchased inputs at both the state and national levels. This reflects the uneven distribution of capital purchases over time and the relative flexibility of production decisions regarding many purchased inputs.

For the decade beginning in the late 1950s, all states outside the northeastern quadrant of the country increased their capital input as more tractors, combines, and farm machines of all types were purchased. In the most recent

TABLE 4.3 Correlation of state indexes with national indexes, 1949–1991

				Classes of Inputs			
	MFP	Output	Input	Land	Labor	Capital	Intermediate Inputs
Alabama	0.98	0.98	0.85	0.98	0.99	0.84	0.98
Arizona	0.96	0.97	−0.04	0.45	0.80	0.78	0.90
Arkansas	0.99	0.98	0.46	0.90	0.99	0.49	0.96
California	0.98	0.98	−0.48	0.73	0.77	0.75	0.98
Colorado	0.96	0.97	−0.34	−0.39	0.99	0.60	0.97
Connecticut	0.94	−0.77	0.69	0.96	0.98	0.25	−0.68
Delaware	0.96	0.96	−0.42	0.77	0.99	0.38	0.79
Florida	0.92	0.97	−0.43	0.97	0.67	0.35	0.98
Georgia	0.98	0.97	0.81	0.97	0.99	0.52	0.98
Idaho	0.98	0.98	−0.13	−0.54	0.94	0.68	0.98
Illinois	0.95	0.92	0.79	−0.48	0.99	0.74	0.96
Indiana	0.97	0.95	0.90	0.88	0.99	0.86	0.99
Iowa	0.96	0.95	0.39	−0.28	0.98	0.74	0.97
Kansas	0.94	0.95	−0.22	−0.94	1.00	0.86	0.96
Kentucky	0.97	0.92	0.76	0.98	0.99	0.28	0.99
Louisiana	0.97	0.95	0.88	0.91	1.00	0.89	0.97
Maine	0.92	0.41	0.77	0.96	0.97	0.27	0.22
Maryland	0.99	0.98	0.47	0.95	0.99	0.95	0.95
Massachusetts	0.93	−0.71	0.55	0.96	0.96	0.02	−0.88
Michigan	0.97	0.89	0.73	0.94	1.00	0.56	0.94
Minnesota	0.98	0.97	0.76	0.94	0.98	0.83	0.98
Mississippi	0.98	0.90	0.77	0.90	0.99	0.81	0.94
Missouri	0.95	0.89	0.88	0.71	0.99	0.75	0.95
Montana	0.76	0.80	0.10	−0.83	0.99	0.60	0.97
Nebraska	0.97	0.99	−0.39	−0.84	0.99	0.77	0.98
Nevada	0.93	0.94	−0.03	0.46	0.55	0.06	0.95
New Hampshire	0.81	−0.89	0.53	0.97	0.95	−0.03	−0.81
New Jersey	0.89	−0.80	0.63	0.96	0.99	0.11	−0.88
New Mexico	0.98	0.97	0.35	0.40	0.86	0.84	0.95
New York	0.98	0.68	0.74	0.95	0.99	0.34	0.51
North Carolina	0.96	0.95	0.86	0.97	0.97	0.80	0.99
North Dakota	0.90	0.86	0.82	0.07	0.98	0.74	0.95
Ohio	0.96	0.91	0.88	0.96	0.99	0.67	0.98
Oklahoma	0.98	0.97	0.30	0.04	0.96	0.45	0.97
Oregon	0.98	0.96	−0.14	0.88	0.86	0.78	0.90
Pennsylvania	0.98	0.91	0.63	0.95	1.00	0.45	0.85
Rhode Island	0.92	−0.30	0.63	0.96	0.96	0.04	−0.79
South Carolina	0.98	0.82	0.77	0.96	1.00	0.65	0.89
South Dakota	0.95	0.92	0.79	0.78	0.97	0.80	0.96
Tennessee	0.97	0.94	0.77	0.98	1.00	0.24	0.93
Texas	0.97	0.97	0.05	−0.33	0.97	0.54	0.98

(continued)

TABLE 4.3 *Continued*

	MFP	Output	Input	Land	Labor	Capital	Intermediate Inputs
				classes	Classes of Inputs		

	MFP	Output	Input	Land	Labor	Capital	Intermediate Inputs
Utah	0.97	0.93	0.82	0.85	0.99	0.59	0.93
Vermont	0.92	0.42	0.55	0.98	0.96	0.34	0.84
Virginia	0.97	0.87	0.71	0.98	1.00	0.06	0.93
Washington	0.96	0.95	−0.47	−0.30	0.92	0.77	0.93
West Virginia	0.94	−0.55	0.56	0.97	0.99	−0.05	−0.44
Wisconsin	0.98	0.95	0.66	0.97	1.00	0.75	0.95
Wyoming	0.85	0.87	0.19	0.17	0.98	0.44	0.93

SOURCE: Authors' calculations.

decade, only a handful of geographically scattered states saw an increase in capital services. The patterns of investment in the intermediate years are quite varied across states. With different investment patterns, the cumulative differences in capital services can be quite large. In 1991 Florida was using 2.6 times as much capital as it did in 1949; Arkansas and California each used roughly 1.5 times as much as they did in 1949. In contrast, capital services in 1991 in New York and Pennsylvania had dropped, respectively, to 60 percent and 90 percent of services employed in 1949 (Figure 4.3c).

Although the national trend indicates that purchased inputs were the fastest-growing component of agricultural inputs, this was not so for all states. In 1949 purchased inputs accounted for a national average of 23 percent of total input costs; by 1991 U.S farmers committed about 37 percent of their total costs to these inputs. But for northeastern states such as Connecticut, Massachusetts, New Hampshire, New Jersey, and Rhode Island and the Appalachian state of West Virginia, purchased inputs were smaller in real terms in 1991 than in 1949 (Figure 4.3d). Interestingly, agriculture in these states became more productive despite a contraction in output; the rate of decline in agricultural output in all these states was more than offset by the decline in aggregate inputs, so that measured MFP grew by more than 1 percent per year.

Quality Changes

Figures 4.4a and 4.4b provide an indication of the magnitudes of changes in the quality of land, labor, and some components of capital at the national level. Here we have an implicit quality index that represents a quality-adjusted Divisia index of a particular class of inputs as well as a measure of inputs that simply sums the various components of the respective input aggregate. For labor the unadjusted total is the sum of all hours in agriculture, whether hired, family, or various classes of operator labor; for land it is the total acres in agriculture; and for tractors and combines it is an unweighted sum of machine inventories.

FIGURE 4.2a Selected state and national output indexes, 1949–1991

Index (1949 = 100)

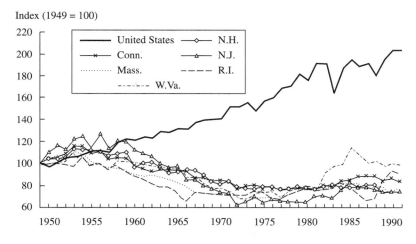

SOURCE: Authors' calculations.

FIGURE 4.2b Selected state and national input indexes, 1949–1991

Index (1949 = 100)

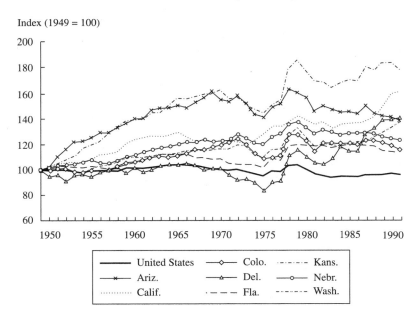

SOURCE: Authors' calculations.

FIGURE 4.3a Selected state and national land indexes, 1949–1991

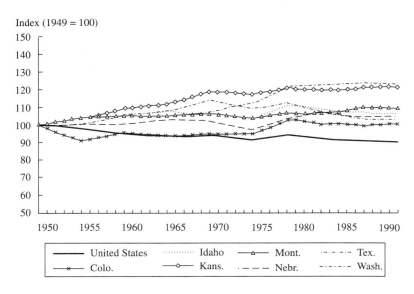

FIGURE 4.3b Selected state and national labor indexes, 1949–1991

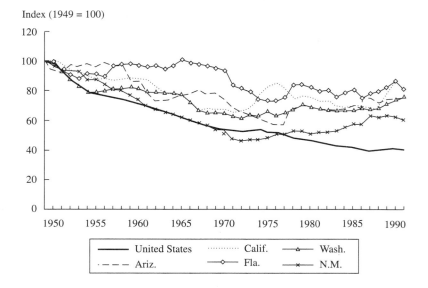

FIGURE 4.3c Selected state and national capital indexes, 1949–1991

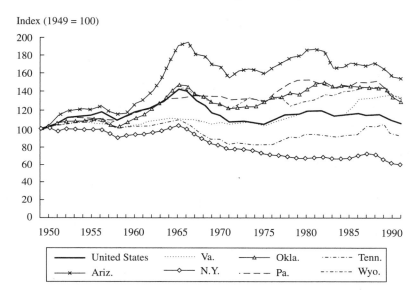

FIGURE 4.3d Selected state and national purchased input indexes, 1949–1991

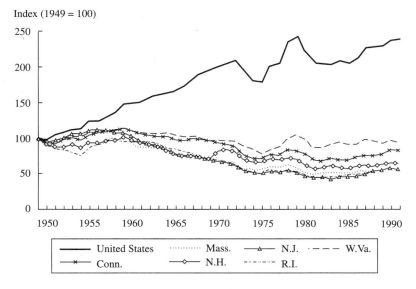

SOURCE: Authors' calculations.

FIGURE 4.4a Implicit land and labor quality indexes, 1949–1991

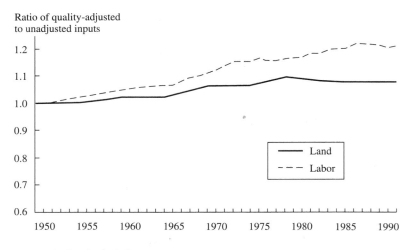

SOURCE: Authors' calculations.

FIGURE 4.4b Implicit tractor and combine quality indexes, 1949–1991

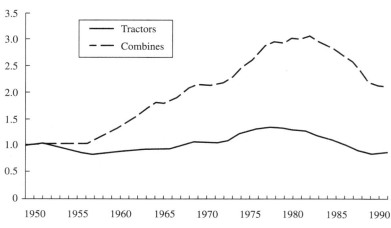

SOURCE: Authors' calculations.

As the composition of the labor force changed to include more-experienced and better-educated farmers, the quality of labor in U.S. agriculture rose by 20 percent in the post–World War II era (Figure 4.4a). Total hours in agriculture in 1991 represented only one-third of the total hours worked in 1949, but accounting for changes in the composition of these hours substantially slows the measured rate of decline in labor input. Our quality-adjusted index of the labor used in U.S. agriculture fell by 2.21 percent per year, compared with 2.68 percent per year for the quality-unadjusted series.

The age and especially the education profiles of farm operators that we have incorporated into our measure of labor changed quite a bit over time. In 1949, 72 percent of the hours worked by farm operators could be attributed to operators with no more than eight years of schooling; in 1991, it was only 12 percent. In 1949, less than 5 percent of operator hours were worked by operators with any college-level education; in 1991 it was 37 percent. The growing share of hours worked by better-educated farm operators partially offsets the decline in total hours worked by all farm labor types.

The mix of labor in agriculture varied substantially in economically significant ways across states and over time; consequently, quality adjustment does not have equally large effects on the measurement of labor inputs in all states. For example, the mix of labor used in California did not change much over our sample. Hired labor always accounted for close to 60 percent of the total cost of labor. Farm operators in California were on average better educated in 1991 than in 1949, but their share in the total labor input was smaller, so that this improvement in operator labor did not affect the total measured labor input as dramatically as it did for the country as a whole. This contrasts sharply with the Great Lakes states, where operator labor accounted for the lion's share of total labor costs. Over the postwar period, operator costs constituted 70 percent of the total, and quality adjustment reduced the measured drop in labor inputs by nearly 0.4 percent.

The effect of disaggregating land types is similar to the effect for labor but muted. Nationally, the rate of decline in land use drops from 0.47 percent to 0.30 percent per year when one controls for the quality mix of land. This is due, in part, to the doubling of irrigated acres in U.S. agriculture over the period from 1949 to 1991. Because irrigated acres still account for a small share of the total, the primary reason for the different picture given by quality adjustment is that, except for the most recent decade in our sample, the acres of land taken out of agriculture were more likely to be lower-quality pasture- and rangeland. In the most recent decade of the series, that trend was reversed in a majority of states and regions, as some relatively high-priced cropland was taken out of agriculture at a faster rate.

It is easy to summarize the implications of quality adjustment of just these two components of agricultural inputs for productivity measurement. Disaggregation to control for the changes in the quality mix within labor and land inputs will *reduce* measured productivity gains in U.S. agriculture because in both these categories average input quality rose, so that quality adjustments meant a greater increase (or smaller decline) in input use over time. The effect of quality adjustment of capital inputs is harder to demonstrate or predict because the alternative to using disaggregated data is much less obvious. If tractors are to be added to combines, there is no economically appealing way to do so without making use of prices and hence some degree of embodied quality adjustment.

For a specific capital class such as tractors, we can take every tractor on every farm to be identical and construct an index of the number of tractors on-farm by scaling yearly totals with base-year inventories. This is analogous to constructing an unadjusted land index, taking all acres in agriculture to be identical. In Figure 4.4b we contrast such an index with a quality-adjusted tractor index that adjusts tractor inventories in each state using what is known about the average age and horsepower of tractors on-farm. We also construct a similar index of combines using information on the relative quality of combines purchased.

Using either index of tractor inventories, the number of tractors on U.S. farms has increased, but quality adjustment halves the measured average rate of growth over our sample by 0.4 percent per year to an average of 0.43 percent per year. Taking service flows to be proportional to these inventories, quality adjustment of tractors would reduce the measured increase in capital services and so *increase* measured growth in productivity over the time period. This is driven primarily by the large drop we measure in tractor services in the 1980s. Tractor sales fell in the country as a whole since the early 1980s, as did the average horsepower of tractors sold.

Figure 4.4b demonstrates a dramatic increase in the quality of combines on U.S. farms. The overall quality of these machines doubled from 1949 to 1991, and during the early 1980s the quality index was three times higher than it was in the immediate post–World War II years. The change in this index reflects a number of aspects. Like tractors, the average age of combines declined during the 1960s and 1970s as sales of these machines accelerated. Slower sales in the 1980s caused an aging in the stock of combines on U.S. farms in the late 1980s. Complementing the effects of accelerating sales in the earlier years (and no doubt a causal factor in this acceleration) was a major technological change, the shift from pull-type to self-propelled combines. In the early years of our sample, virtually all the combines on farms were pull-type machines that were hitched to tractors when in use. Unpublished figures on sales of pull-type combines continued through 1971, but the stock on farms is now almost entirely self-propelled machines. Unlike tractors, the capacity (as indexed by horsepower rating and bin size) of these combines increased fairly steadily, but sales did not follow this same trend.

For any capital group, erratic patterns of investment make it unlikely that quality adjustment will have uniform effects in all time periods or regions. For example, increased tractor and combine purchases in the early 1970s implied only modest increases in the undifferentiated stock of tractors and combines on farms in most states and regions. Because the average quality of tractors and combines was increasing and the average age of tractors on farms was falling in this period, the decade's average annual growth rate in the quality-adjusted tractor stock is far more impressive than that of the unadjusted stock of tractors and combines.

Conclusion

The data reported here represent our efforts to construct a highly disaggregated series of national and state-specific output, input, and MFP measures. In developing these measures we gave special attention to accounting for quality changes embodied in conventional inputs such as land, labor, and capital. Although still subject to data limitations, results suggest that the efforts to incorporate greater detail have yielded fresh perspectives on the pattern of technical change in U.S. agriculture during the post–World War II period. First, accounting for quality change in inputs reduces the national rate of growth in agricultural productivity but does not have a uniform effect on state-specific productivity measures. Second, the use of state-specific data provides ample evidence that the patterns of growth and development within the United States have been quite diverse. Studies of any facet of agricultural production or policy should benefit from similar efforts to deepen the cross-sectional detail in published statistical series, since that information obviously contains some interesting variation that might take decades to uncover in time-series data.

Our efforts to account for quality change in inputs can reduce measured productivity growth but have not explained all the movements in aggregate output. Some of these changes could undoubtedly be tied to technological innovations stemming from industrial R&D; some may represent the effects of the public provision of infrastructure, institutions, and research and extension services. Disentangling the technological from the institutional sources of growth and identifying the public versus private roles will still prove to be difficult. Nevertheless, the extent of variation we have uncovered in state-level data makes us optimistic about finding new empirical insights to guide public policy.

5 Cereal-Crop Productivity in Developing Countries: Past Trends and Future Prospects

PRABHU L. PINGALI AND PAUL W. HEISEY

The past three decades have seen extraordinary growth in cereal-crop productivity in the developing world. Productivity growth has been significant for rice in Asia, wheat in irrigated and favorable production environments worldwide, and maize in Mesoamerica and selected parts of Africa and Asia. A combination of high rates of investment in crop research and appropriate policy support fueled this land productivity. These elements of a Green Revolution strategy improved productivity despite increasing land scarcity and high land values.

In the post–Green Revolution period, increased inputs and, most recently, technical change have sustained productivity growth, particularly in Asia.[1] Recent signs indicate, however, that productivity growth of the primary cereals—rice and wheat—has slowed, especially in the intensively cultivated lowlands of Asia. Degradation of the land resource base resulting from intensive cultivation and a slackening of infrastructure and research investments have curtailed productivity growth. Future increases in productivity growth will require substantial research investments to shift the yield frontier and make cereal-crop production more profitable through greater input efficiency.

A synthesis of the existing evidence on cereal-crop productivity in developing countries and a discussion of future growth follow. Not unexpectedly, the vast majority of studies have measured productivity in terms of yield per hectare. A substantially smaller number of studies use other partial-factor productivity indicators, and a few measure total-factor productivity (TFP) trends.[2] Fewer still are the studies that decompose TFP growth to identify the contributing factors, such as research, policies, and investments in infrastructure. While concerns may exist about data quality, aggregation procedures, and methods used for measuring productivity, comparisons across countries and continents show some rather striking similarities in productivity trends.

---

1. The post–Green Revolution period is difficult to date, but it began in the early to mid-1970s in the most advanced Green Revolution areas.

2. Most of the literature uses the term "total-factor productivity." It is used here as well, even though in most empirical situations some of the factors that produce agricultural output (for example, environmental services) are not measured (Alston, Norton, and Pardey 1995).

56

Partial-Factor Productivity: A Review of the Evidence

Cereal-Crop Productivity Performance and Sources of Growth

Increasing cereal-crop productivity through the application of modern science has been most successful in land-scarce economies, particularly in Asia. Partial productivity and TFP studies conducted in Asia attest to the contribution of biological innovations to increased food production and alleviation of food scarcity. The returns to investments in agricultural research and irrigation infrastructure have been highest in areas of acute land scarcity but good market infrastructure. Rising land values and the rapid adoption of land-augmenting technical change have been the primary factors contributing to productivity growth in much of Asia for both rice and wheat.

The published literature for Latin America and Africa is scant by comparison, but the available evidence suggests a more mixed record. Cereal yields have increased markedly in some Latin American and African countries but varied in others. Given lower population densities compared with Asia, the extent to which governments have invested in market infrastructure and emphasized export-oriented trade has determined the rate of productivity growth. As the demand for cereals became more elastic, through improved access to domestic and export markets, cereal output became more profitable and expanded through the adoption of productivity-enhancing technical change. Cereal-crop productivity growth in Argentina, Brazil, and South Africa can be attributed to the explicit export orientation of the agricultural sectors in these countries.

Cereal-crop output and productivity growth rates have been particularly low in Sub-Saharan Africa over the past three decades. In many parts of the region rapid population growth outstripped the more modest gains in food-crop production. Relative land abundance compared with Asia, poor market infrastructure, and inward-focused trade policy contributed to the modest yield performance of the cereal-crop sector in Sub-Saharan Africa. Farmers in the region, facing an inelastic demand for basic cereals, had little incentive to invest in productivity-promoting technology.

Yield Growth in Rice, Wheat, and Maize

Yield growth is still the most commonly used indicator of productivity growth in developing-country agriculture. Yield growth rates for rice, wheat, and maize are reported in Table 5.1. Rapid yield growth was the primary contributor to rice output growth in 1965–80, a result of the adoption of modern rice varieties. Rice yield growth in Asia declined sharply in the 1980s, however, from an annual rate of 2.84 percent in 1976–85 to 1.39 percent during the 10-year period beginning in 1986. Yield growth in the past decade has been 1.5 percent per year.

For all developing countries, excluding China and India, the two largest wheat producers, wheat yields grew at an average annual rate of 2.09 percent between 1956 and 1995. Wheat yields in China and India grew at a much more rapid rate over this period, especially during the Green Revolution period. Although rates of growth in wheat yields in these countries have declined more recently, they have averaged a minimum of 2 percent per year. Wheat yields in South and East Asia (again excluding China and India) grew at an annual average rate of 2.60 percent over the period 1956–95, displaying much the same pattern over time as India but with greater reductions in recent years. Latin America lagged behind with a yield growth rate of 1.80 percent per year. In West Asia and North Africa and Sub-Saharan Africa yield growth has varied over time and displayed a less consistent pattern.

Maize performed the worst of the three major cereal crops during 1956–95, with particularly poor growth rates in Sub-Saharan Africa (Table 5.1). Maize yields in developing countries, excluding the commercialized producers —China, Brazil, Argentina, Chile, and South Africa—which plant a majority of their maize area to hybrids, grew at less than 2 percent a year between 1956 and 1995. Moreover, maize growth rates differed from those for rice and wheat, strengthening in some regions toward the end of this period and fluctuating more particularly in Sub-Saharan Africa. The predominantly rainfed nature of maize production in Africa, along with its subsistence orientation, accounts for the crop's low and variable rate of growth in the region over the past three decades.

Changes in Partial-Factor Productivity of Land and Labor

Asian economies that started with low land and labor productivities in the 1950s and early 1960s are on a trajectory toward high land and labor productivities. The extent of movement toward high land and labor productivities is conditioned by the extent of land scarcity and the level of economic development. Comparisons of land and labor productivities for Latin America and Africa do not show a clear pattern.

Increases in land productivity have come about from the intensification of agricultural production and the adoption of yield-enhancing technologies, especially modern, high-yielding varieties (HYVs) and fertilizers. The transition from low-yield, land-extensive cultivation systems to land-intensive, double- and triple-crop systems is most profitable only in those societies in which the land frontier has been exhausted (Boserup 1965; Hayami and Ruttan 1985; Pingali and Binswanger 1987). Where population densities are low, the returns to intensification are high only if export markets are available and accessible. Otherwise, labor and other costs associated with intensive agriculture are substantially higher than the incremental returns to intensification. This holds true even with the adoption of labor-saving technologies.

TABLE 5.1 Annual rates of growth in yield for major cereals in developing countries, 1956–1995

Region/Country	1956–95	1956–65	1966–75	1976–85	1986–95
	(percentage per year)				
Rice					
Asia	1.83	0.72	1.83	2.84	1.39
Southeast Asia	2.16	1.07	2.86	3.57	2.48
South Asia	1.49	0.01	1.93	2.89	2.48
China	2.70	1.29	1.45	4.89	1.39
India	2.02	1.41	2.25	2.79	3.00
Wheat					
Less-developed countries (excluding China and India)	2.09	1.51	2.35	2.32	1.12
South, East, and Southeast Asia (excluding China and India)	2.60	0.90	5.04	2.19	1.43
West Asia and North Africa	2.10	0.68	1.87	1.43	1.07
Latin America	1.80	3.54	1.90	4.58	1.59
Sub-Saharan Africa	2.44	2.79	3.56	−0.06	1.93
China	4.58	−0.70	4.66	7.32	2.08
India	3.45	2.33	4.59	3.58	2.58
Maize					
Less-developed countries (excluding China, Brazil, Argentina, Chile)	1.65	1.75	1.01	3.00	2.05
South, East, and Southeast Asia (excluding China)	1.70	1.23	1.43	2.96	2.26
West Asia and North Africa	2.75	3.74	1.85	2.52	2.28
Latin America (excluding Brazil, Argentina, Chile)	2.26	3.14	1.48	3.70	3.01
Sub-Saharan Africa (excluding South Africa)	1.04	0.41	1.93	−0.26	0.17
China	3.83	0.09	4.10	4.84	3.30
Brazil	1.68	0.68	1.47	2.62	4.29
Argentina	2.61	0.29	2.43	2.29	3.58
South Africa	1.81	1.08	4.67	−3.46	−2.27

SOURCE: Authors' calculations from Food and Agriculture Organization (FAO) data; http://apps.fao.org/cgi_bin/nph-db.pl?subset-agriculture.

Much of South and Southeast Asia made the transition to land-intensive production systems in the 1950s and 1960s. East Asia made this transition earlier (Barker and Herdt 1985; Bray 1986). A cross-sectional comparison of Asian countries shows that the use of irrigation, HYVs of cereal crops, especially rice and wheat, and fertilizer is positively related to population density (Pingali, Hossain, and Gerpacio 1997).

Agroclimatic population densities also affect land use and technology adoption patterns. An apparently land-abundant country such as Niger, for example, has an extremely high agroclimatic population density because most of its land is of very poor quality.

The available evidence relating population pressure to land augmentation outside Asia is fragmentary and mixed. Block's (1993) study of Sub-Saharan Africa shows that, indeed, output grew the most in densely populated eastern Africa during 1963–88. Likewise, Thirtle, Hadley, and Townsend (1995) demonstrate high growth rates in agricultural-sector TFP in densely populated Rwanda and Burundi. Beyond that, however, few apparent relations exist between agroclimatic population densities and regional growth in TFP. The lack of further relationship may stem in part from the widely differing population pressures among African countries grouped in the same subregion. Another explanation could be that countries with low land quality, such as many of those in the Sahel, have relatively high populations relative to available fertile land but fewer agricultural technology options at present (Sanders, Shapiro, and Ramaswamy 1996).

Increases in labor productivity in Asia are associated with the increasing adoption of labor-saving technologies, both as a means of saving on the higher labor needs of intensification and a means of economizing on labor as its opportunity cost rises with economic growth. The movement from single-crop cultivation systems to double- and triple-crop systems increases the demand for labor and also increases the demand for timely completion of farming operations (Barker and Cordova 1978). A recent comparison of labor requirements in the irrigated and rainfed rice production systems in six Asian countries indicates that adoption of modern varieties in favorable environments significantly increases labor use per hectare by raising labor requirements for crop care, harvesting, and threshing (David and Otsuka 1994).

Initially, the switch to modern varieties is profitable, even with higher labor requirements per hectare, because the labor requirements per ton of paddy are lower compared with those for traditional varieties (Barker and Cordova 1978). Over time, however, increasing labor demand for peak-period operations leads to a rise in real wages for these operations, even in densely populated, labor-surplus countries such as India (Bardhan 1970; Lal 1976) and Indonesia (Naylor 1992). The rise in wages is further exacerbated by the concurrent growth in the rural nonfarm sector and increasing employment opportunities in the urban sector, as happened in Japan and Korea and is now taking place in Southeast Asia.

Widespread adoption of labor-saving mechanical and chemical technologies alleviates the growing labor constraints and contributes substantially to overall productivity growth (Sidhu and Byerlee 1992). The most notable confirmation of this hypothesis comes from the now developed Japan, where labor productivity has risen substantially in the past 30 years but land productivity has shown almost no increase (Craig, Pardey, and Roseboom 1997; Hayami and Ruttan 1985).

Changes in Input Use for Cereals

The assessment of overall growth in cereal-crop productivity requires information on trends in use of other (that is, nonland, nonlabor) factors of production, such as fertilizers, and trends in crop-specific TFP. The issue is one of identifying whether the rate of growth in output is greater than the rate of growth in aggregate input use.

In the case of rice, national data across Asia indicate that the rate of growth in yields has been substantially smaller than the rate of growth in fertilizer use over the past three decades (Pingali et al. 1997). Consider three intensively cultivated rice bowls of Southeast Asia—central Luzon, the Philippines; central plains, Thailand; and West Java, Indonesia—for the period 1980–89. In Central Luzon, a 13 percent yield increase over a 10-year period was achieved with a 21 percent increase in fertilizers and a 34 percent increase in seeds. In the Central Plains yields increased by 6.5 percent, while fertilizer rates increased by 24 percent and pesticides by 53 percent. Similarly for West Java, yields increased by 23 percent, while fertilizer use increased by 65 percent and pesticide use by 69 percent (Pingali 1992).

In the case of wheat, factor-use trends were assessed by Sidhu and Byerlee (1992) for the Indian Punjab between 1972 and 1989 and Kumar and Mruthyunjaya (1992) for five major Indian wheat-producing states between 1971 and 1989. These states constitute 80 percent of India's wheat area and just under 90 percent of wheat production. Kumar and Mruthyunjaya found that the use of modern inputs of fertilizer and machine power grew during this period in all the states studied, and at faster rates in the irrigated heartland. Manure use fell in most states, but pesticide use rose in some. Labor use fell in all states; animal labor fell precipitously. Seeding rates rose in three of the five states. (Sidhu and Byerlee [1992] found trends in the Punjab that were consistent with Kumar and Mruthyunjaya for that state.)

By the late 1980s, the most advanced post–Green Revolution areas of Asia, such as the Punjab of India and Central Luzon of the Philippines, had reached a point of sharply diminishing returns to further intensification with conventional inputs and had entered a second post–Green Revolution phase characterized by the use of better knowledge and management skills instead of ever higher levels of conventional inputs (Byerlee and Pingali 1994). In this post–Green Revolution phase, productivity gains accrued from the timing and method rather than the amount of input use (Byerlee 1987; Pingali, Moya, and Velasco 1990). Over time, technical knowledge and management skill have become the primary determinants of differences in productivity and profits among farmers.

Varietal selection, fertilizer timing and placement, water use, and pesticide application are some areas in which efficiency gains can lower unit production costs. It should be recognized, however, that the adoption of knowledge-intensive technologies requires farmers to trade reductions in inputs against a higher time commitment to management and supervision. A farmer's incentives for adopting techniques that increase input efficiency thus depend on the relation between price of inputs and the opportunity cost of time.

For both South and Southeast Asia, the primary unexploited avenue for further productivity growth is in enhancing input efficiency through the use of knowledge-based technologies. The importance of input efficiency in Asia has been reinforced by evidence of significant problems in sustaining the quality of the resource base for intensive rice production systems (Cassman and Pingali 1995; Pingali and Rosegrant 1993). These sustainability problems are most evident in the rapid decline in partial-factor productivities, especially for nitrogen fertilizer, and the leveling off and decline in the growth of TFP. In other words, the yield gains achieved in the post–Green Revolution period are being maintained by increasingly higher quantities of inputs to compensate for degradation of the lowland resource base (Byerlee and Siddiq 1994; Cassman and Pingali 1995).

TFP Growth in Developing-Country Agriculture

The partial-factor productivity measures discussed earlier do not provide a complete picture of the impact of technological change on cereal-crop production systems. A partial productivity measure such as yield may increase over time because of some fundamental change in the production process or because of the increased use of inputs such as fertilizer or water. TFP trends over time can help clear up the ambiguities about sources of yield growth. TFP is calculated by dividing an output index by an input index. This allows changes in output over time to be partitioned into changes resulting from increased input use and changes in TFP. A few studies (for example, Arnade 1992; Fan 1991; Thirtle, Hadley, and Townsend 1995) divide TFP further, into a technical progress component and an efficiency gain component. These simple decompositions will be the basis for most of the following discussion.[3]

---

3. Nonetheless, there are many complicating issues and alternative approaches to the analysis of TFP. The first is to bear in mind the relationship between TFP and the aggregate agricultural

Empirical Studies of TFP Growth in Developing-Country Agriculture

Few examples exist of crop-specific TFP measurements. The exceptions include Cassman and Pingali (1995) and Pardey et al. (1992) for rice and Sidhu and Byerlee (1992) and Kumar and Mruthyunjaya (1992) for wheat. A number of TFP studies, however, track productivity growth for the aggregate crops sector or the aggregate agricultural sector. TFP estimates for aggregate crop output are widely available for Asia. Studies for Latin America and Africa, with a few exceptions, estimate TFP for the aggregate agricultural sector. Because technical change in developing-country agriculture is known to have affected cereal staples, to a considerable extent these aggregate TFP estimates partially reflect the technical change that has taken place in cereal production.

Several observations emerge from Table 5.2, which compares TFP estimates for agriculture in developed countries. First, agricultural output growth in developing countries has been overwhelmingly positive and positively related to growth in TFP (see Figure 5.1). On average, 40–45 percent of measured output growth in the studies reported in Table 5.2 results from growth in TFP. In many industrialized countries, on the other hand, growth in TFP has accounted for all the growth in agricultural output in a simple accounting framework; input use in agriculture has actually contracted (see, for example, Ball et al. 1997; Cox, Mullen, and Hu 1996; Narayanan 1996; Shane, Roe, and Gopinath 1998). Preliminary broad hypotheses relating TFP growth and output growth are summarized in Figure 5.2.

Second, some studies (for example, Fernandez-Cornejo and Shumway 1997; Rosegrant and Evenson 1995) show higher growth rates in TFP at times

---

production function (Hayami and Ruttan 1985; Lal and Yotopoulos 1989; Trueblood 1991). If the underlying production function is not constant returns to scale, changes in aggregate output may be caused by scale effects as well as by changes in input levels, technical progress, and changes in efficiency (Arnade 1992; Capalbo 1988). Furthermore, it is almost always impossible to define and measure all the inputs and outputs in the agricultural production process (Alston, Norton, and Pardey 1995).

Second, aggregation procedures and shifts in relative prices can be problematic for studies that make intercountry comparisons, or for analyses that compare the agricultural sector with other sectors in the same country. Two major approaches to output aggregation for international comparisons are the physical "wheat units" aggregation (Hayami and Ruttan 1985) and the method of first creating an index of real national-level output, then converting it to a common currency using exchange rates based on agricultural purchasing power parities (PPP) (Pardey, Roseboom, and Craig 1992).

Quality differences and quality changes in outputs, and particularly in inputs, can cause both conceptual and measurement problems. One major issue is the endogeneity of land and labor quality to past investments in infrastructure and education. A related issue is whether input quality differences in a given period or over time are accounted for by price differentials (Arnade 1994; Binswanger, Khandker, and Rosenzweig 1993; Craig, Pardey, and Roseboom 1997).

Finally, data limitations often hamper attempts to empiricize some of the more complex constructs pertaining to changes over time in agricultural output, input use, technical change, efficiency, and the like. This is a particular problem for developing countries.

TABLE 5.2 Evidence on productivity growth in developing-country agriculture for all crops, 1947–1991

Country	Time Period	Output Growth	Input Growth	TFP Growth	Aggregation Procedures	Indexing Methods	Reference
		(percentage per year)					
India	1950–60	3.9	2.0	1.9	Wheat units		Galgalikar and Alshi (1987)
	1961–70	2.8	1.8	1.0			As above
	1971–80	2.9	1.8	1.1	Wheat units		As above
	1950–80	2.9	1.8	1.1	Wheat units		As above
	1956–67	2.2	1.1	1.1		Törnqvist–Theil TFP	Rosegrant and Evenson (1995)
	1967–76	2.7	1.3	1.4		As above	As above
	1976–86	2.1	1.0	1.1		As above	As above
	1956–65			0.81		Törnqvist–Theil TFP	Rosegrant and Evenson (1993)
	1965–75			1.22		As above	As above
	1975–85			0.98		As above	As above
Pakistan	1950–55	1.8	1.6	0.22	Wheat units		Ahmed (1987)
	1955–60	2.3	1.8	0.60			
	1960–65	3.7	2.4	1.40			
	1965–70	5.1	2.3	2.78			
	1970–78	2.7	2.3	0.47			
	1978–83	4.0	2.4	1.58			
Pakistan	1956–65			1.65		Törnqvist–Theil TFP	Rosegrant and Evenson (1993)
	1965–75			1.86		As above	As above
	1975–85			−0.36		As above	As above
Philippines	1950–60	5.0	3.5	1.5			David, Barker, and Palacpac (1987)
	1960–70	3.2	2.4	0.8			
	1970–80	6.3	4.6	1.7			
Thailand	1951–61	7.4	3.0	4.4	Wheat units		Budhaka (1987)

Country	Period						Author
Bangladesh	1961–71	4.5	3.0	1.5	Törnqvist-Theil		Dey and Evenson (1991)
	1971–81	5.4	3.5	1.9			
	1960–70			1.3			
	1970–80			–0.09			
	1980–89			0.79			
Republic of Taiwan	1951–66	4.6	2.5	2.1	Laspeyres index (annual chain formula)	Constant prices 1965–67: base period	Yueh-eh Chen in APO (1987)
	1951–58	4.4	2.5	1.9			
	1958–62	2.7	1.6	1.1			
	1962–66	6.6	3.1	3.5			
	1966–75	1.5	0.4	1.1			
	1966–71	1.7	–0.1	1.8			
	1971–75	1.3	1.1	0.2			
	1975–81	0.2	2.5	2.7			
	1975–78	1.1	–2.1	3.2			
	1978–81	–0.7	–2.9	2.2			
	1951–81	2.7	0.8	1.9			
China	a) 1965–79			0.19	Production elasticities		S. Fan (1990)
	1980–86			3.18			
	1965–85			1.14			
	b) 1965–79			2.23	Factor shares		S. Fan (1990)
	1980–86			5.15			
	1965–85			3.11			
	1970–78			–0.71			Kalirajan et al. (1996)
	1978–84			1.24			
	1984–87			0.91			
Brazil	1968–87	3.96	2.25	1.71	Törnqvist (unchained) constant returns to scale	Price weights	Arnade (1992)

(continued)

TABLE 5.2 *Continued*

Country	Time Period	Output Growth	Input Growth	TFP Growth	Aggregation Procedures	Indexing Methods	Reference
Mexico (all agriculture)	1960–91	4.1	1.3	2.8	Price weights	Törnqvist (chained)	Fernandez-Cornejo and Shumway (1997)
South Africa (all agriculture)	1947–91	3.0	1.8	1.2	Revenue shares	Törnqvist (chained)	Thirtle et al. (1993a)
Zimbabwe (commercial agriculture)	1970–89	2.86	−0.56	3.43	Price weights	Törnqvist (chained)	Thirtle et al. (1993b)
Zimbabwe (communal agriculture)	1975–90	7.32	2.56	4.76	Price weights	Törnqvist (chained)	Thirtle et al. (1993b)

For the following countries, estimates are for aggregate agriculture (crops and livestock)

Country	Time Period	Output Growth	Input Growth	TFP Growth	Aggregation Procedures	Indexing Methods	Reference
Burkina Faso	1971–86	3.77	2.20	1.57	ppp conversion	Malmquist index (chained)	Thirtle, Hadley, and Townsend (1995)
Burundi	1971–86	1.24	−1.44	2.68	ppp conversion	Malmquist index (chained)	Thirtle, Hadley, and Townsend (1995)
Cameroon	1971–86	1.65	0.67	0.98	ppp conversion	Malmquist index (chained)	Thirtle, Hadley, and Townsend (1995)
Central African Republic	1971–86	2.16	0.40	1.76	ppp conversion	Malmquist index (chained)	Thirtle, Hadley, and Townsend (1995)
Congo	1971–86	2.01	3.41	−1.40	ppp conversion	Malmquist index (chained)	Thirtle, Hadley, and Townsend (1995)
Ethiopia	1971–86	1.30	0.56	0.74	ppp conversion	Malmquist index (chained)	Thirtle, Hadley, and Townsend (1995)
Ghana	1971–86	−0.49	−1.07	0.58	ppp conversion	Malmquist index (chained)	Thirtle, Hadley, and Townsend (1995)
Côte d'Ivoire	1971–86	3.92	2.62	1.30	ppp conversion	Malmquist index (chained)	Thirtle, Hadley, and Townsend (1995)

Country	Period					
Kenya	1971–86	3.25	2.66	0.59	ppp conversion	Malmquist index (chained)	Thirtle, Hadley, and Townsend (1995)
Malawi	1971–86	2.41	1.84	0.57	ppp conversion	Malmquist index (chained)	Thirtle, Hadley, and Townsend (1995)
Mali	1971–86	3.31	1.11	2.20	ppp conversion	Malmquist index (chained)	Thirtle, Hadley, and Townsend (1995)
Nigeria	1971–86	1.40	0.39	1.01	ppp conversion	Malmquist index (chained)	Thirtle, Hadley, and Townsend (1995)
Rwanda	1971–86	3.98	0.82	3.16	ppp conversion	Malmquist index (chained)	Thirtle, Hadley, and Townsend (1995)
Senegal	1971–86	0	0.04	−0.04	ppp conversion	Malmquist index (chained)	Thirtle, Hadley, and Townsend (1995)
Sierra Leone	1971–86	1.59	1.27	0.32	ppp conversion	Malmquist index (chained)	Thirtle, Hadley, and Townsend (1995)
Sudan	1971–86	1.93	2.24	−0.31	ppp conversion	Malmquist index (chained)	Thirtle, Hadley, and Townsend (1995)
Tanzania	1971–86	3.19	1.15	2.04	ppp conversion	Malmquist index (chained)	Thirtle, Hadley, and Townsend (1995)
Togo	1971–86	1.73	1.65	0.08	ppp conversion	Malmquist index (chained)	Thirtle, Hadley, and Townsend (1995)
Zambia	1971–86	0.89	1.87	−0.98	ppp conversion	Malmquist index (chained)	Thirtle, Hadley, and Townsend (1995)
Zaire	1971–86	2.28	0.74	1.54	ppp conversion	Malmquist index (chained)	Thirtle, Hadley, and Townsend (1995)
Zimbabwe	1971–86	1.08	0.78	0.30	ppp conversion	Malmquist index (chained)	Thirtle, Hadley, and Townsend (1995)

NOTE: ppp denotes purchasing power parity.

FIGURE 5.1 Contribution of TFP growth to output growth in developing-country agriculture

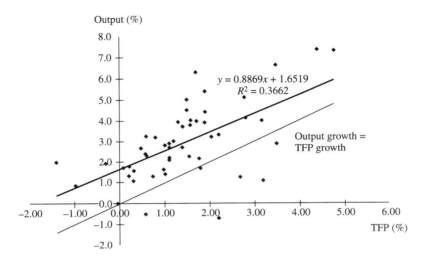

SOURCE: Table 5.2.

of known, rapid technological change, such as the rapid diffusion of HYVs and fertilizer. In other countries, TFP growth rates were high *before* classic Green Revolutions; and in still others, TFP grew rapidly where no such easily defined Green Revolutions took place. Studies using greater disaggregation (for example, Murgai 1997; Sidhu and Byerlee 1992) sometimes show that TFP growth

FIGURE 5.2 Hypothetical output growth and TFP contribution to output growth by factor endowments and market infrastructure

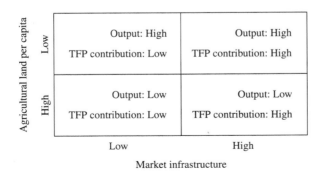

SOURCE: Arnade (1994).

rates can be higher in immediate post–Green Revolution periods than during the initial diffusion of seed-fertilizer technology. These studies suggest that TFP growth decreases during technology diffusion because of extremely rapid input growth during such periods. In post–Green Revolution periods, TFP can grow more rapidly because input growth slackens while the efficiency of input use increases. Still other authors of disaggregated studies (for example, Ali 1998; Ali and Velasco 1993; Cassman and Pingali 1995) find evidence of agricultural resource degradation accompanying recent slow growth or negative trends in TFP. Some studies (for example, Arnade 1992; Block 1993; Fan 1991; Kalirajan, Obwona, and Zhao 1996; Lin 1992) discover relatively short periods of rapid increases in agricultural TFP associated with major policy reforms. In all these cases, TFP evidence can provide strong support to an author's argument but cannot clinch the case. The discussion now turns to some of the empirical studies that analyze causes of differences in growth rates over time and across regions and the relative importance of those causes.

Sources of TFP Growth in Developing-Country Agriculture

Table 5.3 reports the results of studies that formally decompose sources of growth in agricultural TFP in developing countries or use regression analysis to explore these sources without a formal decomposition. Though the studies cover different periods and countries and use different methodologies, several common themes emerge.

The studies show the importance of agricultural research. This is the most commonly cited source of productivity growth, and its effect is nearly always found to be positive and quantitatively important. A few authors (for example, Evenson and McKinsey 1991; Fernandez-Cornejo and Shumway 1997; Rosegrant and Evenson 1995) analyze the effects of direct research and research spillovers separately; Evenson and colleagues sometimes further distinguish between public and private research.

Relatively few studies look at efficiency changes over time, although a slightly larger number look at the related area of the effects of policy changes. These studies (for example, Arnade 1992; Fan 1991; Lin 1992; Thirtle, Hadley, and Townsend 1995), as well as related studies that do not formally decompose TFP growth (Block 1993; Kalirajan, Obwona, and Zhao 1996), suggest that relatively strong gains through technical change can sometimes be partially or even totally offset through increased inefficiencies. They also find that policy reform can have a strong positive effect on productivity growth. This effect, however, is usually relatively short term (three to five years).

Infrastructure is another less studied but interesting and complicated determinant of TFP growth in developing-country agriculture. Some proxy variables for infrastructure include market density and irrigation. In the studies cited in Table 5.3, these proxy variables have mixed but usually positive effects. Accounting for infrastructural effects on TFP growth is an important

TABLE 5.3 Decomposition of agricultural productivity growth, 1950–1990

Country or Region	Time Period	Crop or Sector	Sources	Annual Growth	Share TFP Growth Explained	Reference
China	1965–85	Aggregate agriculture	Institutional change		62.9	S. Fan (1991)
			Technological change		37.1	
	1978–84	Aggregate agriculture	Household farming reform		46.89	J.Y. Lin (1992)
			Multicropping		1.94	
			Ratio of nongrain crops		3.69	
	1984–87	Aggregate agriculture	Household farming reform	0		
			Multicropping	20.90		
			Ratio of nongrain crops	27.79		
India	1971–88	Rice	Research	5.86	57.2	Kumar and Rosegrant (1994)
			Markets	5.60	14.4	
			P_2O_5:N ratio	1.87	9.9	
			Agricultural terms of trade	−1.56	18.9	
			Canal share in total irrigation	−0.56	0.3	
India (5 states)	1970–88	Wheat	Market infrastructure		High	Kumar and Mruthyunjaya (1992)
			Literacy		Negative	
			Research		High	
			Mechanization		High	
			January–March rainfall		Intermediate	

Region	Period	Type	Variable	Value	Value	Source
India (10 states)	1972–82	Crops	HYV expansion	38?		Evenson and McKinsey (1991)
			Public research	18?		
			Private research	36?		
			Irrigation	<1?		
			Markets	1?		
India	1956–87	Crops	Modern varieties	7		Rosegrant and Evenson (1991)
			Foreign research	25		
			Domestic public research	25		
			Domestic private research	15		
			Extension	33		
			Infrastructure	10		
			Residual	–15		
India (irrigated districts)	1956–64	Crops	HYV area	0	0	Fan and Hazell (1997)
			Road density	1.94	Low	
			Literacy	2.55	Negative	
			Irrigation	0	0	
	1967–77		HYV area	19.58	High	
			Road density	3.94	Low	
			Literacy	2.05	Negative	
			Irrigation	0.12	Low	
	1978–90		HYV area	3.38	Negative	Fan and Hazell (1997)
			Road density	2.87	Low	
			Literacy	2.29	Negative	
			Irrigation	1.20	Medium	
India (rainfed districts)	1956–64	Crops	HYV area	0	0	
			Road density	2.60	Low	
			Literacy	2.44	Negative	
			Irrigation	0.93	High	

(continued)

TABLE 5.3 *Continued*

Country or Region	Time Period	Crop or Sector	Sources	Annual Growth	Share TFP Growth Explained	Reference
India (rainfed districts) (*continued*)	1967–77		HYV area	20.41	High	Dholakia and Dholakia (1993)
			Road density	5.45	Low	
			Literacy	1.90	Negative	
			Irrigation	3.64	High	
	1978–90		HYV area	4.92	Low	
			Road density	3.30	Low	
			Literacy	1.91	Negative	
			Irrigation	3.29	High	
India	1950–88	Aggregate agriculture	Use of modern inputs (irrigation, fertilizer, HYV)		High	
Pakistan	1955–85	Crops	Modern varieties		Important	Rosegrant and Evenson (1993)
			Research		Important	
			Infrastructure		Important	
			Human capital		Important	
Brazil	1968–89	Crops	Efficiency changes		–3,100	Arnade (1992)
			Technical progress		800	
			Scale effects		2,200	
	1980–83	Crops	Efficiency changes		38	
			Technical progress		16	
			Scale effects		46	

Country/Region	Years	Sector	Factor	Value	Source
	1984–87	Crops	Efficiency changes	−1,325	
			Technical progress	375	
			Scale effects	1,050	
Sub-Saharan Africa—22 countries	1971–86	Aggregate agriculture	Efficiency changes	−60	Thirtle, Hadley, and Townsend (1995)
			Technical progress	160	
Sub-Saharan Africa—22 countries	1971–86	Aggregate agriculture	Modern inputs	Low	Thirtle, Hadley, and Townsend (1995)
			Infrastructure	High	
			Research, extension, and education	High	
			Policy	High	
			Weather	High	
Sub-Saharan Africa—22 countries	1971–86	Aggregate agriculture (technical progress only)	Tractor	Positive	Thirtle, Hadley, and Townsend (1995)
			Labor/land ratio	Positive	
			Research	Positive	
			Secondary education	Positive	
Zimbabwe	1970–89	Commercial agriculture	Research and extension	>90%	Thirtle et al. (1993b)

example of the problem of endogeneity. Do markets and irrigation investment tend to flow to areas with relatively high agricultural potential and thus to areas where, a priori, one would expect TFP growth to be higher?[4]

Finally, the few studies that have looked at the relationships between education or agricultural extension and TFP generally have found mixed effects and even found the opposite of the expected sign. In these cases, as in the others cited earlier, factors that affect TFP are often chosen as the result of a particular research interest. Few studies begin with an explicit theoretical consideration of what factors might drive TFP changes in agriculture, other than the common presupposition that investment in knowledge generation, through agricultural research, contributes to technical progress. Though a consensus exists that agricultural research and infrastructure, as well as improvements in agricultural efficiency, drive growth in agricultural TFP, a number of unanswered questions remain about the sources of such growth.[5]

A comprehensive approach to analyzing TFP growth in developing-country agriculture awaits considerable future research.

Prospects for Further Cereal Productivity Growth

Virtually all future output growth in Asia must come from increased yield per unit of land because the opportunities for further area expansion are minimal. This is increasingly the case for many countries in Africa and Latin America as well. In other countries, such as Brazil, Sudan, Zambia, or Angola, potential for land expansion at the margin still exists. In general, evidence continues to mount that the growth in cereal yields has leveled off, especially in the irrigated lowlands of Asia. There is a danger that yields will decline in the future (Pingali et al. 1990). When countries are stratified by cropping intensities, it turns out that the rate of deceleration in yields is higher for countries with higher cropping intensities (Pingali et al. 1997). These countries invariably have exhausted the land frontier where output growth was sought through land-augmenting technical change. China, Korea, and the Philippines are examples. But some countries experienced rapid yield growth during the 1980s. The growth came from an increase in intensification in low-intensity countries such as Laos, Nepal, and Cambodia. India and Vietnam were exceptions to the declining trends. In the former case, an increase in irrigation infrastructure in the 1980s boosted yields (Rosegrant and Pingali 1994), and in the latter case policy reforms of the mid-1980s contributed to growth increases (Pingali and Xuan 1992).

---

4. In a paper accounting for output growth, not TFP growth, in India, Binswanger, Khandker, and Rosenzweig (1993) argue that this is indeed the case.

5. Agricultural production function studies using nonconventional inputs suggest that better results might be obtained if technical education were used rather than general education (Trueblood 1991).

The plateauing of cereal yields that hit most of the developing countries occurred because the yield gap between technological potential and farm-level yields has narrowed considerably and because of unfavorable relative prices and the deterioration of the land resource base. World cereal prices have trended down in real terms since 1900 (Mitchell and Ingco 1995). In the case of rice, the declining price has shifted land out of rice and into more profitable cropping alternatives and slowed the growth in input use and yields. Probably more important in the long run, the declining world price has caused a slow-down in investment in rice research and irrigation infrastructure (these issues are discussed in detail in Rosegrant and Pingali 1994). Investment in research on other cereal crops such as wheat has also decreased (Maredia and Byerlee, 1999; Traxler, Byerlee, and Jain 1996).

Exploitable Yield Potential

What exactly does exploitable yield potential mean? The agronomic yield potential, determined on experiment stations, which often reside on the best land in a region and have reliable irrigation water supply, is the maximum achievable yield with no physical, biological, and economic constraints. This maximum experimental yield (which also indicates the technology potential) reflects the knowledge frontier and best-known management practices at any given time. When the objective is changed from maximizing yields to max-imizing profits, the yields obtained by experiment station researchers are sig-nificantly lower than the maximum attainable yields (Herdt 1988). For a given location and set of prices, the yield that maximizes profit is called the exploit-able yield potential.

Although national average yields are used to gauge farm-level perfor-mance, a more reasonable measure of farm performance is the yield from provinces or districts where particular technologies and environments domi-nate. Consider the state of the Punjab, the most important agricultural state in India and the center of the Green Revolution for rice and wheat. The average rice yield in the Punjab is around 5 metric tons per hectare, which is more than twice the Indian national average and only around 2 tons lower than the technological potential. A comparison of experiment station yields with farmer yields in the same geographic area that minimizes agroclimatic and biophysi-cal differences shows that the gap between what is achievable and what is actually achieved is small. Studies in the Philippines have shown that more than a third of the farmers in the "rice bowl" provinces of Laguna and Nueva Ecija have been matching the best yields on neighboring experiment stations since 1980 (Pingali, Moya, and Velasco 1990).

In the high-potential irrigated rice areas across Asia, the economically exploitable gap between the technology frontier and farmer performance is small. Given current technology and relative price levels, it is not profitable for farmers in these environments to bridge this gap further. Accordingly the yield gains in the "rice granary" provinces across Asia have leveled off. Dramatic shifts in productivity resembling the growth of the 1960s and 1970s can occur in these high-potential areas only if new rice varieties with substantial improvement in yield potential are developed.

In intensively cultivated irrigated wheat areas, such as the Yaqui Valley of Mexico or in parts of Asia, a similar reduction of the economically exploitable yield gap can be observed. In other areas, including other parts of irrigated Asia such as Pakistan, economically exploitable yield increases in wheat are still possible. There are far fewer regions in the developing world where maize appears to be near its economic yield potential.

Intensification-Induced Decline in Cereal Crop Productivity

Does intensification of land use, independent of world price effects, lead to a long-term decline in cereal-crop productivity? Pingali et al. (1997) argue that the practice of intensive rice monoculture contributes to the degradation of the paddy resource base and hence to declining productivity. A positive relationship between intensification and productivity declines for wheat is most apparent where wheat is grown in rotation with another cereal, such as in the rice-wheat systems in Asia. Intensive maize production is more likely to be associated with productivity declines in hilly areas prone to erosion or in parts of eastern and southern Africa, such as Malawi, where a near maize monoculture has arisen.

Long-term experiment-station data show that under intensive rice monoculture systems productivity is difficult to sustain, even with the best scientific management (Cassman and Pingali 1993). One should, therefore, expect similar declines in productivity in the intensively cultivated irrigated lowlands of Asia that have been under rice monoculture systems over the past two decades.

At the farm level, declining yield trends are difficult to observe because input levels are not held constant over time. However, in areas where intensive rice monoculture has been practiced over the past two to three decades, stagnant yields, declining trends in partial-factor productivities, especially for fertilizers, or declining trends in TFPs are evident (Cassman and Pingali 1993; Pingali 1992; Pingali, Moya, and Velasco 1990).

Prospects for Shifting the Yield Frontier in Cereals

Pingali, Hossain, and Gerpacio (1997) have presented evidence that the yield potential of modern semidwarf rice varieties has remained relatively stagnant since the release of IR-8 in 1965. While subsequent varieties have shown marked improvement in pest resistance, grain quality, and reduced crop duration, yields have increased only marginally. Recent progress in plant-breeding research indicates that the yield frontier could be shifted significantly both in the medium and longer terms. In the medium term, yield increases of around 20 percent may be possible through the adoption of hybrid rice (Virmani, Khush, and Pingali 1993). The longer-term prognosis is for a "new plant type" that could yield about 12.5–13 metric tons per hectare and, if used as a parent for improved hybrids, could increase this yield to 15 metric tons per hectare (Khush 1995). While the prospects are good for the generation of new seed technologies, research and adaptation work is by no means complete. High levels of research investments need to continue in order to make widespread farmer adoption a reality. To secure productivity growth in rice, the new seed technologies ought to be complemented by continued investments in irrigation and other rice-related infrastructure. Moreover, profitable adoption of new seed technologies will require intense use of inputs, especially fertilizers and herbicides, otherwise yield will fall short of the potential of the new varieties. The implications of input intensification are discussed below.

In contrast to rice, the yield potential in wheat has continued to shift up by about 1 percent per year in irrigated areas since the Green Revolution.[6] Data for rainfed environments are less extensive and more varied in quality but show nonetheless that the rate of genetic improvement in general has been slower than for irrigated environments (Byerlee and Moya 1993). Evidence on continued yield progress in irrigated areas is mixed, however. Traxler et al. (1995) suggest that though the latest advanced lines have continued to increase yield potential for the most favorable, irrigated environments, the actual rate of increase has begun to decline. (Yield variance has declined as well.) Sayre, Rajaram, and Fischer (1997) argue that genetic rates of gain in wheat yield have not decelerated.

There are three major avenues for raising the yield frontier in wheat. The first is the "conventional" breeding methods of crossing and selection. Gains from conventional breeding are likely to continue for many developing-country environments for the next two decades or more (Evenson and Rosegrant 1995), but the research costs are likely to be higher than in the past. Several untested routes for increasing conventional breeding efficiency show promise. Heterosis is one, though it is less understood for wheat than it is for rice or maize. Another route incorporates insights from wheat physiology. Research is already manipulating plant type, exploiting genetic variation in growth stages, and taking advantage of new techniques that allow more rapid assessment of favorable characteristics such as leaf canopy temperature (Reynolds, Rajaram, and McNab 1996).

A second way to shift the yield frontier in wheat is to incorporate genetic material from wild and weedy plant types using wide-crossing techniques. Of the three major cereals, wheat may be most advantageously placed to use this technique, in terms of both knowledge and availability of secondary and tertiary gene pools (Mujeeb-Kazi and Hettel 1995). In the near term, wheat vari-

---

6. In the special acid-soil environment of Brazil, breeders have made even more rapid progress, increasing wheat yield potential by 2 to 3 percent per year over a 20-year period.

eties resulting from wide crosses are most likely to resist abiotic and biotic stresses, thus shifting the expected yield frontier under stress conditions. Longer-term goals include increasing photosynthetic efficiency.

The third approach to shifting the yield frontier uses new biotechnologies. Biotechnologies in wheat science probably lag behind those for maize and rice (Dalrymple and Srivastava 1994), partly because they attract relatively little private-sector interest but require large investments. Many experts contend that genetic transformation in wheat is unlikely to make a major impact for several decades. But two biotechnology niches may show more rapid impact: the interface with conventional breeding, using molecular markers to clarify the inheritance of yield components and traits such as time until flowering (Snape 1996), and the use of doubled haploids to produce pure lines in a single generation.

In principle, technology transfer from the industrialized nations could shift the yield frontier for maize more readily than that for wheat and rice in the developing world. This sort of transfer, however, is most likely to occur in China or other parts of Asia where rapidly expanding demand for feed maize will make the crop increasingly profitable. Consequently, large private-sector seed companies should be willing to make the necessary investments given the appropriate institutional environment.

It is far less likely that this kind of transfer will occur in regions that continue to rely heavily on maize for food, such as eastern and southern Africa or Mesoamerica. On the other hand, the currently known ways of shifting the yield frontier have not been exhausted in these areas. Accordingly, public-sector research support, innovative new ways of diffusing improved maize germplasm among farmers, and, in Mesoamerica, the ability of plant breeders to maintain or incorporate traits important to farmers in the zone of origin for the crop need to become priorities. Two areas in which maize has been improved considerably are resistance to biotic and abiotic stresses. Apomixis, in which a plant reproduces asexually, therefore obviating the need to replace hybrid seed every year but maintaining the yield advantage of hybrid maize, is a technological option with a much longer horizon. Even so, scientists are closer to transferring a gene for apomixis to maize than they are to rice or wheat.

It is important to note that the biotechnology most likely to have immediate commercial impact on all cereals in developing countries involves simple traits likely to be controlled by a single gene. Many quantitative traits of commercial importance are polygenic. In areas such as yield, conventional plant breeders have recognized and exploited this for a long time. But basic molecular biology is just beginning to unravel the mysteries of gene interaction. Given the investments required and the political support necessary for such basic research, the first fruits of this understanding are likely to come in medicine in industrialized countries. Over the long run, however, applications to agriculture and cereal staples may be forthcoming. Even where transgenic crops are available, their farm-level adoption may be constrained by regulatory impediments that restrict access. Intellectual property rights may further limit access to materials developed through biotechnology.

Sustaining Profits through Improvements in Input Efficiency

The evidence presented so far suggests that farmers are nearing the conventional yield frontier in intensive multicrop systems in many areas. On the other hand, studies of economic efficiency in developing-country agriculture usually find that many farmers, even in these areas, are technically inefficient (Ali and Byerlee 1991). Differences in time period, location, and methodology may cause some of the discrepancy between these two views. Our previous discussion of knowledge-intensive technologies has suggested some of the ways in which technical efficiency might be improved.

Meeting the long-term demand for cereals not only requires a shift in the yield frontier but also necessitates fundamental changes in the way fertilizers, pesticides, and labor are used. In order to sustain cereal productivity growth while conserving the resource base, production increases may have to be achieved with less than proportionate increases in chemical inputs. Recent advances in fertilizer and pesticide technology could help meet these dual goals.

Changes in fertilizer application, especially in terms of timing and application methods, could contribute to a significant reduction in nutrient losses and improvement in plant nutrient uptake. Such efficiency gains may reduce the overall fertilizer requirements for sustaining productivity growth. Recent evidence indicates that insecticides have had a very modest impact on rice production, despite the fact that insecticides are used on rice more than on the other major cereals. Farm-level experiences with integrated pest management (IPM) show that the judicious use of insecticides could lead to substantial reductions in its application without a reduction in rice yields.

While the growth in fertilizer and insecticide use can be managed through the adoption of efficiency-enhancing technologies, herbicide use may be harder to control. Indeed, it is expected to increase dramatically across Asia for the foreseeable future. Growth in herbicide use is closely linked to increasing wage rates and therefore to the substitution of chemical control for manual weeding. For rice, rapidly rising wages also contribute to the shift from the labor-intensive transplanting operation to direct seeding, a switch that cannot be made without the use of herbicides. Growing water scarcity in irrigated rice systems also contributes to the increased use of herbicides. Opportunities for reducing herbicide use through efficiency improvements are limited in tropical rice systems. *Phalaris minor* is the major grassy weed affecting wheat production in the rice-wheat systems of Asia. Mixed strategies featuring rotations, bed planting, and judicious use of chemicals are currently the most promising options for weed control. Weed problems in wheat are less pronounced where wheat is grown in other rotations.

Although efficiency-enhancing technologies are available for fertilizers and insecticides and savings in input costs per unit of output are possible, the adoption of these technologies comes at a significant cost of farmer time. Most efficiency-enhancing technologies are knowledge-intensive and require substantial time for learning, decisionmaking, and supervision. The monetary cost savings associated with the adoption of these technologies ought to be weighed against the demand of farmers' increasingly expensive time. Finally, the profitability of adopting efficiency-enhancing technologies will be lower in countries where the relative prices of inputs are kept lower through explicit or implicit subsidies.

Over the past three decades Asia has seen an unprecedented shift to mechanization of agriculture, especially in the high-potential irrigated environments. The adoption of mechanical technologies alleviated the labor bottlenecks associated with intensification, helped enhance agricultural productivity, and lowered the unit cost of production, even in the densely populated countries of Asia. Economic growth and commercialization of agriculture are leading to further mechanization, including the spread of rice mechanization in Southeast Asia and a shift to larger machines. The mechanization process, part of the labor-substitution phase of technological change in cereal crop production, in many ways is a more recent development than land-augmenting technology and therefore an opportunity for increased efficiency as farmers become more knowledgeable and better machines become available.

Mechanization has been most pronounced in some countries of Latin America, where labor is the limiting factor. But where land is relatively abundant in Africa, many factors constrain mechanization, including the current length of fallow period, length of growing season, and animal disease constraints (Pingali, Bigot, and Binswanger 1987).

The likelihood that significant input inefficiencies will accompany technical change in cereal systems that are less intensified than in Asia has already been noted. In many parts of Sub-Saharan Africa, however, infrastructure constraints and higher input-output price ratios will keep economic gain from land-augmented yield growth considerably lower than it was in the land-augmentation phase in Green Revolution Asia. As a result, input-use efficiency may become an issue earlier in the diffusion process for such technology in Africa than it did in Asia (Heisey and Smale 1995).

Two major investment possibilities outside the agricultural sector will affect the degree to which input-use efficiencies contribute to greater cereal productivity. The first is investment in improved farmer education (Byerlee 1987; Byerlee and Pingali 1994). In addition to raising productivity, better education may also increase opportunities available in areas with intensive systems and rapid income growth. This would raise the opportunity cost of time, making greater input use more profitable but also counteracting the drive to technical efficiency.

The other investment is in agricultural research. The main concern for researchers is that the cost of developing knowledge-intensive technologies may be high relative to their likely impacts because such technologies are fairly location-specific (Traxler and Byerlee 1992). Advances in crop modeling and geographic information systems (GIS) may help to alleviate some of the constraints of location specificity. In one sense the areas of inquiry that may improve input-use efficiency are quite similar to the innovations in biotechnology that may shift the yield frontier—both are promising but relatively untried.

Conclusion

Driven by increasing land scarcity or high land values, cereal-crop productivity in the developing world has increased tremendously in the past 30 years or more. The most notable and widely cited evidence has been large increases in yields. A few studies that have made international comparisons (for example, Arnade 1994) have suggested that during rapid periods of technological change, TFPs have sometimes declined in developing countries owing to significant technical inefficiencies. However, the majority of analyses of single-country or crop-specific TFP indicate increasing TFP over various periods in the past 30 years. Nonetheless, there is some evidence that in the most intensively cultivated areas, particularly those with a double or triple cereal rotation, resource base limitations may now be leading to a slackening of productivity growth.

Productivity changes have occurred through a sequence of land augmentation, labor substitution, and knowledge improvement. Different developing countries and regions are at different stages in this process, making observation and analysis of the transformation more difficult, but the underlying processes are clear. Agricultural research; better farmer knowledge, through both greater experience and improved education; infrastructure and market development; and policy reform have all contributed to productivity changes. The punctuated nature of the gains from infrastructure and policy changes makes the need for continuous investment in research and farmer education all the more important, but long-term declines in world prices of cereals and structural adjustment within developing economies have often led to decreases in these investments in recent years.

Though significant methodological advances have been made in productivity measurement in recent years, there is still room for improvement in methods and in use of the methods now available. The need for better measurement of the factors of production and a sharpening of the analysis of how the causes of productivity growth function and interact is particularly acute in the developing countries. Future analysis will also have to be increasingly cognizant of the growing integration of world cereal markets.

Continued gains in cereal productivity are essential to meet demand growth, driven by both population and income increases. Productivity growth will be forthcoming only through improvements in yield and input-use efficiency. At the same time, attention must be paid to conserving the resource base. The kind of growth in productivity that is needed will be forthcoming only if investments in agricultural research and education are maintained or increased. But in an era of serious constraints on these types of investments, better knowledge of the specific effects of specific investments in particular places and times is necessary to allow resources to be reallocated and to increase the marginal returns of resources.

PART III

Research, Productivity, and Natural Resources

6   A Skeptical View of Sustainable Development

WILFRED BECKERMAN

The past few years have seen a great expansion of bureaucratic activity dedicated to the pursuit of "sustainable development"—a slogan used to justify policies that are mistakenly believed to reconcile economic growth with equity and concern for the environment. The environment makes a major contribution to human welfare in all sorts of ways—for example, as a source of materials and food, a locus of spiritual and aesthetic satisfaction, and a venue for leisure activities. But many of the policies urged on governments in the name of sustainable development will harm the environment in particular, as well as the general welfare of society as a whole, including that of future generations.

First, in a very general sense, as soon as one examines more carefully the principle of sustainable development, it becomes clear that it is either meaningless or morally repugnant, and in any case nonoperational. It constitutes an attempt to replace the time-honored economist's concept of welfare maximization, from which precise theoretical criteria for policy action can be derived and which reflects widely acceptable ethical judgments, with a confused and morally highly contentious principle. As two eminent authorities have written of it, "it would be difficult to find another field of research endeavor in the social sciences that has displayed such intellectual regress" (Dasgupta and Mäler 1990).

Second, being unconstrained by the discipline of economic theory, environmental pressure groups tend to urge governments to adopt draconian regulations to protect the environment, despite the fact that, in general, these are much more costly than recourse to market-based mechanisms. Hence, whatever level of resources any nation is prepared to devote to environmental protection, less such protection will be obtained. At a more general level, this pressure for greater regulation has been reflected in a major expansion of bureaucratic institutions to promote sustainable development, both nationally and internationally, often accompanied by protectionist regulations that impede international trade in the name of sustainable development.

Third, despite occasional lip service to the contrary, environmentalist pressure groups and prominent environmental campaigners tend to be hostile to economic growth, although this is a necessary and sufficient condition for improving the environment for the vast majority of the world population.[1]

Fourth, environmentalist pressure groups make much of the alleged special concern of sustainable development with intergenerational equity, which they interpret to imply greater intergenerational equality of welfare. In fact, the standard definitions of sustainable development do not imply greater intergenerational equality of welfare at all. Furthermore, our obligations to future generations should be seen in humanitarian, rather than egalitarian, terms. And since a major component of these obligations is to bequeath to future generations institutions in which human rights and liberties are respected more than is the case today in many countries of the world, there is no conflict between the interests of present and future generations. This contrasts with the sustainable development emphasis on the need to constrain current consumption and growth rates in order to conserve resources for distant generations.

Sustainable Development and the Bureaucratic Expansion

The Brundtland Report was pivotal. This report led to a United Nations resolution in 1989 to hold the Conference on Environment and Development—the gigantic Rio jamboree held in June 1992, otherwise known as the Earth Summit. The Rio conference adopted many resolutions and made many declarations of principle, including the adoption of a major document of several hundred pages, known as Agenda 21, that set out a program of action needed throughout the world "to achieve a more sustainable pattern of development." The plan called for the establishment of a new United Nations Commission on Sustainable Development comprising 53 members, which was set up to monitor progress toward sustainable development.

The United Nations also set up three committees—the Committee on Natural Resources, the Committee on New and Renewable Sources of Energy, and the Committee on Science and Technology for Development. Each of these spawned further committees. For example, the Committee on Natural Resources, whose pronouncements are discussed in more detail later in this chapter, recommended in turn that a Commission on Mining and Materials be established to assess and report on technological progress toward sustainable resource use. It justified the need for this additional commission on the grounds that "continued growth in per capita consumption to levels currently enjoyed by the developed countries for a future global population of 10–12 billion is clearly not sustainable." As I show later in the chapter, this assertion is clearly absurd and flies in the face of all the evidence.

Moreover, in order to meet their Rio obligations to report regularly on their policies to promote sustainable development, more than 100 countries

---

1. See references to Jonathan Porritt, Sir Crispin Tickell, and others in Beckerman (1995a).

have now set up national bodies to consider and advise on sustainable development. The British government, for example, has set up roundtables, panels, committees, and so on to help it prepare its reports to the United Nations Commission on its progress. The United States has set up the President's Council on Sustainable Development, France has its Commission Française du Développement Durable, and so on.

The sustainable development bandwagon, then, has led to the creation of a vast network of commissions and committees and research projects to measure sustainable development and to determine which policies should be adopted to promote it. This inevitably involves an expansion of many national bureaucratic units, which will naturally be reluctant to report that their services are unnecessary and that they themselves should be disbanded. For example, like the other countries at the Rio conference, the United Kingdom committed itself to develop a set of indicators to show whether its development was becoming more sustainable. As part of this effort an interdepartmental working group was set up to consider the matter and report on its findings (Department of the Environment and Government Statistical Service 1996). One of its findings was that it is not at all clear what sustainable development means; therefore it is difficult to know how to measure it or which policies promote it (see, in particular, page 5, paragraph 2.2). Unfortunately, this is not a temporary problem that can be solved by further research. It is inherent in the very concept of sustainable development, as is argued in the next section.

The Concept of Sustainable Development

If so many people and institutions are to be involved in trying to measure sustainable development and work out its policy implications, one would expect there to be some powerful prima facie theoretical reasons for adopting it as a policy objective in place of the old-fashioned economist's objective of maximizing social welfare.[2] One may tolerate a certain amount of theoretical fuzziness in the early developmental stages of any major new policy tool, and one may accept that the empirical basis for its application may be very weak. After all, the framework of modern welfare economics has taken a century to develop to its present state, and all economists are well aware that the gaps in the data required for purposes of applying welfare criteria in specific instances are invariably enormous. But to discard it all in favor of a concept that so flagrantly lacks any clear conceptual promise and—insofar as it can be brought into relation with any empirical observation—is patently at variance with the facts is a totally unscientific endeavor. Yet this is the situation as far as the concept of sustainable development is concerned. As George Eliot put it, "What science has built up over the centuries ignorance can destroy in a day."

---

2. For a more detailed discussion of the conceptual weakness of the objective of sustainable development, see Beckerman (1994, 1995a, 1995b).

The original Brundtland report's famous definition of sustainable development was "development that meets the needs of the present without compromising the ability of future generations to meet their own needs" (World Commission on Environment and Development 1987: 43). In the same report, however, it is also stated that "the loss of plant and animal species can greatly limit the options of future generations; so sustainable development requires the conservation of plant and animal species" (43). But these two criteria—the second of which is often known as "strong sustainability"—can be mutually contradictory. For example, at most stages in history the human race has had to use up the environment in order to meet its own needs. Should it have refrained from doing so in order to conform with the second Brundtland criterion? If the second definition merely means that some vague and undefined conservation of plant and animal species is desirable, it is far too loose a criterion to be of any operational value. However, if it is interpreted to mean—as it often is—that *all* species have to be conserved, it is not only obviously physically impossible but also morally repugnant, for it would require unlimited diversion of resources to this end and, hence, astronomic sacrifice of human welfare.

When it soon became obvious—though not to "hard ecologists"—that the "strong" concept of sustainable development was morally repugnant, as well as totally impracticable, many environmentalists shifted their ground. A new version was adopted, known in the literature as "weak sustainability." This allows for some natural resources to be run down as long as adequate compensation is provided in the form of increases in other resources, perhaps even in the form of human-generated capital. But what constitutes adequate compensation? How many more schools or hospitals or houses or factories or machines are required to compensate for using up some mineral resources or forests or clean atmosphere? The answer, it turned out, was that the acceptability of the substitution had to be judged by its contribution to sustaining human welfare. This was a crucial shift, for it meant that the advocates of sustainable development had retreated to the economist's favorite terrain of welfare maximization.

However, if we are now concerned with welfare irrespective of whether it is derived from natural or human-generated capital, in what way does the concept of sustainable development differ from the conventional economist's concern with maximizing social welfare? The answer lies in the second crucial feature of the standard definition of sustainable development: the stipulation that welfare must not be allowed to decline in the future.

For example, in his 1992 authoritative and extensive survey John Pezzey concluded that most definitions still "understand sustainability to mean sustaining an improvement (or at least maintenance) in the quality of life, rather than just sustaining the existence of life," and he went on to adopt as a "standard definition of sustainable development" (11) one according to which per capita welfare must never decline. The same definition is adopted in the editorial introduction to a more recent extensive collection of articles on sustainable development, where it is stated that "consequently, non-negative change in economic welfare per capita becomes the intertemporal equity objective" (Faucheux, Pearce, and Proops 1996:4). Sustainable development is also sometimes interpreted as meaning that per capita welfare must never fall below that enjoyed by the current generation (Howarth and Norgaard 1992).

However, this is not an improvement on the conventional economist's approach at all. In fact, it is positively regressive. Whether the maximization of social welfare requires the path of development over time to rise or fall, temporarily or otherwise, during the time period in question is irrelevant. All that matters is whether the policy adopted gives the maximum social welfare over the whole of the selected time period. If a local or transitory decline in welfare does not affect aggregate welfare overall, why bother about it? And if it does affect welfare, why can it not be included in the concept of welfare we are trying to maximize?[3]

In Figure 6.1, two paths of development are shown. Path SD represents a sustainable development path in that there is no decline in welfare at any point. Path MSW shows the path that would maximize social welfare over the whole time period in question. The generation alive at the end of the period is generation *n*. In Figure 6.1a it can be seen that under SD generation *n* is much worse off than if path MSW had been followed, although this path is ruled out by the sustainable development criterion. If generation *n* could be aware of the alternatives facing us at the beginning of the period, it would be unlikely to thank us for having chosen path SD instead of path MSW. In Figure 6.1b, generation *n* is much better off than if we had followed path MSW. But on any statistical measure of inequality—such as some variant of the degree of dispersion about the mean—the degree of intergenerational inequality is much greater under SD than under MSW, so that the equity concern alleged to be unique to sustainable development would be violated.

Of course, it can be argued that, given the practical prospects, as distinct from theoretical possibilities, what we really ought to be concerned with is neither of the foregoing scenarios but one such as that illustrated in Figure 6.2. In this figure, the MSW path rises for a time, but its subsequent decline on account of our having used up too many resources (including clean air) leaves generation *n* worse off than we are now. And, it would be argued, the fact that this path maximizes welfare over the whole period is of little compensation to the members of generation *n*, since they are not the same people as the members of earlier generations—such as generation *j*—whose welfare levels are much higher. In other words, when different generations are included in the

---

3. There are one or two other complications concerning the difference between *changes* in the level of welfare and the *level* of welfare. These do not, however, affect the argument, and they are explored in more detail in Beckerman (1994, 1995a).

FIGURE 6.1 Effect of development path on welfare per capita: Scenarios 1 and 2

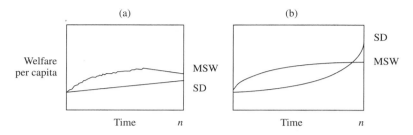

FIGURE 6.2 Effect of development path on welfare per capita: Scenario 3

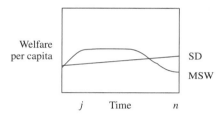

maximization exercise, the conventional economic model of how any given individual maximizes lifetime consumption (or welfare) no longer suffices.

Now this is perfectly true, and it brings us a little closer to a serious discussion of the implications of sustainable development for inequality. As is shown in the next section, the standard definitions of sustainable development are no more intergenerationally egalitarian than the objective of maximizing cumulative welfare over time, and no case can be made for intergenerational egalitarianism.

Sustainable Development and Intergenerational Equity

As indicated earlier in this chapter, the objective of sustainable development is often contrasted with the standard economist's concern with maximizing the future stream of, say, consumption or economic welfare over some relevant time period. For example, Robert Goodin writes that the objective of sustainable development "contrasts with the directive of ordinary expected-utility maximization to go for the highest total payoff without regard to its distribution interpersonally or intertemporally" (1983:13). This is perfectly true. Frank Ramsey's seminal article on optimal growth stated explicitly that distributional considerations were ignored (1928:544). And the same abstraction from distributional considerations was also explicitly endorsed in Solow's exposition of modern growth theory (1970:81).

By contrast, sustainable development is usually defended on the grounds of its greater concern with intergenerational equity.[4] Now "equity" is not, of course, the same as "equality," since egalitarian principles are not the only possible kind of principles of equity. Nevertheless, most—if not all—theories of equity or distributive justice contain, as a crucial ingredient, some appeal to the desirability of equality of something or other.[5] What it is that should be distributed equally is, of course, a subject of considerable dispute, and candidates for an appropriate equilisand include welfare, preference satisfaction, opportunities, capabilities, Rawlsian "primary goods," functionings, and economic resources—all with possible variations, such as the exclusion of allowance for "expensive" tastes.

In the present context it does not seem necessary to spend much time on quite common definitions of sustainable development that rule out any decline in welfare below that enjoyed by the current generation, for it is difficult to see why one should attach crucial normative significance to the current level of welfare. It cannot be argued that, by some extraordinary coincidence, the present average standard of living constitutes some minimum subsistence level below which future generations must not be allowed to fall. Past generations seem to have survived with far less, as do about half the people in the world today (depending on which precise concept of the average one adopts). And if the rule is to be interpreted, instead, as one that needs to be adjusted over time—that is, each generation is under moral obligation to ensure that successor generations will not fall below the level of welfare that it has reached, however high that may be—then it is really transposing into the more general rule that precludes any decline in welfare in any period. So it is on this latter quasi-standard rule that we shall concentrate. Not that this need take up much time either, since it is trivially obvious that it cannot be intergenerationally egalitarian at all. It would permit welfare to rise continuously, which, over time, could obviously lead to great inequality between generations—as has happened in the past up to the present time.

More generally it is obvious that "going up" is a purely formal feature of some variable that implies neither a more equal distribution of the variable in question nor a more desirable development than "going down" (consider a staircase or high blood pressure). However, it may be argued that this argument is irrelevant because we are not comparing different possible world histories that may have started from different levels of welfare. At this point in time we

---

4. Innumerable advocates of sustainable development subscribe to variants of Norgaard's view that "sustainability is primarily an issue of intergenerational equity" (1992).

5. It is for this reason that scattered throughout the vast literature on justice and equity are learned discussions of the relationship in the original Greek language between the words *justice* and *equality.*

are choosing, it would be argued, between two feasible future development paths starting from the same present level. This is, perhaps, the reasoning behind the interpretation of sustainable development that takes the form of excluding any decline in welfare below the present level. But this argument gives the game away.

It is true, of course, that, starting from any particular level, if we want to maximize something good, such as welfare, it is better for it to go up—or even remain stable—than to go down. But that is only because, and insofar as, we expect that this will lead to total welfare over the future being greater than it would otherwise be. So in the end all that one is really concerned with is the total welfare over some future time period, and the purely technical characteristic of "going up" or "going down" is incidental.[6]

This means that, faced with the choice between two technically feasible development paths over some given future time period, if one path includes a period of declining welfare and the other does not, but the former leads to higher total welfare over the whole period, then that is the path that should be chosen. If, instead, we reject it on (perhaps mistaken) egalitarian grounds, we must have forgotten why we tend to prefer periods of rising rather than falling welfare, and we are making a choice that is inconsistent with our underlying objective of maximizing welfare.

And it is perfectly feasible, as in Figure 6.3, for a sustainable development path to lead not only to greater intergenerational inequality but also to lower total welfare than does a path starting from the same level and containing a period of declining welfare. It seems unlikely that any ethical principle to justify this would be easy to find.

But the real error in the objective of sustainable development does not lie in the fact that, contrary to the supposition of most of its proponents, it is no way egalitarian, for, as I have argued in detail elsewhere (Beckerman 1997, 1998; Beckerman and Pasek 2001), there is no case for intergenerational egalitarianism anyway. My three main objections to intergenerational egalitarianism can be summarized as follows:

1. The most common arguments for egalitarianism at any point in time are instrumental ones, such as that greater inequality—for example, of income or status—creates envy, reduces social cohesion, or confers excessive power of some people over others. Clearly, none of these arguments can apply between generations.
2. The notion that greater equality across generations can have some intrinsic value, even though there is no entity or society to which it can be valuable, stretches the metaphysical notion of a "society" or the concept of values in the absence of valuers beyond reasonable limits.

---

6. Nozick (1989:100–102) advances an argument couched in graphic terms similar to those used here but arriving at the opposite conclusion. I discuss his arguments in Beckerman (1998) and Beckerman and Pasek (2001).

FIGURE 6.3 Effect of development path on welfare per capita: Scenario 4

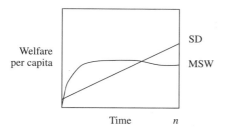

3. Equality (like going up) is a purely formal characteristic of a variable, and what one really wants to reduce is not inequality per se but the poverty and suffering that we see in the world around us (see also Beckerman 1979; Frankfurt 1997; Raz 1986). This is closely related to my next point.

Even though intergenerational egalitarianism should be rejected as an objective, this does not mean that we have no obligations to future generations. I believe we do but that these comprise mainly two things, though the first of them is of little practical importance. This is to avoid policies that, by depriving them of some resource that could be finite and important, could plunge future generations into poverty. This is a purely humanitarian objective of avoiding actions that might deprive future generations of basic needs. It is not, however, an egalitarian objective. It does not take the form of a strictly egalitarian proposition such as "Given a finite amount, G, of some good and n people, every person should receive one nth of G."

But while we should accept that, *in theory,* we have a humanitarian obligation to avoid policies that could lead to future generations living in dire poverty on account of our having used up too much of some supposedly finite resource, in practice this possibility can be virtually ignored, as argued in the next section. It is based on assumptions that fly in the face of the facts that have a bearing on the alternative scenarios facing humanity.

The second and more important obligation to future generations is to bequeath to them a just society. As shown below, this objective is not compatible with many policies proposed in the name of "sustainable development."

The Facts about Sustainability

Given space and time constraints, this chapter concentrates on only two of the many scare stories associated with the notion that we should be worried about the sustainability of continued economic growth: (1) we shall run out of mineral resources, and (2) the growth of the food supply will be unable to match the expected growth of world population.

Minerals

I consider the case of minerals for three main reasons. First, the "finite re-sources" school of thought represents a clear-cut case of failure to grasp the theory of the way society adapts to changes in supplies and demands of any resource. Second, it is a strange combination of both a failure of imagination and failure to respect well-known facts. Third, it is a striking example of the intrusion of regulation into international trade under the banner of sustainable development.

As mentioned earlier, one of the newly created international bodies set up in connection with the concern over sustainable development is the Committee on Natural Resources, which in turn has recommended the creation of a Com-mission on Mining and Minerals to tackle the problem of overcoming the constraint that finite mineral resources would place on sustainable develop-ment. The history of false predictions of this nature goes back to ancient Greece.[7] One of the best known of such predictions was the famous 1972 report to the Club of Rome, entitled *The Limits to Growth.* Yet this blatantly flawed report was referred to in the recent (draft) report of the Committee on Natural Resources as "a landmark in the debate on sustainability" (1996:3).

It is true that by its use of a computer the Club of Rome report appeared to improve on earlier—and all falsified—predictions. But this merely misled people such as the Bishop of Kingston (1971), who wrote at the time, "The computer is adding precision to what used to be regarded as mere prophecy by cranky ecologists." (But why a bishop should be so contemptuous of prophets is a mystery to me.) By comparing estimates of known reserves of many minerals with annual rates of consumption, the Club of Rome's computer showed that at current rates of consumption the existing reserves would soon all be used up. Well, we are now in a position to see what actually happened.

In a 1995 book (and elsewhere) I have shown a table that compared the 1970 estimates of reserves of key metals and primary fuels as given in the Club of Rome's *The Limits to Growth* with the 1989 figures and the estimates of how much of the metals in question had been consumed in the 19 years that had elapsed (Beckerman 1995a:53).[8] My table showed that the 1989 reserves were much greater than those reported in 1970, for all the items covered, despite the fact that cumulative consumption during the intervening years had been large relative to initial 1970 reserves. In fact, for two of the items shown (namely, lead and oil) more had been consumed in the period 1970–89 than had been recorded in "known reserves" in 1970. And for two others (natural gas and zinc) consumption during the period 1970–89 had been just about as great as the initial level of known reserves. Indeed, for all the products listed, known

---

7. For details, see Beckerman (1974:3).
8. In the U.S. edition, *Through Green-Colored Glasses* (Washington, D.C.: Cato Institute, 1996), see p. 60.

reserves were greater than they had been at the beginning of the period despite the relatively very high levels of consumption during the period.[9]

Clearly, it was totally absurd to use estimates of "known reserves" in the way that the Club of Rome and others have done, since these represent only those reserves that have been judged to be worth seeking out, given the prices of the minerals in question. If there was a long-run failure of supply to meet demand, the price would rise, and this would set in motion a chain reaction that would include shifting to substitutes, exploration for more reserves, and the development of improved extraction technologies.

These lessons of the past, however, did not prevent the international Committee on Natural Resources from concluding that "there will be critical management problems throughout the twenty-first century as the global population continues to increase. Prudent management, according to the precautionary principle, clearly requires further knowledge of the sustainability of supply . . . beyond the present horizon of sustainability. . . . It is likely that there will be real problems of meeting demand over the next century" (1996: 18).

However, the committee did appear to absorb one lesson from the past, namely, that the reliance on estimates of existing known reserves is fatally flawed, for it tried to go a step further and recommended that "global estimates of Undiscovered Resources be made . . . so that the horizon of sustainability can be extended and maximum warning obtained of potential mineral shocks" (18).

It is not at all clear, however, in what way such surveys would be superior to the price mechanism as a means of providing warning signals about future changes in supplies and demands. Throughout the course of human history the demands for and supplies of materials have followed varying trends, with accompanying changes in relative prices. There is no reason to believe that, in the future, it is the market mechanism that will fail while predictions made by some new international bureaucratic institution will perform better.

Food and Population

My second example is the alleged impossibility of increasing world food supply enough to feed the expected increase in world population. I take this example not only because it is somewhat closer to the interests of this volume than my first one but also because it differs from it in one crucial respect: the operation of the price mechanism to equilibrate demand and supply is not necessarily adequate as far as food is concerned. A shortage of food leading to

---

9. Other crushing refutations of the more recent predictions of the imminent exhaustion of nonrenewable resources include the well-known $1,000 bet that Paul Ehrlich made in 1980 with the economist Julian Simon. Ehrlich bet that by the end of the decade five products chosen by Ehrlich himself would have higher prices (reflecting increasing shortages). In the event, by the end of the decade the prices of all five products had fallen. And, as Stephen Moore (1992) has shown, Ehrlich would have lost the bet almost irrespective of which set of five products he had selected. See also Simon (1996) for an extensive analysis of the flaws in the "scarce resources" hypothesis.

a rise in its price means that some people may starve. Beyond a point there is no substitute for food. So it is more important in the case of food to determine how much substance there really is in the widespread predictions that the trend in demand will outstrip the trend in supply.

In 1968 the distinguished biologist Paul Ehrlich published a book that began: "The battle to feed all of humanity is over. In the 1970s the world will undergo famines—hundreds of millions of people are going to starve to death in spite of any crack programs embarked upon now" (1968:i). During the following two decades, of course, world food supply grew faster than population, as it has done consistently since Malthus made his famous predictions of unavoidable starvation two hundred years ago. This has not induced Professor Ehrlich to change his views at all. The same applied to Lester Brown, president of the Worldwatch Institute, who has also been predicting imminent worldwide famine for nearly 30 years and who has stated, as recently as 1994, that "seldom has the world faced an unfolding emergency whose dimensions are as clear as the growing imbalance between food and people" (Brown 1994:196).

Nor does the experience of the postwar period deter Sir Crispin Tickell, the chairman of the United Kingdom Panel on Sustainable Development, who even commends Brown's constantly falsified predictions to us. Sir Crispin is particularly worried that the coming expansion of the world population, unaccompanied by a corresponding expansion of the world food supply, will lead to a greatly increased international flow of refugees and possibly international conflicts as the richer countries try to stem the inflow of the starving hordes from famine-stricken regions. Sir Crispin's scenario not only flies in the face of the evidence concerning food and population; it also fails to recognize that almost all the refugees in recent years are the result of ethnic strife and civil wars, while international migration is largely the result of people seeking higher incomes, not fleeing areas of famine.

Brown does, at least, concede that food output per capita has been growing over the past few decades, but he claims to detect a "watershed year" in 1984 that marked an abrupt reversal of the trend. It is true that the upward trend in world per capita food output leveled off around the mid-1980s, but this is hardly surprising in view of the emergence of huge surpluses of some food products in some parts of the world and the problems this created of disposing of them without disrupting established markets and with minimum cost to the taxpayers of the countries in which they were produced. These trends naturally dampened the enthusiasm for increasing food output in many of the major food-producing areas of the world.

The long upward trend in food output per capita was, unsurprisingly, accompanied by a steep fall in the relative price of food. For example, between 1953–55 and 1983–85 the price of rice fell by 42 percent, wheat by 57 percent, sorghum by 39 percent, and maize by 37 percent (Sen 1994). Thus, as Amartya Sen (1994:67) points out, "When we take into account the persistent cheapening of food prices, we have good grounds to suggest that food output is being held back by a lack of effective demand in the market. The imaginary crisis in food production, contradicted as it is by the upward trends of total and regional food output per head, is thus further debunked by an analysis of the economic incentives to produce more food."

This desirable and normal operation of market forces is also confirmed by the noticeable differences among regions in developments in food output. For example, between 1979–81 and 1991–93 food output per capita rose by 3 percent for the world as a whole. But it rose by only 2 percent in Europe and fell by about 5 percent in the United States—that is, the two regions where surpluses had been a major problem (Sen 1994). By contrast, it rose by 22 percent in Asia as a whole, including 23 percent in India and 39 percent in China—that is, in countries where there had been large population increases. The assertion, therefore, that although global food production may still be rising in line with population it is not rising in the areas most in need is quite the reverse of the truth (Dyson 1994; Sen 1994).

The one major exception to this trend is, of course, Africa, where food production per capita fell by 6 percent over the same period. But in Africa the food problem has not been the result of population pressures. It has been the result mainly of wars (including civil wars and ethnic conflicts), dictatorship, and political chaos. This was the case, for example, with the mass starvation in Ethiopia in the 1980s or in Somalia at the end of the 1980s and early 1990s and, more recently, in Rwanda. In other words, the main cause of recent famines— as with the Soviet famine of 1934 or the Chinese famine of 1958–61—was human evil and stupidity, not environmental catastrophe.

So unfounded is the assertion that there is any foreseeable danger of famine on account of increasing population that it is perhaps unnecessary to scrutinize the evidence even further. As one authoritative voice put it, "Perhaps the only neo-Malthusian claim that can be substantiated is that world population growth has been outpacing cereal production since about 1984. Plainly, this has *not* been primarily caused by the scale or speed of contemporary world population growth. . . . The explanation lies largely in surplus cereal supply relative to effective demand leading to deliberate production cut-backs. Similarly it is *not* true that population growth is outpacing cereal production in all world regions (far from it). It is *not* true that world cereal yield increments are slowing down and it is *not* true that world food production is lagging behind demographic growth (quite the contrary)" (Dyson 1995:32).

Welfare versus "Wilfare": Bequeathing a Just Society

Thus although, in theory, a humanitarian approach to our obligations to the future means that we should avoid action that might deprive future generations of basic needs (an objective that bears some resemblance to sustainable development), it is not a component of our obligations that is of much (if any) practical importance. A far more important component of our obligations to future generations concerns the institutions that we bequeath to them. It is sometimes forgotten that, according to Rawls, "the just savings principle can be regarded as an understanding between generations to carry their fair share of the burden of realizing and preserving a just society" (1972:288–99). It is not just a matter of the amount of capital that we bequeath to future generations. We should shift our attention to a completely different component of our obligations to future generations, namely, to try to ensure that they will live in a more decent and civilized society than the one in which the majority of the world's inhabitants currently live.[10]

What horrifies most of us about the past is not the acute poverty in which earlier societies lived on account of the low level of development, but reminders of the atrocities, persecution, humiliation, and suffering inflicted by some sections of the world population on others. In other words, we should be much more concerned with the extent to which we bequeath political and social institutions that respect human rights and effectively protect personal liberty than with the number of species of beetles or supplies of copper that posterity will inherit. If bodies such as the United Nations Commission on Human Rights or the Inter-American Commission on Human Rights were given a fraction of the publicity and resources accorded to environmental bodies and international jamborees such as the Rio conference of 1992, far more concrete contributions would be made to human welfare.

Furthermore, respect for human rights is not a finite resource that must be shared out between generations. Hence, as regards the most important obligation to future generations, there is no real conflict of interest between present and future generations. The best one can do for future generations is to improve the respect for basic human rights and the quality of justice and liberty today. Societies that have confidence in the ability of their own institutions to resolve fairly their own internal, and inevitably recurring, conflicts do not have to conjure up artificial conflicts between generations in order to escape from these problems.

Thus the conclusion that we should ignore the emphasis on intergenerational equity that sustainable development is alleged to promote, and concentrate instead on improving the lives of people today, is reached from two different directions. One is that what is important is the humanitarian objective of relieving poverty and deprivation where they are most acute and certain, and this happens to be among large sections of today's population. The other is that we should give at least equal emphasis to the promotion of decent societies in which basic human rights are respected and to the move toward bequeathing just societies to future generations.

---

10. A superb exposition of what is meant by a "decent" society is given in Margalit (1996).

Concern with future generations should thus take the same form as concern with people alive today, namely, give priority to providing them with what I shall call "wilfare." The precise content of this cannot be laid down for all time (or space), but the essential point is that it comprises two components. These bear some resemblance to the two components of Rawls's two basic principles of justice at any point in time, "primary goods" and liberty, but without his lexicographic priority for the latter and without the egalitarian element in the rules governing the distribution of primary goods. "Wilfare" is what one should try to ensure is provided to people of any generation, and it comprises whatever minimum level of (1) personal and publicly provided goods and services and (2) human rights and liberties is essential to the self-respect and opportunities for personal fulfillment that characterize a decent and civilized society. It is a principle of entitlement, not an egalitarian principle relating to the way that some supposedly scarce resource is to be shared out between generations.

Conclusion

I hope that I have demonstrated that the objective of pursuing "sustainable development," urged on us from all sides, is intellectually incoherent, based as it is on flawed logic and a belief in disaster scenarios that fly in the face of all evidence. Such slogans are dangerous, as they can be invoked to justify all sorts of policies that are bad for society, both today and in the future.

Society is constantly faced with the need to make choices about the allocation of scarce resources among competing ends. Economics, described as "the logic of choice," provides a theoretical structure, constructed out of precise concepts and held together by a logical framework, designed to help make such choices in a rational manner. Over the past two centuries the structure has been refined and clarified, as have been the methods of practical application. Its shortcomings and limitations are well known to its practitioners—as are the shortcomings of medical science or, indeed, of any respectable branch of human learning. Sustainable development, as an alternative objective, is a step backward into vague and confused rhetoric, and it should be exposed for the nonsense that it is. It is founded on sloppy thinking, and its vagueness means that it can be used to justify any policies that pressure groups advocate, including some that are easily shown to be bad for efficiency or equity or both. Its shortcomings are not even perceived by its advocates.

Furthermore, the respect paid to the concept of sustainable development leads to excessive tolerance among environmentalists for the activities carried out under the banner of sustainable development by antirational groups that often resort to ecoterrorism. The past few decades have witnessed innumerable examples of how easily human activities can become dominated by irrational dogmas and appeals to mystical slogans and how disastrous the consequences may be. They have demonstrated that the real conflicts facing us are between people, not between people and the environment.

One important illustration of this is the claim made by advocates of sustainable development that they occupy the moral high ground because they are more concerned with intergenerational egalitarianism than is the usual economist's objective of maximizing welfare over time. But it has been shown here that there is nothing particularly intergenerationally equitable about the objective of sustainable development. Furthermore, the usual arguments in favor of egalitarianism at any moment cannot be transposed to the intergenerational context. But this does not relieve us of any need to consider our moral obligations to future generations.

In general these should be guided by the objective of moving toward just institutions and a "decent" society. Such an objective calls for no constraint on present living standards or on continued economic growth. There is thus no conflict of interest between generations because there is no fixed supply of "just institutions" that must be shared out among generations. The widespread institutionalized hardship and violation of basic human rights in the world today are indisputable facts, not matters of speculation about distant futures based on assertions that, as has been shown, run counter to both economic theory and historical fact.

7 Measuring Factor Productivity Changes under Regulated Open-Access Resource Use

JAMES WILEN AND FRANCES HOMANS

It is probably fair to say that most analysis of innovation and technical change has been conducted in settings in which the maintained assumptions include competitive behavior, complete markets, and well-defined property rights for inputs and outputs. At the same time, the economics profession devotes considerable attention precisely to those circumstances in which these preconditions to efficiency may be lacking—namely, instances of market failure, externalities, and public goods. This is particularly true in environmental and resource economics, in which the conceptual underpinnings of welfare analysis focus on market failure in its many guises.

One early analysis of an important class of market failures was provided nearly 50 years ago by H. S. Gordon in his oft-cited paper on open-access fisheries. As Gordon (1954) pointed out, natural populations can be viewed as productive assets, much like farmland. Unlike farmland, however, many important renewable-resource populations are unowned and therefore subject to the rule of capture in an open-access setting. Since there is no landlord empowered to collect rents from prospective users of the asset, entry occurs over and beyond the amount necessary to maximize rents. In most cases, this will lead to excessive harvests, a reduction of the population to a low level (or complete extinction), an excessive amount of variable inputs, and dissipation of the rent or surplus that would normally accrue to the resource owner.

This chapter examines some issues associated with measuring factor productivity in a setting in which an open-access renewable resource is used in production. In the next section we discuss some stylized facts about such industries. We then develop a simple model that accounts for some of the features highlighted and propose a novel way to measure factor productivity in the fourth section. The fifth section presents an application of the proposed measurement scheme, and the last section concludes and summarizes.

Some Stylized Facts about Renewable Resource Use

A quick scan of the literature in economics that deals with renewable resources gives the impression that there are really only two institutional settings within which renewable-resource use takes place. At one end of the spectrum are open-access settings in which entry is free and unfettered to all and in which no one exerts any control collectively over the behavior of individual users. This is the world described by H. S. Gordon, in which the likely equilibrium is one in which the resource stock is driven to a low level and economic rents are completely dissipated by entry of excess inputs. At the other end of the spectrum depicted in the literature is the sole-owner setting, in which it is assumed that a foresightful decisionmaker optimizes use by choosing a dynamically optimal use path that maximizes the present value of resource rents. This latter paradigm is often depicted in the literature as the ideal, toward which it is suggested open-access resources ought to be guided by appropriate choice of interventionist policies, whether they are taxes, individual quotas, or other private property rights schemes.

A hard look at the real world, however, reveals that there really are not too many instances of either pure open-access common property or sole-owner, optimized resource use. In fact, most renewable-resource use takes place in a setting that might be called *regulated open access* or *regulated restricted access.* By regulated open access we mean that access to the resource is open to all, but only under certain conditions regarding conventions of use. By regulated restricted access, we mean that use is restricted to a particular group, also subject to conditions of use. Conditional use restrictions are the key component of these institutions, and the precise nature of these use restrictions sometimes emerges from the bottom up, but more often they are imposed from the top down. Anthropologists and sociologists have drawn much attention to instances of bottom-up regulated commons use whereby a local community spontaneously devises and enforces rules of use aimed at sustaining the resource (for example, see Ostrom 1990; Ostrom et al. 1994). Examples include many "self-regulated" resources such as irrigation districts, near-shore fisheries, agroforestry systems, and groundwater basins. More prevalent are institutionalized settings of regulations whereby a nation, state, or regional government allows participation but with certain rules and regulations set regarding allowable harvesting gear, open areas, season length restrictions, and so on. These are common in air basins, watersheds, forests, and fisheries.

What is the importance of this to the problem of measuring and understanding the forces that determine factor productivity? Basically the importance is that one cannot hope to understand what is happening to technological change and factor productivity without understanding the nature of the regulatory system. Economic agents in regulated open- (or restricted-) access settings behave in a manner heavily influenced by the regulatory structure within which they operate. One might be tempted, at first, simply to sidestep complications by treating regulations as fixed and exogenous constraints on available technology. However, this would be insufficient in most settings for several reasons. First, regulatory restrictions are seldom static. They change with both changes in industry behavior and with changes in exogenous environmental conditions affecting the inherent productivity of the resource. They change, of course, because regulators are themselves rational actors. Agencies (or local groups) charged with managing common-property resources are goal oriented and purposeful. Regulations are thus endogenous, and understanding the dynamics of regulations calls for understanding the behavior of regulators, both their inherent goal structure and the manner in which they use regulatory instruments at their disposal. A second problem with treating regulations as simple exogenous constraints is that regulations themselves often condition the set of technological options chosen by resource users. This happens in an obvious manner when regulatory constraints restrict technology sets available to users. It is common, for example, to prohibit certain types of harvesting technologies (for example, dynamite or poisons in coral reefs or hunting using spotter planes). More generally, to the extent that technological development responds to regulatory constraints as well as prices and other economic variables, the path of innovation will itself reflect the whole history of regulatory decisions. The point, then, is that serious modeling and measurement of productivity, technical change, and innovation in most resource-using settings must not only recognize the importance of the regulatory structure but also elevate its importance in the modeling and empirical work to a level on par with that of industry behavior, resource characteristics, and technology description.

In this chapter, we present a characterization of the relationship between industry behavior, regulatory behavior, and technology in a simple model of renewable resource use.[1] To foreshadow our results, we develop a model of industry behavior that is conditional on biological parameters, expectations of regulatory rules, and technology. Then we develop a simple model of the behavior of a regulatory agency, assuming that regulations are purposeful and goal-driven. The equilibrium in this model is a joint one in which both the industry and regulators act in a manner to produce an equilibrium in which their expectations are fulfilled. Lying behind the equilibrium is the nature of harvesting technology. In this model, we show how exogenous changes in technology influence both the industry's and the regulatory sector's behavior. This then allows us to examine the impact of technological change in an indirect way, by observing how regulators react to it in changing their policies to address their goals. The empirical usefulness of this approach is demonstrated using an example of the North Pacific halibut industry.

---

1. This model derives its basic structure from Homans (1993), Homans and Wilen (1997), and Wilen (1985).

A Model of Regulated Renewable Resource Use

We consider a simple biological setting in which each calendar year is divided up into a harvesting season and a period over which no harvesting is allowed. The focus of the model is the sequence of temporary equilibria that occur within each season. Transition of the system between seasons can be motivated by assuming that species growth and recruitment to the next year's initial fishable biomass depends on the biomass remaining after the harvesting season is over. For now we simply assume that an initial (pre-season) biomass level $X(0) = X_0$ is known and given at the beginning of each season. Assume also that over the duration of the harvesting season the biomass evolves according to:

$$\dot{X}(t) = -qEX(t), \qquad (7.1)$$

where E represents instantaneous harvesting capacity on the fishing grounds and q a "catchability" coefficient. This model is standard in the fisheries biology literature and is attributable to Schaefer (1957) and Beverton and Holt (1957).[2] We assume that the industry commits a fixed amount of capacity E that is constant over any given season. The catchability coefficient basically captures the extent of technology here, and we assume that it is also fixed during any given year but can vary among seasons. With the above biological growth equation, we can solve for the end-of-season biomass after T days have elapsed by integrating (1) to get:

$$X(T) = X(0)\exp(-qET). \qquad (7.2)$$

Ignoring natural mortality over the harvesting season, we can deduce that the total harvest over the season will be the difference between initial and ending biomass or

$$H = X(0) - X(T) = X(0)[1 - \exp(-qET)]. \qquad (7.3)$$

This is, in effect, the seasonal harvest production function for the industry derived from standard assumptions made in fisheries biology. Note that the biomass level aids in harvesting; for a given level of applied fishing capacity, the more dense the biomass, the larger will be the aggregate harvest. Note also that, contrary to a standard economics production function such as the Cobb-Douglas, one can capture the entire biomass only with an infinite amount of the other input. Finally, note that implicitly there is perfect substitution between harvesting capacity and time. Holding biomass density constant, it is assumed that one can take the same amount in six months with half the gear as one might take in three months with a full complement of gear.

---

2. For an exposition, see, for example, Clark (1976).

Now, given these preliminary assumptions about biology and harvesting technology, we can turn to industry behavior. We assume that there are variable costs v per unit time associated with utilizing harvesting capacity, so that total variable costs over the season are vET. We also assume fixed costs f associated with each unit of capacity E committed over the season. In practice, fisheries biologists often measure E as an index of standardized gear units fished, such as net tows in a trawl fishery, vessel days in a troll fishery, diver hours in a dive fishery, and so on. We will be using such a measure in our empirical example; it is then convenient to consider other inputs as applied with a Leontief technology, with f and v accounting for these auxiliary inputs as well as those associated directly with the primary unit of gear measured.

With the production and cost structures defined, we can now turn to specifying a theory of input determination. Clearly the appropriate theory depends on the institutional setting, and it is sensible as a first step to assume that, since this is an open-access resource, the industry commits an amount of effort such that (undiscounted) seasonal rents are dissipated.[3] Since most fisheries operate with a skipper/owner determining entry, and since remuneration is typically done with a share system, we also need to incorporate the fact that entry-relevant returns will be based on some share to the skipper/owner entrepreneur. Designate the share going to compensate for the fixed gear and associated proportional inputs s, and the former-vessel price of output P. Then the rent-dissipating harvesting capacity will be the amount of effort that satisfies the implicit equation:

$$\text{Rents} = s\{PX(0)[1 - \exp(-qET)] - vET\} - fE = 0. \qquad (7.4)$$

Note that we are assuming the skipper/owner share is taken net of variable costs vET, which is normal practice. Although this equation cannot be solved explicitly for E, it yields a rent-dissipating equilibrium capacity that we can write implicitly as:

$$E = E(T; X(0), P, v, f, q, s). \qquad (7.5)$$

This is written to emphasize that the industry makes its capacity decisions contingent on profitability over the season, which in turn is affected by the season length chosen by the regulators and dependent on price/cost parameters and the technology parameter. While regulators typically have at their disposal many policy instruments with which to control harvesting capacity, in what follows we will be depicting the regulators as using one instrument, namely, the season length, T, to control the impact of harvesting capacity on the biomass.

---

3. See, for instance, the models by Gordon (1954), who assumes that rents are dissipated instantly and fully, and the models of Smith (1968), who assumes that the rent dissipation process is dynamic with some sluggishness.

What should we assume about the behavior of regulators? Although various possibilities have been suggested in the literature, we assume that regulatory structures are dominated by technocrats whose concern is related to resource "health." Evidence in fisheries suggests that those who actually make and implement policy are most often biologists whose inherent concern is to ensure that the biomass is at or even above some "safe" level. We model this by assuming that regulators follow a two-stage process whereby in each season they first measure initial pre-season biomass and decide how much they will allow to be taken, consistent with the desire to guide the fishery toward a healthy biomass level. Assume that regulators aim to cause the harvest not to exceed Q where Q is a predetermined function of the initial biomass so that $Q = Q[X(0)]$. Generally we would expect a direct functional relationship between the initial biomass and quota, so that larger biomass levels allow larger harvest quotas to be set. We also might observe a fishery away from its long-run desired "safe" level, and in this case the quota rule would presumably be set to promote dynamic adjustment to the ideal stock level.

Once the quota target is established in the first stage, regulators must employ instruments at their disposal to reach that goal. In our model, since we assume that the season length is the only instrument at their disposal, we depict the second stage of the regulatory process to be one in which, given a harvesting capacity E, biomass $X(0)$, and quota Q regulators choose T so that:

$$Q = Q[X(0)] = H = X(0)[1 - \exp(-qET)]. \qquad (7.6)$$

This can be solved explicitly for T so that we can write:

$$T = (1/qE)[\ln(X(0)/(X(0) - Q)]. \qquad (7.7)$$

Note that, with the quota assumed to follow some rule $Q(X(0))$, the season-length choice decision reduces to some function:

$$T = T(E;X(0),Q(X(0)),q). \qquad (7.8)$$

Given a predetermined initial biomass and knowledge of the technology summarized in the catchability coefficient, regulators thus choose the season length that ensures that their quota goal is not exceeded. Equation (7.8), when combined with equation (7.5) describing the industry equilibrium, gives us a joint regulated open-access equilibrium in which each party's behavior reflects fundamental incentives. The equilibrium is depicted in Figure 7.1. Note that the rent-dissipating level of harvesting capacity is generally an increasing function of the expected season length, since longer seasons mean more harvesting and higher rents, ceteris paribus, which are dissipated away by excess entry of capacity. Note also that the regulatory equilibrium is described by a rectangular hyperbola in E and T. This arises because we assume that regulators are only concerned about attaining the desired harvest and not whether it is achieved with many units of gear operating over a short season or fewer units operating

FIGURE 7.1 Regulated open-access equilibrium

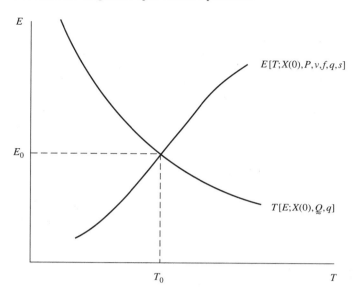

over a longer season. The system is in a joint equilibrium when both the industry is in a rent-dissipating equilibrium given the season length set by regulators, and regulators have set a season length that achieves their season-quota target, given some initial biomass.

This model has several attributes that make it preferable to the typical open-access model generally used to describe renewable-resource use. First, it incorporates the regulatory sector in a nontrivial manner. Second, the regulatory sector is assumed to be purposeful in that it follows goals and sets policies according to both goals and industry behavior. Third, the equilibrium is a joint regulatory sector/industry equilibrium, which involves both the inputs chosen by the industry and the policy instruments chosen by the regulatory sector. Finally, this model is in much closer accord with what we observe empirically. For many open-access resources, populations have not been driven to insupportably low levels. In commercial fisheries, for example, although the rent dissipation hypothesis of Gordon probably holds generally, it is often not at the very low bioeconomic levels he and Vernon Smith predicted under pure open access. Many fisheries are perfectly healthy biologically and in fact close to or exceeding maximum sustainable yield. These are generally ones where managers have been willing and able to exert the statutory authority that mandates protection of the resource. At the same time, even with managed fisheries that are successfully held at high biomass levels, few are earning significant rents because these are still being dissipated away in a process in which industries add capacity, which is then stifled by regulators, and so on.

Measuring Factor Productivity

If we are correct in depicting the nature of most regulated open-access settings in this manner, where regulators are assumed to be limiting output by choosing policy instruments to stifle capacity, then observing the behavior of regulators can be a powerful aid to understanding exactly how technology is evolving in the industry. A simple example makes this clear. Suppose that regulators have been able to guide a renewable resource to a position close to their ideal "safe" steady state by choosing and enforcing certain harvest quotas continually over a period. Then, in any subsequent season, in order to maintain harvest at the target in the face of capacity-increasing technical change, the regulators will of necessity have to react to increased harvesting power by tightening regulatory instruments. Hence for every increase in potential capacity we should witness a corresponding tightening of regulatory restrictions. The pattern of changes in restrictions should, in a perfect world, tell us something about the pattern of increases in harvesting capacity induced by technical change. In a real world example, of course, many more variables would be changing, and hence one would have to pay close attention to other forces in order to filter out any "pure" productivity-enhancing technical change.

To illustrate with a simple case, consider equation (7.7) above, which depicts the level of the instrument (season length) that will meet the goal of $\underset{\sim}{Q}$ set by regulators, given both an initial stock level $X(0)$ and an expected capacity commitment, $E,$ by the industry. Assume that over time the quota chosen has been exactly the level necessary to ensure that next period's initial biomass is exactly $X(0)$, so that the biomass and quota targets are assumed to be in a long-run steady state. This is a special case in which $X(0)$ and $\underset{\sim}{Q}$ remain fixed so that we can focus on fundamental relationships between the technology and behavior of the industry and the regulator. Now let $q,$ the catchability coefficient, be some function of time, $q(t)$, representing changes in the technology of harvesting where t indexes consecutive seasons.[4] If both $\underset{\sim}{Q}$ and X remain unchanged from season to season (because the steady-state goal is achieved in each season), then we know from (7.7) that:

$$d\ln(qET)/dt = (\dot{q}/q) + (\dot{E}/E) + (\dot{T}/T) = 0. \tag{7.9}$$

This shows clearly that any change in either exogenous technical change $(\dot{q}/q)$ or in the amount of capacity $(\dot{E}/E)$ must be met by corresponding changes in the regulatory instrument $(\dot{T}/T)$ in order to hold harvest at the target.

---

4. We are ignoring any complexities associated with the discrete nature of the between-seasons transition and treating all between-season changes in variables as if they were continuous.

In this special case where biomass and quota are constant, changes in the technology parameter can be measured simply by measuring changes in the other two inputs, one chosen by the industry and the other by the regulatory agency. Because we are assuming that regulators successfully hold total harvests constant, total-factor productivity (TFP) exerted on the grounds must also be constant, and any changes in components of potential productivity must be matched by changes in other components. Importantly, since regulations are endogenous, any changes in q and E between seasons must be stifled by regulators to ensure that the quota is met continuously. As a result of this endogeneity, the above relationship may be particularly useful when economic researchers can easily observe regulator behavior but not capacity choice.[5] Since we are assuming that regulatory behavior mirrors capacity choice, successful regulators must react in order to hold harvests to the desired (constant) levels implied by their quota rules. To see how these assumptions are useful, consider the industry decision regarding capacity choice depicted in (7.4). If we log differentiate this, assuming that Q, $X(0)$, and the price/cost parameters are constant, we can determine the relationship between E and T and q that must hold when the industry is in a rent-dissipating equilibrium.[6] Solving this relationship for $(\dot{E}/E)$ and substituting this behavioral condition into (7.9) yields a reduced-form equation that depicts how regulations must respond in the regulated equilibrium to any productivity changes depicted by changes in $q(t)$ between seasons. This turns out to be:

$$(\dot{q}/q) = -[(\dot{E}/E) + (\dot{T}/T)] = -(\dot{T}/T)[1 - (svT/(svT + f))].\qquad(7.10)$$

Equation (7.10) shows that the rate of disembodied technical change $(\dot{q}/q)$ is proportional to the rate of change in the regulatory instrument, with the factor of proportionality associated with the share and the costs of fixed and variable factors. The interpretation of the above measure of factor productivity is straightforward and easily illustrated with a graph. If factor productivity changes, by increasing the catchability coefficient q between seasons, for example, then both curves in Figure 7.1 will shift, resulting in a new equilibrium as shown in Figure 7.2. A higher technology parameter causes, ceteris paribus, more pressure for capacity to enter because potential rents-per-unit capacity rises. This is shown by the upward shift of the industry equilibrium curve. At the same time, a higher catchability coefficient means that regulators

---

5. This is typical in fact. Most regulatory agencies see their task as primarily ensuring biological health of the resource, and only secondarily do they worry about the economic health of the industry. Hence the types of information usually gathered focus on biological variables such as stock assessment data and regulatory decisions made and not variables such as prices and costs.

6. Since revenues remain constant, we need only differentiate costs. By assumption, their rate of change is zero, and so we must have $(\dot{E}/E) = -(\dot{T}/T)[svT/(svT + f)]$. This implicitly defines how T must change when E changes in order to hold the industry in a rent-dissipating equilibrium that also freezes harvest levels.

FIGURE 7.2 Technological change in a regulated open-access equilibrium

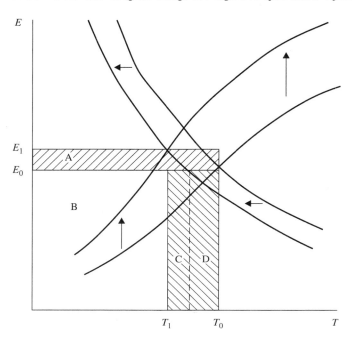

must restrain the impact of any amount of total capacity over the season (ET) even more vigorously in order to ensure that the fixed harvest target is not exceeded. This is shown by an inward shift of the regulatory curve. In essence, there are two effects of technological change, one boosting productivity of each unit of capacity, and the other drawing more units of capacity into the fishery as a result of higher potential rents.

Equation (7.10) shows that there are two ways to measure technological change by observing industry and regulator behavior. One is to measure the (negative of the) sum of rates of change of both inputs E and T between seasonal equilibriums. Using the initial equilibrium (E_0, T_0) as the base, the negative of the sum of the percentage changes of E and T can be approximated by:

$$\dot{q}/q \approx \{[(E_1 - E_0)T_0 + (T_1 - T_0)E_0]/[E_0 T_0)]\}. \tag{7.11}$$

This is shown on the graph by the area given by the boxes:

$$-\{[A/(B + C + D)] - [(C + D)/(B + C + D)]\}.$$

In this example, the percentage change in the regulatory instrument is negative (the season length is shortened), and the change in capacity is positive (since higher potential rents attract capacity). Technical change is measured as the (negative of the) sum of these opposite-signed effects. It is important to note that the proper measure of technical change is not the full amount of the percentage change in the regulatory instrument, since some of the total regulatory response is associated with having to stifle additional effort drawn in by the more productive technology.

Another way to measure technical change, corresponding to the right-hand side of equation (7.10) above, is to measure the overall tightening of regulations, netting out the indirect effect associated with the extra entry drawn in by the more productive technology. The overall regulatory impact is given by the areas $(C + D)/(B + C + D)$, and this is multiplied by a fraction less than one to net out the "pure" increase in productivity per unit of input. The appropriate fraction is $[D/(C + D)]$, which nets out the extra regulatory instrument tightening $[C/(B + C + D)]$ associated with the increase in aggregate inputs in the industry. The net change in the regulatory instrument associated with the productivity increase per unit capacity is thus $[D/(B + C + D)]$, which is equal to the first measure outlined above when areas A and C converge. Note finally that all these geometric representations are depicted with the initial equilibrium as the base for computing percentage changes. If, instead, the final equilibrium is used as the base from which percentage changes are computed, similar geometric representations may be derived. These geometric measures converge as $(\dot{q}/q)$ becomes infinitesimal.

This simplified model in which it is assumed that biomass and harvests are held at their safe levels continuously may be too simple to depict a more reasonable setting in which regulators are in sequences of temporary equilibriums moving toward the "safe" stock goal for the biomass over the long run. In this case, the quota will be adjusting gradually over time in accord with the quota rule $Q(X)$, and the biomass will be asymptotically approaching the safe stock level. When the biomass is below the long-run equilibrium, the quota will be set below the biological yield, and the biomass will grow between periods. Thus, both the industry equilibrium curves and the regulatory equilibrium curves will be shifting between seasons as the biomass and quota approach the long-run equilibrium. In general, the combinations of these shifts are complicated. As biomass rises, for example, the industry equilibrium curve shifts up. The regulator equilibrium shifts inward as a result of the direct effect of higher biomass levels, but outward as a result of the indirect effect that allows a higher quota.

Measuring factor-productivity changes in this more general setting is also made more difficult in practice by random shocks and errors in decisionmaking by either the regulators, the industry, or both. The stylized model discussed above depicts interaction in a manner much like a market that "clears" to determine capacity and season length perfectly in each season. In reality, even if the industry and regulators were behaving essentially as we depict, the data from any given year would likely be, at best, in the neighborhood of the joint equilibrium. There are thus several computational approaches that one might use, depending on one's belief about how close to equilibrium each group of agents is. We develop one that is consistent with equation (7.10) above but allowing for changes in the quota and biomass.

Differentiating the rent-dissipating equation (7.4) but this time allowing for changes in X and Q, we have:

$$(\dot{X}/X) + qET\exp(-qET)(X/H)[(\dot{q}/q) + (\dot{E}/E) + (\dot{T}/T)] - (\dot{E}/E) -$$
$$(\dot{T}/T)(svET/sPH) = 0. \qquad (7.12)$$

This implicit equation in $\dot{E}/E$ shows that the rent-dissipating rate of change of capacity between seasons will depend on the rate of change of biomass (which serves as an "input" with a unitary output elasticity) and the combined rates of change of the technology parameter and the regulated season length. Note that the term in front of the brackets is essentially a "share" term. In standard analyses of technical change (for example, Solow 1957), if the production function is homogenous of degree one, and if inputs are chosen by a competitive industry, we can compute these shares using factor-remuneration data, or if the function is Cobb-Douglas, we can use output elasticities. In the case at hand, the production function is not homogeneous of degree one, nor are inputs chosen to maximize profits or minimize costs. Hence we cannot use these tricks to measure the "share."

To understand this "share" term and options for measuring it, note that it can be written as:

$$R(E;T,q) = (MP_E/AP_E) = qET/(\exp(qET) - 1), \qquad (7.13)$$

where we use R to indicate the ratio of marginal to average product of capacity E (or, since they are perfect substitutes, of T or of q). It can easily be seen that the ratio of marginal to average product is bounded between one and zero as ET goes from zero to infinity. However, this term will not in general be a constant, since E and T (and possibly q) will be changing from season to season in the regulated equilibrium as the biomass and quota are adjusted by regulators. In fact, in a regulated open-access equilibrium, regulators determine total capacity, ET. Hence, one option that suggests itself is to use the regulatory instrument choice rule in equation (7.7) to substitute out the share term expressed as a function of total capacity, ET, by replacing it with

$$R(E;T,q) = \{\ln[X/(X - Q)]\}[(X - Q)/Q], \qquad (7.14)$$

which is a function of the biomass and quota level. Using (7.14) to replace (7.13), inserting in (7.12), and solving for $\dot{E}/E$ thus gives us:

$$(\dot{E}/E) = [1 - R]^{-1} \{(\dot{X}/X) + R(\dot{q}/q) - (\dot{T}/T)[(svT/(svT + f)) - R]\}. \qquad (7.15)$$

The expression in (7.15) could be used directly by solving for $(\dot{q}/q)$ and using data on harvests, biomass, quota targets, capacity, and season lengths.

However, since this is basically a "primal" model derived by differentiating the rent-dissipation equation, it does not contain all the additional information associated with the manner in which regulators are hypothesized to react between seasons in response to changes in technology, biomass, and capacity. The regulatory behavior assumptions can be incorporated by differentiating (7.7) and allowing quota to change with biomass according to the quota rule, so that:

$$\dot{T}/T = -(\dot{q}/q) - (\dot{E}/E) - (1/R)(\dot{X}/X)[1 - (dQ/dX)(X/Q)]. \qquad (7.16)$$

This expression connects changes in the regulatory instrument $(\dot{T}/T)$ to its three determinants. One set of forces is associated with growth in biomass between seasons and the requisite changes in the overall quota allowed as a result. This is given in the expression in brackets on the right-hand side of equation (7.16). This expression shows that, ceteris paribus, as the biomass grows the regulatory instrument will have to be changed in a manner that reflects the offsetting effects of the impact of larger biomass as a productive input and as a determinant of the allowable quota. In addition, when technical change or entry of capacity occurs, these forces will also be reflected in regulatory decisions as depicted in the first two terms in (7.16).

Since equation (7.15) describes how capacity will change between seasons in response to fundamental driving variables, including technical change, we can insert (7.15) into (7.16) and substitute out $(\dot{E}/E)$. The resulting equation can then be rearranged to derive a reduced-form equation with $(\dot{q}/q)$ on the left-hand side and exogenous variables and the equilibrium rates of change of the regulatory instrument on the right-hand side. In particular, we can rearrange (7.15) and (7.16) to get:

$$(\dot{q}/q) = [(\dot{Q}/Q) - (\dot{X}/X)]\{[(Q/(X - Q))/\ln[X/(X - Q)]\}$$
$$- (\dot{Q}/Q) - (\dot{T}/T)[1 - (svT/(svT + f))]. \qquad (7.17)$$

This is basically an implicit equation that expresses the way regulations will change to reflect factor-productivity changes and changes in the biomass given the corresponding quota rule. Alternatively, if we know how regulators' behavior changes and how the biomass and quota rule are changing, we can infer how productivity must be changing as the system adjusts from one temporary regulated equilibrium to another over time. This equation is the generalization of (7.10) above, which was derived under the assumption that the system was locked into its long-run, "safe," biomass steady state, with constant harvests and unchanging biomass levels.

To recap to this point, the model developed in this section depicts the evolution of a harvesting industry that is regulated by an agency that chooses policy instruments to guide the biomass toward some "safe" stock level. The industry takes these instruments as given and enters until seasonal rents are dissipated. The regulatory agency takes the industry's behavior as given and then determines the optimal policy instrument conditional on the biomass level and quota-target rule for that season. The key feature of this model is that it allows us to measure changes in factor productivity by observing the actions of the regulators who are, in fact, trying to contain the impact of such factor-productivity changes on the biomass. Factor-productivity growth can be measured in a manner that filters for the many-faceted influences of biomass changes, as well as the increases in capacity that are mirrored by purposeful changes in the policy instrument used by regulators. The expressions are relatively simple to compute, given estimates of the biomass, harvest quota, and season length. An additional virtue is that the required data are very much like those typically available and published by regulatory agencies charged with managing resources, with the exception of the variables related to fixed and variable costs.

Application: The North Pacific Halibut Fishery, 1935–1978

In this section we discuss an application of the above model to the North Pacific halibut fishery. This fishery is particularly suitable to a test of the model for several reasons. First, the fishery has been managed intensively since the 1930s, and a considerable amount of data exists, including good estimates of the biomass of halibut. Second, both the fishing technology and the method of regulation have remained relatively static and close to the framework outlined earlier. In particular, the fishery is conducted mainly as a long-line fishery, and the only regulations that have been imposed over much of the past 60 years are season-length restrictions. Fishing with long-line gear is particularly simple. Each unit of gear (called a "skate") is about 1,800 feet long, with hooks spaced approximately every 18 feet. Vessels carrying long-line gear arrive on the grounds and then bait the hooks and lay out strings of long lines with buoys attached to each end. After a certain number of hours have elapsed, the vessel returns, and crew retrieve the long line, disgorge the hooks from the fish, rebait the line, and begin the process again. Regulatory authorities keep careful count of the rate-of-effort application by measuring the number of "skate soaks," the catch-per-unit effort, and so on.

Over the period under consideration, there were only minor changes in the technology of long-line fishing. Vessels carrying and deploying the skates remained close to the same size. Some vessels operate with diesel engines, and these are close in design to those fishing in the 1930s, whereas others fish with newer engines and hull designs. Winches used to haul skates have improved somewhat, although not dramatically. Navigational gear (loran), bottom finders, and fish finders have improved dramatically, of course, but mainly over the past 10 to15 years. With respect to the basic gear unit, hooks were originally J-shaped, but more recently the industry has switched to so-called circle hooks. Bait use has varied over time, and recently skates have evolved to use

FIGURE 7.3 Biomass and harvest (Management Area 2–scaled)

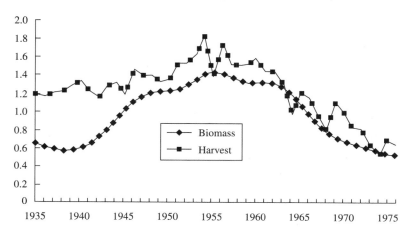

snap-on hooks rather than permanently ganged hooks. Snap-on hooks use less storage space and gear clutter and can also be used to adjust hook spacing.

We have gathered data to compute the more general factor-productivity measurement procedure summarized in (7.17). We have data for the period 1935–77 on biomass, harvest, and season length as well as a variety of other variables including skate soaks and numbers of vessels. Some of these data are disaggregated by vessel size class and by various areas; we aggregate into a single fleet operating over Management Area 2, which lies west of British Columbia and south of Alaska. The period over which we examine the data reveals a considerable amount of variation in the fundamental variables (see Figure 7.3). For example, biomass rose steadily from about 60 million pounds in 1930 to a peak of 135 million pounds in 1956. This increase in biomass was generated by a very active regulatory system, which was imposed in 1930. From the outset, regulators set new and stringent harvest quotas designed to allow the stock to rebuild itself after three decades of overharvesting. The rebuilding was a success as indicated by the biomass doubling between 1930 and the mid-1950s. During this growth period, the number of vessels also doubled as rents began to emerge. As a result of growing fishing capacity, regulators found it necessary to reduce season lengths, reaching a low in the 1950s (see Figure 7.4). Those who fish for a living and industry representatives concerned about the marketing implications of such short seasons managed to implement a "lay-in" program, which required vessels to remain in port for several days per month after landing. This allowed a stretching of the nominal season length in the 1950s, although real fishing time per vessel was still drastically constrained.

FIGURE 7.4 Harvest capacity and season length (scaled)

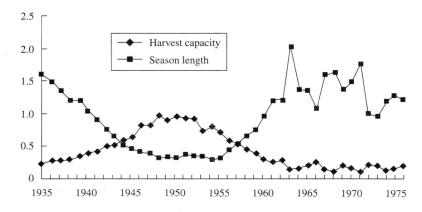

For the most part, biomass remained apparently healthy for the next decade, and then, beginning in 1963, it dropped precipitously to a low of 63 million pounds in 1978. The reasons for the drop are hotly debated, but regardless of the cause, regulators tightened the precision of many of their procedures and steered the fishery through a second rebuilding plan, which continued into the 1980s. During much of this period, while quotas were low, prices improved and capacity remained relatively constant. Regulators held seasons relatively short and fine-tuned them by carefully monitoring capacity and sometimes changing season lengths dramatically from season to season. In more recent times, higher prices brought an influx of capacity at the same time that biomass began to fall again, and during the late 1980s the season length was reduced to around five days. In 1990 the fishery in Area 2 was converted into an individual, quota-based scheme, resulting in a dramatic change in methods and incentives. In this analysis we cover the pre-individual quota period only.

We computed the factor-productivity index in equation (7.17) in order to understand what might have been happening to the productivity of fishing technology over this period that witnessed considerable change. Equation (7.17) was computed over the period 1935–78, using information on biomass, quotas, capacity, and the season length from the International Halibut Commission Management Reports.[7] Equation (7.17) contains a term $[1 - (svT/(svT + f))]$, and since we did not have actual accounting data on the fixed and variable costs associated with gear use, we needed to substitute something for the cost

---

7. The analysis was truncated at 1978 because in that year management was transferred from a joint U.S.-Canadian international committee to one that was primarily Canadian. Thus the nature of both subsequent policies and the data-gathering process changed in a relatively discrete manner in 1978. In 1980, for example, the Canadians introduced a limited entry program, whereas the corresponding Area 3 (which lies off Alaska) remained a regulated open-access fishery.

ratio that multiplies the logarithm of the change in the seasonal policy instrument. As it turns out, using the rent-dissipation equation (7.4), an alternative representation of the ratio in (7.17) in rent-dissipating equilibrium is the ratio $\{1 - [(svET/sPH]\}$. But this is basically one minus the ratio of variable seasonal costs to the skipper/owner entrepreneur's share of total fishing revenues. A study by the Commercial Fisheries Limited Entry Commission of Alaska surveyed a wide range of Alaskan fisheries and found that variable fishing costs (for bait, gasoline, and food) averaged about 20 percent of gross revenues. Hence, as a first approximation, the ratio can be computed as 0.80. We also used values for v and f estimated econometrically in Homans and Wilen (1997). These assume a constant value for q over the period, but they are illustrative for comparison.

The productivity index computed over the 40-year period is shown in Figure 7.5. As can be seen, the index rose at first and then fell during World War II, leveled out during the postwar period, and then sustained a precipitous drop until the mid-1960s. During this period of apparent technical regress, the season length gradually fell, reaching its low in the mid-1950s. Following the precipitous drop in biomass in the mid-1960s, there was considerable exit, and then season lengths began to rise, even in the face of low biomass levels and low quotas. During this period, the index rose gradually until the end of the period of examination.

Since the pattern of technical regress is somewhat unusual, it raises the issue: What could account for this apparent pattern? The first concern, of course, is simply spurious results because of poor data measurement, inappropriate theory, or sensitivity to our rule of thumb regarding the $(svT/(svT + f))$ ratio. We are reasonably confident that the measurement of units of gear application is relatively accurate, as are measurements of season length, harvests, and quota. Fishers have been required to fill out logbooks since the inception of regulations that detail when and where each unit of gear was dropped, how long it was soaked, and what the yield was upon retrieval. This information is used by regulators to monitor stock densities in various areas, and periodic independent checks have shown that fishermen are both honest and diligent about the logbooks. An unknown is how accurate measures of biomass are. Regulators compute indexes of biomass using complicated methods that utilize age-specific samples of catch and research tows designed to sample and measure particular biological parameters. We also believe that the theory used is sensible and, as explained earlier, essentially accurate as a simple representation of the types of regulation and fishing technology used in this particular fishery. The one potentially significant concern is the assumption of instantaneous adjustment in the model of regulatory equilibrium. It is likely that rents are not completely dissipated each year, and it is also likely that regulators are not always exactly able to attain their quota target each year. Without a further parameterization of the model and estimation, one cannot

FIGURE 7.5 Productivity index *q(t)*

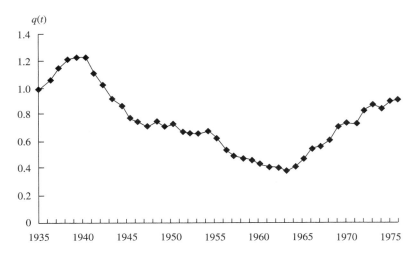

probably go too much further with the data available than was done here, however.

In trying to interpret these results, it should also be noted that the index $q(t)$ is very much a catch-all index that measures many dimensions of the relative catching power of a unit of gear. First of all, it incorporates the impacts of any auxiliary inputs that are associated with units of gear, including labor and vessel capital, which may not be in fixed proportion as we have assumed. We suspect that these impacts are not major issues in this case, however; labor per unit of gear did not change appreciably over the period, vessel capital for these vessels has remained fairly constant, and gear is virtually unchanged. What has changed is the intensity of fishing, however, as fishing seasons were adjusted to check changes in total units of gear deployed as well as any changes in biomass or apparent changes in efficiency. Most industry observers point to the many ways that fishing becomes more frantic and less efficient as seasons are shortened. Some fishing involves "searching" by making test soaks, and as the season shortens, fishermen must search less and commit to areas of lower average productivity. In addition, the geographic distribution of fishing has shifted toward near-shore grounds, and the timing of fishing has been compressed into a period in which fishable biomass may have changed. Fishermen also talk about gear entanglement as more vessels are packed into smaller fishing regions over shorter periods. All of these could serve to reduce factor productivity during periods of declining season length.

The productivity index computed here should thus be regarded as illustrative at this point. We have used a simple index in this chapter, but others are possible using more or less of the theory developed earlier. For example, one could develop a simple "primal" index that only makes assumptions about the harvest capacity function and input changes. The drawback is that such an index would require more information about cost shares, but the advantage is that it would not rely on maintained assumptions we have used to tie various relationships together. On the other hand, it is possible to develop more data-intensive dual measures that require more parameterization and estimation of cost/production function parameters. The model used here is not particularly data-intensive, and it illustrates how it is possible, in principle, to focus mainly on the types of data that regulatory authorities might normally collect and to express the productivity measure in terms of those. The novelty of the approach is in the possibility of inferring patterns of technological change by observing the behavior of regulators whose success depends in part on reacting to such productivity changes.

Conclusion

This chapter takes a first step toward thinking about measuring factor-productivity changes in an industry that uses a natural resource under open access but regulated conditions. We argued at the outset that regulated use is by far the dominant institutional setting for most important common-property resources, many of which are also open access. The importance of the incorporation of regulatory behavior cannot be underestimated. As we suggested earlier, regulations are purposeful, dynamic, and endogenous generally. As a result, it may be possible to develop more structured analyses of these industries by modeling not only production technologies and industry behavior but also the regulatory technology and regulatory behavior. This chapter develops a simple conceptualization of such a system and uses it to explore the implications for measuring factor productivity.

Although the quantitative results of this exercise should not be taken too literally, they are suggestive of some interesting hypotheses about these types of industries. First, is factor-productivity regression plausible in this and in other regulated open-access industries? Should we not generally observe gear productivity to be increasing as new technologies and methods are adopted? There seem to be opposing forces at work. On the one hand, from the individual decisionmaker's standpoint, one way to "beat" the system, at least in the short run, is to adopt productivity-enhancing innovations. This provides a vessel-level demand for new technology, and one would assume that these incentives would be reflected in gear and boat-building innovations. On the other hand, it is the nature of regulated, open-access resource use that there can be no ultimate payoff over the long term when everyone adopts new technology. This is because *aggregate* output must not exceed target levels, and regulators are poised to ensure that this remains the case. In this setting, individuals are locked into a prisoner's dilemma in that if they do adopt and others do not they gain temporarily, but if they do not adopt and others do, they lose immediately. Under these circumstances, everyone will be drawn into adopting new technologies (perhaps earlier than is efficient) that have no ultimate effect on industry output. If innovations save costs, new entry will occur until existing participants' shares fall and total industry costs rise, and rents will eventually be dissipated again.

Moreover, there is another subtle, perverse force operating out of the behavior of regulators. It operates because regulators ultimately must stifle the potential of new technology if it is productivity enhancing in order to avoid overharvesting the quota target. In fact, the hidden goal of managers in this type of setting is effectively one of actually looking for options to reduce the productivity of gear, since their main instrument of control over the harvest, and hence biomass health, is control over aggregate gear application. As the risk of inadvertent overfishing grows, one would expect managers to look for ways to make fishing inefficient in order to spread capacity over time, allow more time to monitor and compute cumulative harvest, and make more accurate decisions regarding season lengths. We have depicted a situation in this chapter whereby the industry "chooses" one input and regulators "choose" another. What may actually be happening in the halibut fishery and reflected in our productivity index is a process of interference between the two inputs so that units of gear, and the period over which gear is applied, are not really perfectly substitutable as assumed in the model. When seasons get very short as gear potential grows, for example, fishermen cannot search efficiently, they may work longer shifts than is sensible, they may incur excessive gear loss or breakage, and so on. All these inefficiencies that are induced by regulatory change might swamp any increases in potential efficiency from innovation, with the net result of apparent technological regress.

This brings up a last point regarding policy in regulated open-access settings. In fisheries as well as other common-property industries, it has not been uncommon over the past 50 years to see, on the one hand, governmental agencies promoting, subsidizing, and investing in productivity-enhancing technology and, on the other hand, different agencies spending considerable sums trying to contain excess capacity by regulation. This seems perverse, at best, and a good example of different agencies conducting uncoordinated policy. It also seems wasteful because the gains that might be generated by technological change remain only potential rather than realized gains until the property rights problems are fixed. Over the past two decades there has been growing recognition among economists that piecemeal policies aimed at the symptoms of incomplete property do not work over the long run. Partly because of this recognition, there has been a wave of recent interest in wholesale changes in property rights systems designed to avoid such wastes. Most nations have moved toward limited entry in valuable fisheries. These programs can contain some rent dissipation, but when harvesting technology is flexible, constraining one input often invites expansion across other dimensions. The newest institutional innovation designed to "solve" common-property problems is the so-called individual transferable quota (ITQ), pioneered in Iceland, New Zealand, and Australia. ITQs give each fisherman a transferable right to a fraction of the biologically determined safe harvest level. Unlike limited entry programs, ITQs directly attack the problem first identified by Gordon (incentives associated with lack of ownership) rather than the symptoms (overcapacity) by creating property rights. Needless to say, these new institutions are being watched with some interest by fisheries policy analysts and those with an interest in using natural resources in a manner that generates the surpluses of which they are capable. The losses from inefficiencies are not small; recent estimates suggest that upwards of $80 billion per year is being wasted in the world's commercial fisheries under inefficient open-access and regulated open-access institutions.

8 Soil Change and Agriculture in Two Developing Countries

PETER LINDERT

Development agencies are increasingly committed to monitoring gains and losses in natural resource assets. The United Nations and the World Bank have set guidelines for incorporating environmental accounts into the traditional measures of national product (Ahmed et al., 1989). Although environmental investments and depreciation are inherently harder to quantify than conventional market products, there is no denying that our view of economic progress is in danger of either overoptimism or overpessimism if it fails to measure changes in the stock of natural resources. The usual fear about our conventional accounts is that they are too optimistic, since conventional gross domestic product (GDP) measures fail to deduct values for the depreciation of a vital resource. There is growing global awareness that resource depletion needs to be measured and priced. It must also be combated, sooner or later, because many natural resources cannot be depleted indefinitely without eliminating the net social benefits from economic growth.

Concern about the stock of cultivable soil as a natural asset has always focused on the desocializing and developing countries, and probably with good reason. Poorer countries are more threatened by any deterioration of food supply, and they are less able to wait for the delayed benefits from investments in soil and forest conservation, fertilizer, and water control.

This chapter is an attempt to improve the debate over the soil-degradation consequences of developing-country agriculture on several fronts. First, some inadequacies in recent writings on soil-degradation trends are noted. In the second section, "Cause and Effect in Time and Space," the requirements for a good empirical test of how agriculture and the soil really interact over the long run are rethought. That section sets the stage for new historical soil data from China and Indonesia—two countries that have been in the spotlight throughout the soil-degradation debate. Such historical data are available, though not always in ideal form. They offer information about the long-imagined trends in soil quality. Some kinds of soil nutrients have been depleted, while others have improved. The sensitive balance involving water control and pH has swung in different directions at different times. The topsoil, meanwhile, is probably not becoming thinner for whole agricultural heartlands.

If the soil endowment seems to have been depleted in some respects but augmented in others, how does the net balance work out? To weigh the effects of various soil characteristics on agricultural yields requires careful statistical work. The section "Cross-Sectional Estimates of the Soil-Agriculture Links in China" draws on a companion article to show that soil depletion leaves less of an imprint on yields than soil augmentation.

Going to the trouble of estimating the mutual feedbacks between soil and agricultural performance brings further benefits in the section titled "Will Development Mine the Soil?" It suggests that shifting agriculture away from staple grains—as economic development does—may itself be a soil-improving shift. This environmental Engel effect will turn out to be one of three ways in which development may preserve agriculture's soil endowment.

"Well-Known" Soil-Degradation Trends: The Single Snapshot as a Motion Picture

Two opposing majority views seem to prevail on the issue of soil degradation. As with so many social issues, the majority view among those who write on the subject is pessimistic (for example, Brown 1995; Dregne 1982; Eckholm 1976; Orleans 1992; Smil 1984). By contrast, the likely view of the silent majority is that soil degradation is only a secondary concern. That the more outspoken side of the debate tends toward pessimism seems natural enough: the incentive to commit time and reputation to writing on an issue is stronger for those who feel that society needs to be warned about that particular issue.

Yet neither those who silently ignore soil degradation nor those who warn about it have gathered systematic time-series evidence on what those trends really are. The available displays of evidence fall far short of establishing what has happened to our soil endowment for two main reasons: most such displays lack any time-series dimension, and all of them are haphazard, sketchy, and unpersuasive.

It might seem that the soil-degradation trends are well known, even on a global scale. After all, one can look them up in statistical volumes, such as those published by the World Resources Institute or Worldwatch. There one finds not only the broad rate of soil degradation but also a global geography of where it is most or least severe.

Doubts about the "well-known" trends begin to emerge when one goes to the sources used to present the summary view of soil trends.[1] The single document that shapes most of the current global conjectures is the *1991 World Map of the Status of Human-Induced Soil Degradation,* compiled for the

---

1. Many of Part II's criticisms of the most-cited estimates have been made in different ways by other authors. On the global estimates, with additional focus on evidence from the United States, see Crosson and Stout (1983), and Crosson (1985, 1995). For a critical review of the Indonesian evidence, see Diemont et al. (1991).

United Nations Environment Program and other agencies as part of the ongoing Global Assessment of Soil Degradation (GLASOD) (Oldeman et al. 1991). The map, with its accompanying explanatory handbook, offers a rich harvest. It shows more than just the soil-degradation trends and where they are occurring around the globe. It names the processes of degradation, with heavy emphasis on wind and water erosion. It also tells us their cause, as evident in the "Human-Induced" part of the title. Some who cite the map (for example, World Resources Institute and Worldwatch) infer that the map even tells us *when* these trends have been occurring—namely, "since 1945." The mention of "when" should set off a warning light, even if the mentions of causes and places have not. How could the GLASOD team in the Netherlands know how good the soil was in the past? There was no global soil survey in 1945, nor has there ever been one worth the name, until the GLASOD mapping effort. How can we know that a change has taken place without at least two dates between which to measure the change?

Another wave of doubt surrounds the "Human-Induced" idea. If we do not know when the soil changed, how can we know why it changed? Soil scientists work hard to sort out human from natural contributions to erosion and other soil changes even at the local level. To globalize the effort, the GLASOD team used the best resources available on a global scale. That is, it sent data requests to experts around the world. It asked each to consider their local terrain, climate, current soil state, and other conditions and to produce from these a judgment of how fast the different kinds of soil degradation might be occurring.

What this yields, however, is not data on how the soil has changed over time, or why, but a set of *predictions* on how much degradation *might* occur for that kind of terrain, climate, and so forth, given the available side evidence from field experiments around the world. The predictions could easily miss the mark. The soil is constantly being affected by humans in complex ways. And as the "Cause and Effect in Time and Space" section of this chapter reemphasizes, humans are reacting to the condition of the soil itself, in ways that are meant to change the soil. None of the available predictions and simulations captures this complexity of human responses.

The basic flaw in the often-used evidence on soil trends, then, is that it tries to measure changes over time without data over time. It is an attempt to run a whole movie from a single snapshot. The same is true of other summary judgments, whether they mean to sweep the globe or to focus on a single region or country. None of them is based on any quantitative history of the soil. The problem grows most acute where the most is asserted about trends. Over the past 20 years those most-debated places have tended to be Sahelian Africa, northwest China, northwest India, and the humid tropics. In all cases the necessary time-series data are lacking. This chapter seeks to fill the gap for two of these target regions.

The other main point to be made about the vast assertive literature on soil-degradation trends, both globally and in connection with China and Indonesia, is that it is skimpy and often of dismissably low quality. It falls far short of delivering even clear evidence of the soil trends themselves, let alone their economic implications. Here is a catalog of the key questions ignored or badly handled by most of the literature:

Deterioration When?

Most writers cite an accumulated degree of degradation without giving a clear starting date. If we are to interpret the role of humans in any soil trend, it matters greatly whether the degradation dates from the dawn of earth, or the dawn of agriculture, or 1957, or 1977. A photograph of the Grand Canyon does not show that farmers are depleting the soil today.

Where?

The abundant literature on erosion often neglects to explain how much of the lost tonnage comes from, or what share of the affected area matches, the places where humans have intervened. For example, some authors cite tons of soil flowing into rivers and the ocean without telling us what share was lost from cultivated lands. Others misleadingly mix data from different places, for example, multiplying a tonnage of soil lost from arid semideserts such as China's loess plateau by a figure on yield lost per ton of topsoil on artificially scraped experimental fields in the fertile plains.

Lost, Fallow, or Converted?

A decline in cultivated area does not necessarily show soil degradation or even a drop in the supply of land available to agriculture. Even soils that are improving can go out of cultivation if the relative prices of farm products drop or if farm wage rates rise faster than farm labor productivity. Such trends are very possible, since economic progress shifts demand away from agricultural products (Engel's law) and raises wages in response to economywide productivity trends. A rise in cultivated area is equally ambiguous as an indicator of soil quality.

In fact, it is surprising to see how often the changes in cultivated area are cited as evidence of trends in soil quality. By themselves, trends in cultivated area can never resolve a debate between pessimists and optimists:

Trend we see—	A pessimist can say—	An optimist can say—
Cultivated area rose	Population pressure forced desperate resort to working poor lands	Progress reclaims and improves new lands
Cultivated area fell	Degraded lands had to be abandoned	Progress pulls valuable labor and capital away from marginal lands

To be useful, the figures on land-area trends must be supplemented by information on land price trends and causal factors.

Gross or Net Soil Loss?

Some indicators, such as soil tonnage flows in rivers, reflect gross soil losses, often from unknown places, and not the net decline in soil depth or in soil nutrients at any one place. The distinction is crucial where tillage and fertilization are separate influences on soil depth and quality.

Predictions or History?

To repeat, virtually all estimates of current soil trends, including every available map of soil-degradation trends, are in fact not data. Rather, they are experts' predictions, derived by combining data on slope, climate, and land use with what happens to such soils under experimental conditions. Sometimes it is refined into "expert opinion," as in the GLASOD map, but it is still not based on any observation before the mid-1980s. For China, the only approximation to an actual time series is that series since 1975 by China's Ministry of Water Resources and Electrical Power, giving areas damaged or in danger (Huang and Rozelle 1995). But the areas cited are not specific to farmland, and the abruptness of their occasional year-to-year jumps, especially in 1984–85, suggests changes in official definitions rather than changes in soil condition.

Cause and Effect in Time and Space

To raise the scientific standard of the debate over soil trends requires some hard thinking about our empirical strategy. A key step is to confront the difficulties of sorting out how soil conditions and agricultural performance affect each other over time and between places.

The Simultaneous Soil-Agriculture System

The most formidable barrier to estimating what we have done to the land and what difference its condition makes to our agriculture is the mutuality of their interactions. People shape the soil that feeds them.[2] This well-known mutuality poses a tough challenge for statistical analysis. It is harder to reach unbiased estimates of two causal links between a pair of variables than it is to estimate a one-way causal link. The barriers to estimating how soil affects agriculture and vice versa, and the choices available to us, can be illustrated with a very simplified algebraic statement of the soil-agricultural system.

---

2. For a sampling of how authors in the nineteenth century noted and reacted to the human control over soil quality, see Hayami and Ruttan (1985:45–50).

The bare essentials of the soil-agriculture system can be portrayed with this pair of simultaneous equation sets:

$$A = a_o + a_1 X_a + a_2 S + e_a \qquad (8.1)$$

$$S = b_o + b_1 X_s + b_2 A + b_3 L(A) + e_s. \qquad (8.2)$$

In the first set of equations A represents a vector of agricultural outcomes (outputs, crop planting areas); X_a is a vector of nonsoil influences on those outcomes, such as human-controlled inputs (labor, fertilizer, irrigation, seed varieties, equipment, draft animals, and so on) and climate; S is a vector of variable soil characteristics that directly affect plant growth, such as soil nutrient levels, organic matter, pH, and topsoil depth; e_a is a random error term, and the a's are sets of coefficients. In the second set of equations X_s represents a vector of relatively fixed determinants of topsoil quality at the soil site, such as parent material, climate, soil classification, terrain, texture, and topsoil depth. The agricultural vector reappears twice here, first in its current values (A) and then as $L(A)$, a vector of its lagged values from the past. The lags are indispensable here, because agricultural practice affects topsoil characteristics only slowly over the years. The b's are coefficients, and e_s is the error term. If we can estimate the coefficients in both equations, we have unlocked the whole system: not only will we know how the truly exogenous forces (X_a and X_s) affect both soil characteristics and agricultural performance, but we can judge the direct effects of soil conditions on performance (a_2) and the direct feedback from agriculture to the soil itself (b_2 and b_3).

The key requirements for empirical success here are measures of all variables that are both reliable and highly variable across some sample. No independent variable can reveal its true influence if it does not vary over the sample, or if it is so closely correlated with another independent variable as to defy sorting out their separate influences.

The ideal experiment for identifying how this system works is easy to describe. To explore the interactions of, say, 10 dimensions of soil quality and 10 dimensions of agricultural performance is a manageable task with a sample of more than 50 years' annual data on more than 40 land areas if government policies, market conditions, property rights institutions, geology, and climate all varied among these places and years in measurable ways.

The readily available sample designs all fall short of this empirical ideal. To see how, and what choices remain open, let us consider each of three main kinds of sample designs.

Controlled Experiments

The best practical design for identifying soil-farming interactions has been generating data for more than 150 years. The long-term experimental plots of Rothamsted, England, in the 1840s, later augmented by the Morrow plots at the University of Illinois and other such plots around the world, have yielded valuable information on how the soil and yields both respond to different farming practices (Frye and Thomas 1991). In terms of our simultaneous-equation framework, experiments in the Rothamsted tradition hold X_s fixed and manipulate X_a and monitor the responses of both A and, in this century, S. After enough years have passed, the whole time path of $L(A)$ is also known, random errors arise, and there is enough information to show how both A and S respond to X_a alone. We have learned, for example, which crop rotations and which fertilizer regimes offer sustainable yields, given their effects on soil conditions.

By their very nature, however, the controlled experiments are far too narrow in scope to answer the question before us here: How do real farm populations, pursuing their own self-interests in different institutional settings, really manage the soil? The problem is not just that humans use a wider range of farm practices and soil amendments, which might only require simulating more dimensions of X_a on the experimental plots. Rather, they vary their management of the soil and their agricultural inputs in response to changes in their economic environment (other parts of X_a) and in response to the condition of the soil itself. Their endogenous practices (more dimensions of A) respond in ways never introduced on any experimental plot. By (wisely) keeping their long-run experiments simple, agronomists have chosen not to attempt the more difficult task of simulating whole farm populations' economic responses over the years.

Short-run agronomic and soil science experiments avoid some of the limits of the long-run experiments but suffer other limits. They avoid the extreme cost of maintaining fixed plots over decades, a cost that limits the long-run plots to tiny size and limited technology. Experiments running only a couple of years can manipulate a much wider range of human practices (more variation in X_a). Yet by losing the long time series they throw away $L(A)$, and by making farm practices exogenous they fail to imitate real behavior.

Conventional Spatial Cross-Sections

By amassing data from large cross-sections of farms or districts in a given year, a long empirical tradition in agricultural economics gets closer to the issues raised here by following the behavior of real economic agents. It takes each place's current agricultural performance as an encapsulation of its own history, effectively using A as a proxy for the unmeasured time path $L(A)$.

This tradition suffers four limitations that are relevant here. The first is the most obvious and least important: current agricultural performance is an imperfect proxy for the $L(A)$ that has shaped the soil now being used. Second, these studies often lack measures of most soil-condition variables (S), reverting instead to available measures of the basic soil background (X_s)—soil classification, climate, terrain, and so forth. Third, with or without data on S, their concern is usually only with the first equation, and not the second, so that they do not try to confront the simultaneity of soil and agriculture. So it is with production-function studies, even those that include the exogenous soil-background variables in X_s.[3] They remain vulnerable to the suspicion that the coefficients on the productivity effects of soil, and perhaps other coefficients as well, are biased by the feedback from agricultural outputs to the condition of the soil.

The final shortcoming of standard cross-sectional studies perhaps needs the most emphasis. These studies usually lack sufficient exogenous variation in the X_a variables, those mostly human influences on agricultural performance, to identify the effects of such interventions. It might seem otherwise. It might seem that cross-sectional agricultural production-function studies have abundant data on the X_a's, in the form of labor inputs, fertilizer inputs, crop choices, and so forth. Yet in most settings these are in fact *endogenous* agricultural variables (within A), simultaneously determined along with agricultural outputs (also in A) by other human variables and by soil conditions. The measures of labor and other inputs are usually not exogenous in a cross-section of places.

The lack of truly exogenous X_a's usually results from the way in which the convenient cross-sectional sample was supplied in the first place. We are typically offered cross-sections of farms or districts *within the same economy and polity,* such as farms in the Midwest or districts of India. The usual cross-sectional approach fails most clearly in a country with well-integrated markets and uniform legal institutions and government policies. In the extreme case of a perfectly integrated country, every place in the cross-section faces the same set of input and output prices and the same set of institutions, tax codes, and subsidies. All spatial variations in the easily measured quantities of agricultural inputs are responses to the X_s's, not exogenous X_a's. In fact, there are few truly exogenous variables to serve as X_a's—perhaps just local climate (which already appears in the X_s vector) and local, nonagricultural economic advantages. Without a strong X_a, neither set of equations can be identified with much confidence in a cross-sectional sample.

Not all cross-sectional efforts to estimate the soil-agriculture system are hopeless, however. One can find a country or region with the right mixture of good data plus economic or institutional drawbacks—a country that has sufficient usable local data despite market imperfections and institutional barriers that make prices, policies, and institutions differ from place to place. Some developing countries fit this description, yielding good spatial variation in the X_a's to complement good data on the other variables. The districts of India would make a good cross-sectional sample of this sort, combining India's district-level agricultural, economic, and political data (and imperfect market integration) with the fruits of the national soil survey of the 1980s and 1990s. China makes another good opportunity at the county (*xian*) level. Not only does China have usable data on all the fronts needed here, but China represents an extreme case in which input supplies and other variables differ widely from

---

3. Good examples are Bhalla (1988) and Peterson (1986).

county to county because government policy has blocked market integration and rationed fertilizer, labor, and other key inputs. In the section "Cross-Sectional Estimates of the Soil-Agriculture Links in China," we make use of this peculiar exogeneity of China's local supplies of agricultural inputs.

Pooling over Many Years and Many Places

To move closer to the ideal experiment sketched earlier, one can try to find countries or regions where all the necessary data reach back many years. The most binding constraint is the supply of data on topsoil quality. This calls for several decades of consistently applied soil surveys to generate a quantitative history of the topsoil's nutrients, pH, and physical composition. Such soil time series can probably be assembled for the United States back to 1930 or even back to 1900 and could be supplemented with good agricultural, economic, climatic, and other data at the county level. That experiment has not been attempted here.

Among developing countries, where concerns about food supply and soil degradation seem more immediate, very few have the necessary soil data before the 1980s. In the next section we examine what appear to be the two richest developing-country soil histories extending back over half a century. Even in these two promising cases, China and Indonesia, the long-run data pool has only the soil data, not a consistent series of economic data, before the 1980s. The time-series approach can estimate only the second set of equations above, those exploring patterns in soil conditions (S).

We can, however, use the time-space distinction as an ally in estimating the determinants of soil quality. For soil data sets that span a few decades, time is the domain of human forces, and the nonhuman determinants of topsoil conditions vary only over space and not over a time period so short. Samples that reach back a half a century or a century are optimal: they are long enough for agriculture and other human interventions to affect topsoil characteristics greatly yet too short for nonhuman forces to change the soil much. In terms of our equations, we can exploit the relative time fixity of X_s and use the time variable to bundle the X_a's together. Time is a stand-in for human soil amendments, just as time often serves as a stand-in for technological change in studies of economic growth. We turn next to this use of new soil-history data sets pooled over decades and over space, before returning to a special cross-sectional opportunity for China.

Soil Quality Trends in China and Indonesia

New Data

Thanks to some pioneering efforts in soil surveying, we can learn much about the physical and chemical state of soils in China and Indonesia since the 1930s.

In China's case, the soil data have come in three waves. For the period 1932–44 (hereafter "the 1930s"), Sino-American teams based in Nanjing and (during the 1940s) Chongqing published several hundred soil profiles from all the parts of China they could survey in such turbulent times (China, 1936–44, vols. 6–24). The second wave, here called "the 1950s," started slowly in 1950 and reached high tide in 1958–61. For this "1950s" wave, we have gleaned a few hundred typical soil profiles from several articles in Chinese, a Sino-Soviet compilation (Kovda 1959), the published but rare volume for the first "National Soil Survey" (1958–61), and a special study of Inner Mongolia in 1961–64. Finally, the ambitious "Second National Soil Survey" of 1981–86 is now available in a mixture of published and in-press province volumes. Through it all, both the intellectual leadership and the measurement techniques remained much the same. The data are rich for the 1980s but much thinner for the first two waves. We were able to use only a few hundred pre-1980 observations for the whole country, and with incomplete detail on land use in particular, to supplement more than a thousand profiles for 1981–86.[4]

For Indonesia, we have more detailed data, thanks to the continuity of procedures and personnel from the colonial era to the present. Dutch-led teams began generating soil-profile samples as early as 1908. The data became quite numerous after 1923, but the coverage of land use remained spotty until 1938. Fortunately, there was an intense and detailed survey covering all islands for the period 1938–41. Regular surveying resumed in the late 1940s and has continued to this day. Pruning down the archive from more than 100,000 soil profiles in various states of preservation yields a sample of 4,562 well-detailed profiles, half from Java and half from other islands.

Before the 1980s the soil characteristics covered by the soil-profile data varied, and a long history is possible only for certain characteristics that were consistently measured. Among the desirable data *not* consistently covered are the "available" levels (as opposed to total levels) of macronutrients, any coverage of micronutrients, cation exchange capacity, or salt content. Almost always available are physical composition (including Al-Fe-Si breakdowns), texture, pH, organic matter, total nitrogen, total phosphorus, total potassium, CaO (for Indonesia), parent material, and a soil classification. The data are presented for different perceived soil "horizons" down to various depths. What we are offered for several decades is a list of variables that is satisfactory, though not ideal. While these indicators fall short of the list of minimum data

---

4. The exact sample sizes vary with the choice of soil characteristic, with data on pH being the most abundant and data on total nitrogen the least abundant. For the details of the samples, their sources, and their limitations, see Lindert, Lu, and Wu (1995).

   As an example of the intellectual continuity of China's soil-science establishment in Nanjing, Professor Li Chingkwei generated some of our primary data as a young field tester on the team involving Professor James Thorp in the 1930s, was a leading organizer of the national soil surveys of 1959–61 and 1981–86, and kindly offered advice on our project in 1993–94.

needed to quantify soil quality (Doran et al. 1994), they figure prominently in such a list. Since we are interested in one particular dimension of soil quality—namely, agricultural productivity—it is fortunate that those who chose which data to gather and present over the decades shared the same priority. Thus most of the soil's effects on yields are predicted fairly well by the few indicators we stress here. Our S vector therefore consists of organic matter, the macronutrient (total NPK) levels, pH, and topsoil depth.[5]

"Comparable" Places

It would be ideal to have repeated measurements of the soil in the exact same thousand or so places over half a century or longer. That has never happened, except on those small long-term experimental plots at Rothamsted and elsewhere. Out in real farmers' fields, it is unlikely that any given plot of a hundred hectares was ever sampled in more than one decade. This raises the concern that the soils being compared at different times are not really comparable. Yet it would be too nihilistic to reject data that are not from the exact same sites, just as it would be wrong to reject comparison of opinion polls over different years on the grounds that they are not the same people. On this soil scientists and statisticians would agree. Soil scientists have always seen predictive value in classifying soils by their characteristics and in using "representative profiles" to stand for the condition for large soil areas.

Historical samples can indeed reveal trends in "similar" soils, but only after a sound statistical procedure has been followed. Historical comparison requires knowing that two different sites are sufficiently "the same" in their broad classes of soil attributes and have the same relationship to the mean values of the variables of interest (pH and nutrients) within each set of "the same" soils in different time periods.

Widespread soil degradation or soil improvement should show up as a downward or upward trend in soil parameters when we "hold other things equal" on our comparison of profiles from different historical eras. Specifically, care has been taken to hold other things equal with a two-step statistical regression procedure. The first stage explores the trends in each soil indicator (our S vector) by holding constant the vegetation, precipitation, parent material, soil class, terrain, texture, and topsoil sample depth. Then, to make sure that all these controls did not miss some important systematic fixed effects, we examined the residuals by district (*xian* for China, *kabupaten* for Indonesia) to find districts whose soil-value "errors" were systematically high or low. Dummy variables for these special districts were then added to the list of things to be held equal, and the regressions were rerun. These precautions seem

---

5. For a general sense of the leading role of these few soil indicators in shaping soil scientists' prediction of yields, see Pierce et al. (1983), Rijsbergen and Wolman (1984), and again Doran et al. (1994).

necessary and sufficient to avoid confusing the effects of time and place on soil quality.[6]

Overall Trends for Cultivated Lands

Careful handling of the soil data reveals some broad trends in the quality of agricultural soils since the 1930s. To feature trends that might hold in other developing countries as well, let us view the trends in each main soil indicator for China and Indonesia side by side. To focus on the effects of human intervention, we concentrate on mineral soils that were cultivated at or before the time the soil-profile data were gathered.

MACRONUTRIENTS.   Different as their geology and climate may be, China and Indonesia shared at least some broad trends in their topsoil endowments of organic matter, nitrogen, phosphorus, and potassium. These trends are summarized in Table 8.1 and Figure 8.1. The numbers represent average trends over broad areas, both to smooth out the fluctuations caused by thinner sampling at the local level and to match the breadth of the debate over soil trends. The averages in Table 8.1 and Figure 8.1 are not simple raw averages. Rather, they are all regression-based noisy conditional averages—that is, they hold the nonhuman site variables (the X_s's) constant, while retaining the statistical "noise" of the regression errors.

If there are endowments that are consistently depleted, or "mined," by agriculture in these two developing countries, those would be the percentages of soil organic matter and total nitrogen. For most regions of China, the trend in organic matter and nitrogen was slightly downward from the 1950s to the 1980s. The depletion since the 1950s was not statistically significant for North China as a whole, though it was statistically significant for total nitrogen in the northeastern Huang-Huai-Hai plain. In the central Chang Jiang (Yangtze) plain, the decline was again slight, though statistically significant for nitrogen at the 10 percent level. The double-cropped rice region on the southeast coast from Fujian to eastern Guanxi shared the same marginally significant decline. Aside from the surprising rise of organic matter and nitrogen shown for the southwestern rice region, most regions show a slight downward trend in organic matter and nitrogen.[7]

Java, too, lost organic matter and (possibly) nitrogen from its topsoil reserves, in this case over the period 1955–90. The decline is statistically

---

6. The estimation techniques are described in more detail in Lindert, Lu, and Wu (1996a, 1996b) and Lindert (1997).

7. The peculiar rise in organic matter and nitrogen (and potassium) in the southwest may have been due to the more favorable trend in organic fertilizers relative to crop intensification in that region than in the rest of the south (Lindert, Lu, and Wu 1996a). Alternatively, it may have been a false rise, if the 1980s data for the southwest were a biased subsample. This bias is possible, since the southwestern data for the 1980s were made available in unpublished form with relatively little documentation.

significant for organic matter. More detailed estimates (in Table 8.3) show that the organic matter in Java's topsoils was already declining for tree-crop soils and grasslands in the earlier 1940–55 period. The odd behavior of the nitrogen (and phosphorus) estimates from 1955 to 1960 is probably due to an uncorrected shift in the soil-sample sites, and the 1955 and 1960 figures should be roughly averaged together in viewing all the Indonesian estimates.

So far, all regions with a long tradition of intensive agriculture seem to have slightly depleted their organic matter and nitrogen. At a glance, trends in the outer islands of Indonesia since 1970 would appear to contradict the view that agriculture depletes organic matter and nitrogen, especially when we remember that the outer islands are a deforestation frontier. Why do Table 8.1 and Figure 8.1 show rises in organic matter and nitrogen for these new-settlement areas between 1970 and 1990? In fact, this outer-island rise after 1970 does not contradict but actually *confirms* the general downward tendency in organic matter and nitrogen as regions continue under cultivation. The likely reason for the recent rise is that time effectively moved backward from 1970 to 1990 in the outer islands. That is, the average tree-crop plot or fallow grassland got *younger,* in the sense of being cultivated for fewer recent years. Between 1970 and 1990, while the expansion of actually harvested area continued to grow at the same rate as over the previous 20 years (2.48 percent a year), the total arable lands expanded at 4.48 percent a year, incorporating vast new unworked areas that were probably described as cultivated land in the soil samples (van der Eng 1996, apps. 4, 8). The average organic matter and nitrogen of these lands will presumably drop once the rate of settlement and forest clearing drops.

Unlike organic matter and nitrogen, topsoil endowments of total phosphorus and potassium were either steady or rising over the last half century of the study. The averages for China show such a rise, especially for potassium, though some of the regional subsamples were thin before the 1980s. The same is true for the intensively farmed and intensively fertilized soils of Java. It is not surprising to see total phosphorus and potassium build up in the topsoil, especially when fertilizer application accelerates. Only tiny fractions of both elements are present in forms available for plant uptake, and much larger shares remain unusable in the soil for many years once applied (especially for phosphorus). The rise in total phosphorus and potassium is therefore predictable but contributes to crop yields more gradually than the visible trend might suggest.

Here again, the outer islands of Indonesia confirm the general tendency, even though they seem at first glance to have the opposite trend since 1970. The post-1970 decline in total phosphorus and potassium on the outer islands reflects the same shift toward more recently cleared and cultivated plots. Again, time moved effectively backward on the outer islands between 1970 and 1990, generating the seeming retreat in the average accumulated phosphorus and potassium.

TABLE 8.1 Average soil characteristics on ever cultivated lands, China and Indonesia since the late 1930s

Region	Average Soil Characteristic				
	(percentage)				
Organic matter					
China	*1932–44*		*1950–64*		*1981–86*
North China[a]	1.48		1.43		1.13
Chang Jiang plain[b]	1.90		2.40		2.30
Southeast China[c]			2.17		2.09
Southwest China[d]			2.11		3.34
Indonesia	*1940*	*1955*	*1960*	*1970*	*1990*
Java[e]	3.44	2.79	2.77	2.34	2.57
Outer islands[f]		3.60	4.37	3.01	3.51
Total nitrogen					
China	*1932–44*		*1950–64*		*1981–86*
North China	0.080		0.088		0.073
Chang Jiang plain			0.085		0.135
Southeast China			0.118		0.107
Southwest China			0.164		0.189
Indonesia	*1940*	*1955*	*1960*	*1970*	*1990*
Java		0.133	0.169	0.138	0.137
Outer islands		0.152	0.192	0.148	0.159
Total phosphorus					
China	*1932–44*		*1950–64*		*1981–86*
North China	0.043		0.050		0.048
Chang Jiang plain	0.040		0.048		0.050
Southeast China			0.040		0.046
Southwest China			0.071		0.058
Indonesia	*1940*	*1955*	*1960*	*1970*	*1990*
Java	0.020	0.029	0.023	0.027	0.033
Outer islands	0.012	0.008	0.008	0.010	0.008
Total potassium					
China	*1932–44*		*1950–64*		*1981–86*
North China	1.257		1.726		1.898
Chang Jiang plain	0.978				1.721
Southeast China			0.759		1.036
Southwest China			0.412		1.068
Indonesia	*1940*	*1955*	*1960*	*1970*	*1990*
Java	0.025	0.024	0.024	0.027	0.031
Outer islands	0.018	0.018	0.021	0.014	0.007

TABLE 8.1 *Continued*

Region	Average Soil Characteristic				
Alkalinity[g]					
China	*1932–44*			*1950–64*	*1981–86*
Northwest China	0.172			0.221	0.147
Acidity[g]					
China	*1932–44*			*1950–64*	*1981–86*
Chang Jiang plain	0.334			0.114	0.306
Southeast China	1.005			0.449	0.479
Southwest China	0.718			0.362	0.412
Indonesia	*1940*	*1955*	*1960*	*1970*	*1990*
Java	0.487	0.355	0.469	0.302	0.520
Outer islands	1.070	1.488	0.987	1.138	1.459

SOURCES: Archival samples described in Lindert (1997, 1999).

NOTES: These averages refer to sites that were "ever-cultivated" in the sense that the data suggest cultivation within the decade ending in the time the site's soil was sampled. "Cultivated" here means the site is either tilled or in productive grasslands or tree-crop stands. The evidence for recent cultivation of sites not currently cultivated is indirect. For China, it consists of miscellaneous geographic information. For Java, the status of recent cultivation and current fallow is inferred from specific mention of these current statuses: all grasslands including imperata (*alang-alang*), scrub bush (*belukar*), and sites explicitly abandoned (e.g., *bekas tegalan*) or fallowed. This definition will probably include a small proportion of never cultivated grasslands and bush. The outer islands averages shown here refer only to land planted in tree crops. For the average characteristics of soils under grasses or primary forest, see Table 8.3.

All averages are based on regressions that hold constant the following attributes of each soil site: land use and vegetation, precipitation, parent material, soil class, terrain, texture, and topsoil sample depth. There are further fixed-effect controls for districts (*xian* in China, *kabupaten* in Indonesia) that appear to be consistent outliers. Most of the procedures used here are detailed in Lindert, Lu, and Wu (1995). The absolute values shown here are base-period sample averages plus regression-predicted changes from the base period to each year shown. The base-period for China is 1981–86, and the base period for Indonesia is 1958–62.

Indonesia's more consistent reporting of land use and vegetation and its larger sample size made it possible to run separate regressions for different land-use systems: paddy (*sawah*), dryland field crops (*tegalan*), tree crops, and fallow. The averages shown here for Java are weighted averages of separate land-system regression predictions. The weights are based on the full sample of profiles between 1923 and 1990. For Java, the averages are based on these sample shares: 0.149 for paddy (*sawah*); 0.448 for field crops (*tegalan*); 0.276 for tree crops; and 0.127 for fallow (shifting cultivation, grasses, and bush), both here and in Table 8.3.

Caveat 1. As emphasized elsewhere, the estimates are subject to varying degrees of error. The percentage standard errors are greater for phosphorus and potassium than for other soil characteristics, since phosphorus and potassium have greater natural variance from site to site. The estimates are also shakier where the samples are thinner. The thinnest samples represented here are those for China's macronutrients (organic matter, nitrogen, phosphorus, potassium) in the 1930s and 1950s. In addition, cells left blank here represent settings for which the sample was too thin even for a guess.

Caveat 2. As discussed elsewhere, the 1980 estimates for phosphorus and potassium in Indonesia seem suspiciously low, an anomaly that withstands a host of side tests and adjustments in the estimates. These circa-1980 estimates are less reliable than the Indonesian estimates for other years

TABLE 8.1 *Continued*

because the same strange dip shows up in the figures for primary forest and other never cultivated lands.

Caveat 3. The total levels of nitrogen, phosphorus, and potassium are less directly related to plant growth than the much smaller "available" shares, for which long time series were unavailable. The total levels are nonetheless traditionally used as an important clue to availability of these macronutrients.

[a]The sample-size-weighted average of the averages for the spring region, the winter-millet region, and the Huang-Huai-Hai plain as mapped in Buck (1937:27) and Lindert, Lu, and Wu (1995).

[b]The simple average of the Yangtze rice-wheat area and the rice-tea area, as mapped in the same sources. The Sichuan basin is excluded from the averages shown here.

[c]The double-cropping rice area as mapped in Buck (1937) and stretching from mid-Fujian to mid-Guangxi.

[d]Southwest rice area as mapped in Buck (1937) and including western Guangxi, Hunnan, and most of Guizhou.

[e]The islands of Java, Madura, and Bali (although very few of the data come from Bali).

[f]All the major islands of Indonesia other than Java, Madura, Bali, and Timor Timur.

[g]Alkalinity is defined as max (pH - 8, 0) and acidity as max (6 - pH, 0) for each individual soil profile.

ALKALINITY AND ACIDITY.   Soil pH is sensitive to human and other influences and can change more rapidly than, say, total phosphorus. Like low levels of nutrients, extreme pH levels can limit crop yields and crop choices. In North China, the wrong water balance can cause alkalinity (pH 8), sodicity (sodium buildup), and salinity. Even where these are mild enough to permit continued cropping, the choice of crops is limited to tolerant crops, generally grasses. A rise in alkalinity, sodicity, and salinity has long been feared in the arid northwest, and today's global maps imply that it is continuing. The available historical data on alkalinity suggest otherwise. As can be seen in Table 8.1, alkalinity was always severe in the northwest. It worsened between the 1930s and the 1950s, but subsequent improvements have returned it to the average level already experienced in the 1930s.[8]

The threat of soil acidity (pH < 6) rises with temperature and humidity. Like alkalinity, it is sensitive to changes in water control, fertilizer mix, and soil amendments. For Central and South China, the half century from the 1930s brought a net abatement of soil acidity, but with a troublesome trend reversal. Part of the improvement achieved by the 1950s and early 1960s was reversed by the 1980s. Similarly for Java, the improvements reaped up to 1970, largely by adapting liming to Indonesian conditions, were reversed thereafter. An issue to be explored is whether Java's post-1970, subsidy-spawned boom in applying

---

8. Alkalinity and salinity were conquered in another area where they were severe in the 1930s. The lowlands along the Jiangsu coast and the Bohai coast had an average pH above 9 in the 1930s and below 7 in the 1980s. So say both the soil-profile data and a comparison of maps from the two eras.

FIGURE 8.1 Average soil characteristics on ever cultivated lands, China and Indonesia since the late 1930s

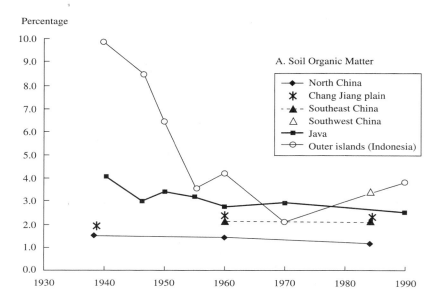

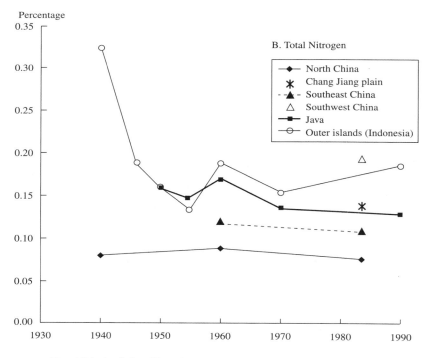

SOURCE: Unpublished soil data files collected by the author.

FIGURE 8.1 *Continued*

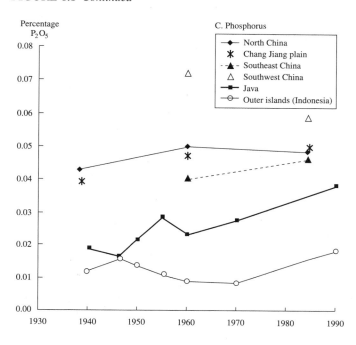

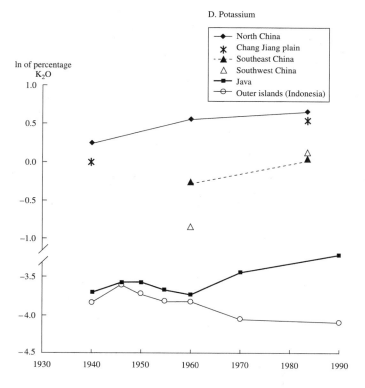

FIGURE 8.1 *Continued*

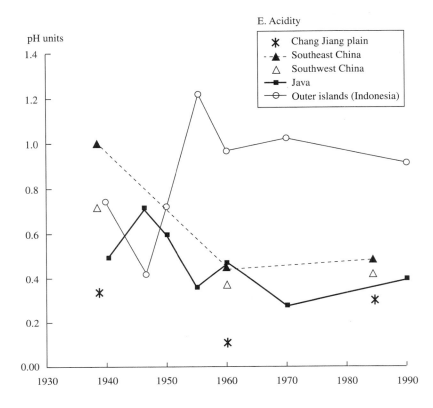

E. Acidity

urea fertilizer raised soil acidity. In the outer islands, especially in the wetter parts of Sumatra and Kalimantan, acidity remains severe for want of the decades of investment in liming and water control that have helped Java, and acid-tolerant tree crops dominate.

TOPSOIL DEPTH.   The dominant soil-degradation fear is, again, erosion. The severity of any trend toward soil loss can be tested in a variety of ways. Since erosion typically lowers topsoil nutrients or worsens pH long before the topsoil vanishes (Lal, Hall, and Miller 1989), a modest test result is already evident in Table 8.1 and Figure 8.1. There was not a clear overall tendency toward nutrient loss or worsening pH, as there would have been if erosion had dominated all other human influences.

Still, one could wish for a more direct measure of topsoil loss. The only available candidate is the thickness of the "A horizon," defined by soil surveyors as the top, relatively homogenous soil layer in the root zone, just below any thin band of loose organic debris. Since most wind and water erosion attacks this band, its becoming thinner over time for soils of given fixed type is at least a partial clue to the net erosion rate.

The raw averages show that the topsoil layers did indeed become thinner in many parts of China and Indonesia. In China, the cultivated lands of the Chang Jiang plain had topsoil horizons that were 5 to 8 centimeters thinner in the 1980s than those sampled half a century earlier. The reduction was smaller, or possibly zero, in other parts of China. Indonesia's topsoil losses are given a closer look in Table 8.2. It would appear that the cultivated topsoils of Java lost 2 centimeters over the half century from 1940 to 1990. At face value, then, the average topsoil thicknesses appear to show that both countries are "losing ground."

A closer look at the original data, however, suggests that the top-layer losses are a false alarm. They are likely to reflect a change in the data-gathering procedure, rather than a true change in the soil. Table 8.2's outer columns provide clues from Indonesia. As the left column suggests, the decline in the topsoil was as prevalent among all soils, including those not cultivated, as it was on cultivated soils. The two trends should have differed if humans are the real erosion culprits.

More telling is the behavior of the odd variable in the right-hand column of Table 8.2, the share of all soil profiles whose top "layer" extended down to a centimeter depth ending in a 0 or a 5. The share ending in 0 or 5 should be near 20 percent if the data gatherers really care to maximize accuracy to the nearest centimeter. Table 8.2 shows that this concern for sharp definition of the topsoil layer is only a recent phenomenon. From the 1920s through the 1960s, data collectors were content to take chemical measurements from top layers that were casually reported as extending down to 20, 35, or even 100 centimeters. In the early years, the purpose of sampling was as much geological as agronomic, inviting deeper samples and rougher depths rather than careful definition of a fairly homogeneous root-zone horizon. In fact, it is only in the last quarter century that Indonesia's data sheets even use such now conventional horizon definitions as "the A horizon." Regression analysis shows that once one has corrected for whether the bottom depth of the topsoil layer ended in a 0 or a 5, there is no significant trend in topsoil thickness. The same change is also evident in the raw data for China. The early reports make much less use of the horizon terminology, whereas the detailed 1980s survey even divides the A horizon into finer soil-science categories (A_o, A_p, and so on). Pending further tests, the tentative conclusion is that the average net loss of topsoil in these two countries was close to 0.

Trends for Different Tropic Use Systems

Overall averages, even carefully standardized averages, hide variation. Convenient averages for all cultivated soils, like those in Tables 8.1 and 8.2, suppress the fact that soil trends differed in different settings. The full variety of soil

TABLE 8.2 Ostensible changes in the thickness of the topsoil layer, Indonesia, 1923–1990

| Period | Average Thickness of Top Horizon | | Shares of Profiles with Bottom Depth Ending (in Centimeters) in 0 or 5 |
	All	Cultivated[a]	
	(centimeters)		(percentage)
Java			
1923–35	24.1	—	96
1936–44	19.6	19.8	94
1947–57	22	23	84
1958–67	18.1	18	77
1968–73	18.7	18.8	64
1974–86	17.6	17.8	41
1987–90	17.6	17.7	41
Outer Islands			
1926–37	15.7	—	66
1938–42	17.1	16.9	75
1947–57	17.4	19.9	76
1958–67	16.1	17.5	72
1968–73	17.1	17.2	62
1974–86	13.6	13.6	39
1987–90	16.6	16.1	38

SOURCE: Indonesian data sets used in Lindert (1997).

[a]Includes *sawah, tegalan* field crops, and tree crops. Excludes pasture, grasslands, and primary forest.

processes cannot be examined here, but the Indonesian data offer enough detail on land use to show how the overall trends in Table 8.1 are the net result of different trends for different land use systems.

As soil scientists would predict, cultivating tropical soils has different effects under different land use systems. Table 8.3 shows separate trends for lowland paddy (*sawah*), upland crop fields (*tegalan*), lands under tree crops, once tilled lands that have become grasslands or brushlands (called "fallow" here), and primary forest, both for Java and for the outer islands in four relatively well-sampled eras.[9]

---

9. The land use systems are defined only approximately here, as in the original data. The term *sawah* (paddy) generally connotes irrigated flatlands, including rice paddy that is seasonally flooded, but not all *sawah* is either irrigated or planted in rice. Terms such as *tegalan* (nonirrigated field crops) or *palawija* (secondary crops) seem to exclude irrigation and rice and seem to refer to uplands but often do not. And not all of the grasslands and bush (*belukar*) here described as fallow have ever been cultivated. The choice of terms is a compromise already made by the recorders of the original data.

Starting with paddy, we find few hints of any net change in organic matter or acidity from 1940 to 1990. Paddy soils did, however, share in the general run-up of phosphorus (measured as P_2O_5 content) and potassium (as K_2O) after 1970. Paddy soils appear stable.

Unlike paddy, the other types of cultivation—upland field crops, tree crops, and fallow—showed a significant drop in soil organic matter in Java. The data for China would probably have shown the same difference had they given more detail on land use. Whatever the consequences of declining organic matter, they are more at issue on lands that are more sloped and less irrigated. For acidity, the current estimates suggest similar movements for all land use types: a decline in acidity up to 1970 and a rise thereafter.

The Indonesian sample also allows us to contrast the levels of soil characteristics between uncultivated and long-cultivated lands, to get a sense of what human settlement and agriculture do to topsoil chemistry. The Indonesian estimates in Table 8.3 show this contrast in two ways: in the difference between primary-forest soils on the outer islands and human-cultivated soils, and the clear contrasts between long-crowded Java and the more recently settled outer islands.

Studying the relatively heavy samplings of primary-forest soils on the outer islands in the period around 1980 shows what is different about their chemistry. They tend to hold higher levels of organic matter and nitrogen, especially relative to the long-worked soils of Java. Deforestation triggers decomposition of organic matter, reducing the ability of the soil to sequester carbon and contributing to atmospheric buildup of CO_2. The initial losses of organic matter, soon followed by nitrogen loss as the carbon/nitrogen ratio tends back to equilibrium, are what cause the well-known downslope in crop yields over the initial years of cropping newly cleared forest areas. On the other hand, a long history of human cultivation brings that buildup of phosphorus and potassium, which is evident in both the higher averages for Java and the contrast between primary-forest and other land use categories.

Overall, then, the soil trends in the two countries are diverse. Some indicators, especially the nexus of organic matter and nitrogen, suggest a trend toward lower soil quality, while others suggest improvement. The statistical reliability of the trends varies. The underlying samples are of limited size and

---

The Indonesian data often contain great detail on the specific crops grown at each site, and not just the general land use systems shown in Table 8.3. One can explore the soil conditions on rubber plantations, in cassava-soybean rotations, in vegetable gardens, and so forth. Trying to do so, however, runs into the difficulty of separating cause and effect between the soil condition and the crop choice. As an extreme example, it turns out that in Java soil nitrogen is lower where nitrogen-fixing legumes are the featured crop. Clearly, this is a case in which the causality runs from the soil condition to the choice of land use. Finding more acidic soils under rubber and teak plantations calls for a similar interpretation. Yet the land use does affect the soil, as it is often intended to do. The underlying difficulty here is that the data cannot give the site's whole history of vegetation and land use but only its current status or this plus occasional remarks about recent uses.

TABLE 8.3 Changes in soil characteristics by land-use type, Indonesia, 1940–1990

Java	1940	1955	1960	1970	1980	1990
			(percentage)			
Organic matter						
Paddy (*sawah*)		2.36	2.36	2.02	2.12	2.23
Tegalan		2.44	2.57	2.34	2.27	2.19
Tree crops	4.62	3.66	3.34	2.62	2.98	3.38
Fallow and grasses	3.68	2.67	2.75	2.12	2.34	2.58
Weighted average	3.44	2.79	2.77	2.34	2.45	2.57
Total nitrogen						
Paddy (*sawah*)		0.124	0.156	0.131	0.128	0.127
Tegalan		0.108	0.167	0.131	0.126	0.122
Tree crops		0.166	0.186	0.155	0.164	0.174
Fallow and grasses		0.157	0.15	0.136	0.128	0.12
Weighted average		0.133	0.169	0.138	0.137	0.137
Total P_2O_5 (mg/100 g)						
Paddy (*sawah*)	55.27	60.93	54.33	50.86	64.19	81.01
Tegalan	52.33	77.51	59.44	76.81	70.62	64.92
Tree crops	34.24	59.68	40.37	48.79	67.97	94.68
Fallow and grasses	32.92	56.3	50.4	54.7	58.17	61.87
Weighted average	45.31	67.42	52.27	62.40	67.35	75.14
Total K_2O (mg/100 g)						
Paddy (*sawah*)	35.55	23.83	23.83	26.19	28.7	31.45
Tegalan	31.31	31.22	35.8	36.81	38.39	40.04
Tree crops	24.93	30.61	22.92	26.3	25.78	25.26
Fallow and grasses	28.17	27.58	24.63	38.81	48.19	59.82
Weighted average	29.78	29.49	29.04	32.58	34.71	37.19
Acidity						
Paddy (*sawah*)	0.54	0.52	0.59	0.27	0.47	0.67
Tegalan	0.34	0.28	0.37	0.21	0.30	0.39
Tree crops	0.63	0.29	0.54	0.40	0.53	0.66
Fallow and grasses	0.63	0.59	0.50	0.45	0.47	0.49
Weighted average	0.49	0.36	0.47	0.3	0.41	0.52
Organic matter						
Tree crops		3.6	4.37	3.01	3.25	3.51
Fallow and grasses		4.32	4	3.4	3.34	3.29
Primary forest					3.4	

continued

TABLE 8.3 *Continued*

Java	1940	1955	1960	1970	1980	1990
Total nitrogen						
Tree crops		0.152	0.192	1.148	0.154	0.159
Fallow and grasses		0.145	0.182	0.14	0.141	0.142
Primary forest					0.23	
Total P$_2$O$_5$ (mg/100 g)						
Tree crops	27.49	18.58	18.43	22.27	20.39	18.77
Fallow and grasses	30.02	30.13	19.28	26.55	27.09	27.64
Primary forest					17.15	
Total K$_2$O (mg/100 g)						
Tree crops	21.45	21.54	24.85	16.59	12.21	8.99
Fallow and grasses	29.01	34.85	27.8	27.95	19.24	13.25
Primary forest					17.51	
Acidity						
Tree crops	1.07	1.49	0.99	1.14	1.3	1.46
Fallow and grasses	0.78	0.97	0.92	0.72	0.93	1.13
Primary forest					1.3	

SOURCE: Centre for Soil and Agroclimatic Research soil-profile in Bogor, the same source used for the Indonesian averages in Lindert (1997).

NOTE: Cells left blank represent subsamples too thin for reliable estimation of a cell average, even though the soil profiles in many of these cells were usable in the underlying regressions. The averages shown in each row are conditional means for the mixes of places sampled in the 1958–62 period for that land use in either Java or the outer islands, with the exception of primary-forest soils where an average for the better-sampled period 1974–86 was used, with an adjustment for the NPK anomaly for 1974–86 data described in Lindert (1997).

Each Java "weighted average" uses the following sample weights to combine the rows: 0.149 for paddy; 0.448 for *tegalan;* 0.276 for tree crops; and 0.127 for fallow (shifting cultivation, grasses, and bush). The weighted average figure for Java's organic matter in 1940 extrapolates back from 1955 on the basis of tree crop lands and fallow only, for use in Figure 8.1.

cannot establish clear trends for many subregions or land-use systems. Fortunately, the data only need to hit a very big target; popular guesses and assertions about soil trends are so broad, and cover such vast geographic areas, that even our limited samples can be used to test them. Table 8.4 summarizes the limited conclusions about trends that can be asserted with statistical confidence here. Any trends not listed should be viewed as still unknown.

TABLE 8.4 Summary of conclusions on soil trends on cultivated lands in China and Indonesia since the 1930s

	Organic Matter	Total Nitrogen	Total Phosphorus	Total Potassium	pH	Thickness of the Topsoil Layer
North China	Down since the 1950s	No clear trend, except down in Huang-Huai-Hai plain since the 1950s	Up during 1930–70	Up since the 1930s. No change in alkalinity in northwest during 1930–90. Improvement on Bohai coast.	No clear change.	Apparent thinning is probably due to definitional changes.
Chang Jiang plain	Possibly down, but the trend is not statistically significant	Down since the 1950s	Up during 1930–70	Up since the 1950s	Acidity abated during 1930–50, then returned to 1930s levels	No clear change. Apparent thinning is probably due to definitional changes.
Southeast China	No trend	Down since the 1950s	Possibly up since the 1950s	Up since the 1950s	Acidity abated during 1930–50, then returned to 1930s levels	No clear change. Apparent thinning is probably due to definitional changes.
Southwest China	Up since the 1950s	Up since the 1950s	Down since the 1950s			No clear change. Apparent thinning is probably due to definitional changes.
Java	Down until 1970, then slightly up resulting in a net drop during 1940–90	No clear trend (few data)	Up since the 1940s	Up since 1960	Acidity down until 1970, then up thereafter	No clear change. Apparent thinning is probably due to definitional changes.
Outer Islands of Indonesia	Down during settlement (to 1970) then no clear trend	No clear trend (few data)	No clear trend	Down since 1970, no clear trend during 1940–70	Up since 1970, no clear trend during 1940–70	No clear change. Apparent thinning is probably due to definitional changes.

SOURCE: Lindert (1997).

Cross-Sectional Estimates of the Soil-Agriculture Links in China

If different soil characteristics have shown different trends, what can we say about the overall net effect of all these trends on agricultural performance? That depends on which effects are stronger, those of the trends toward soil degradation or those of the trends toward improvement. To weigh the different soil tendencies against each other, we need to return to the basic simultaneous soil-agriculture system. We need a proper empirical laboratory. As suggested earlier, we have such a laboratory in the form of a cross-section of counties in China in the mid-1980s. The present section uses the soil data of China's countries in 1981–86 and the agricultural data for China in 1985 to reveal those two kinds of questions posed earlier in equation form: How do soil and other forces combine to determine agricultural performance (A)? and How do agricultural performance and more permanent forces combine to determine the current condition of the soil (S)?

Agronomy and human institutions together define the roles of endogenous and exogenous variables in China's soil-and-agriculture system. Soil conditions affect more than just the current level of yields. They also affect agricultural inputs. In the longest-run perspective, one could view all nonsoil inputs as endogenous by-products of soil geology and climate, which over the centuries govern a region's whole population level and agricultural input intensity as well as its outputs. Thus one could, in Figure 8.2's schematic sketch of causality in the countryside, see everything as flowing from the soil and climate forces featured on the left.

Yet China's agricultural geography is shaped largely by events since the 1930s, particularly the Communist victory in 1949, the waves of policy revolution under Chairman Mao, and the reforms since 1976. It is only a slight exaggeration to say that China before the 1990s lacked not only a land market but also a labor market and a capital market. The tight restrictions on labor mobility have more or less frozen China's demographic geography in place. Before the late 1980s, the same restrictions had even kept farm labor from shifting to nonagricultural production. In a spatial cross-section, the number of laborers available for agriculture is therefore an exogenous variable, as shown by its position on the right-hand edge of Figure 8.2. Also relatively exogenous are irrigation, which is driven by terrain and by the history of public construction campaigns, and the centralized allocation of tangible nonland capital, here represented by electricity use per unit of cultivated land.

Two other input variables may be more endogenous, in that soil quality interacts with policy to determine their levels. The spatial allocation of synthetic fertilizers may respond somewhat to changes in perceived soil responsiveness. The other main influence on fertilizer use is policy, as portrayed in Figure 8.2. Fertilizer is a resource for which provincial governments vie at the national level and county and local governments vie at the provincial level. The

FIGURE 8.2 Causal influences in a cross-section of China's soils and agricultural production, 1980s

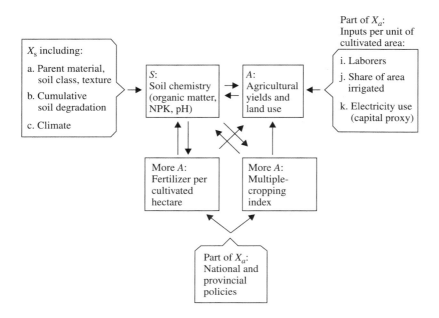

more detailed version of the present model uses province and county attributes as determinants of the lobbying power of subgovernments in augmenting their supplies of subsidized fertilizer.[10] Similarly, the intensity with which laborers and other inputs are thrown into multiple cropping also depends on soil conditions and on the policy environment.

At the center of this causal system, soil conditions and agricultural output are determined jointly. Figure 8.2 shows these interactions.[11] The soil variables "organic matter" and "NPK" are the natural logs for organic matter, total nitrogen, total phosphorus, and total potassium. The natural log specification reflects the belief that the marginal product of absolute nutrient levels declines, but remains positive, as those levels rise. Acidity and alkalinity are also nonlinear, in the sense of being bounded by zero: Acid = max $(0, 6 - pH)$ and Alk = max $(0, pH - 8)$.

---

10. For the full list of independent variables in this and other equations, see Lindert (1996). On fertilizer, irrigation, and technology in general, see Stone (1986 and 1988).

11. A fuller exposition of the model in terms of equations is given in Lindert (1996).

"Laborers" is just a body count of persons employed in agriculture in 1985, per cultivated hectare. To get closer to true labor inputs, we add the multiple-cropping index (MCI) = sown area / cultivated area to the list of variables, as if it were a separate dimension of total labor input. We also add the tonnage of synthetic fertilizer, the irrigated share of total cultivated area, and electricity use per unit of cultivated area.

Two of the agricultural input variables—chemical-fertilizer application and the multiple-cropping index—are endogenous, as mentioned. We imagine that they respond to soil chemistry, which affects both the incentive ("need") for chemical fertilizers and the returns from multiple cropping. They also respond to systematic lobbying-power influences on the allocation of fertilizer and multiple cropping among provinces and among counties within provinces. (Specifically, the underlying lobbying model says that a county's access to fertilizer and to multiple-cropping labor intensity depends politically on its shares of the province's urban population, collective-enterprise production, off-farm purchases, cotton production, and oil production and the province's shares of the same at the national level.) The other input variables, however, are exogenous. We assume that exogenous policy and history combine to dictate the total labor supply, electricity use, and irrigated land area. Policy and history are even assumed to govern the allocation of labor and land area among grain, other main crops, and all other agricultural products.

On the other side of the soil-agricultural interaction, each of the soil parameters in *(S)* is a predicted value, because it in turn depends on agricultural practice. This completes the sketch of Figure 8.2's simultaneous-equation system in which soil and agriculture interact.

The best available data set for exploring these interactions, as noted, is one matching soil-profile data from 1981–86 with agricultural outputs and inputs in 1985 for counties (*xian*).[12] The places do not match perfectly, in that the profiles are taken in particular locations within the county. Of the two grouping approaches available—either average the soil profiles within each county or repeat county-level data for each profile within the county—this chapter uses the latter, a sample of profiles rather than of counties. The samples consist of 266 profiles from 164 counties around North China and 495 profiles from 287 counties in South China. One must take care to interpret these results as cross-sectional, not as an experimental or historical time series. That is, the effect of *x* on *y* here means "how places where *x* occurred differed in their *y*, for both human and other reasons," not "how changing *x* on the same plots changed *y* from one period to the next." The results will help to answer a

---

12. The agricultural data come primarily from the annual agricultural yearbooks, supplemented by the 1982 population atlas of China. I am grateful to G. William Skinner for supplying a computerized version of the 1985 agricultural data and to Bin Zhang and Joann Lu for purging errors from the original data.

TABLE 8.5 Influences on agricultural yields in China, circa 1985

| | Elasticity of the Response of the Gross Value of Agricultural Output per Cultivated Hectare . . . | | | |
| | North China | | South China | |
. . . to Percentage Changes in:	Elasticity	Standard Error	Elasticity	Standard Error
Topsoil conditions				
Organic matter	−0.122	−0.138	0.834	−0.196
Total nitrogen	0.02	−0.161	−0.774	−0.203
Total phosphorus	−0.027	−0.05	−0.059	−0.024
Total potassium	0.017	−0.117	0.08	−0.046
Alkalinity	−0.353	−0.173		
Acidity			−0.223	−0.077
Conventional inputs				
Laborers per cultivated area	0.565	−0.279	0.282	−0.053
Multiple-cropping index	0.234	−0.091	0.257	−0.173
Fertilizer per cultivated area	0.981	−0.96	0.144	−0.049
Irrigated share of cultivated area	−0.014	−0.138	0.184	−0.037
Electricity per cultivated area	0.272	−0.122	0.02	−0.016

SOURCE: Lindert (1999).

NOTE: All outputs are priced in grain equivalents. The multiple-cropping index equals sown area divided by cultivated area. Each coefficient is an implied slope at the mean values of the independent variables. The equations omitted are those that failed the F-test, leaving the dependent variable exogenous for present purposes. In the case of North China, this applies for phosphorus and potassium; in the case of South China, this applies for phosphorus only. There is no equation for acidity in the north, or alkalinity in the south, because these conditions were too rare in the respective examples to warrant their being endogenous variables.

historical question, however: "If China's counties had had their 1930s soil quality instead of their 1980s soil quality, how would yields have been different?"

Tables 8.5 and 8.6 report the results for two-stage least squares regressions on the simultaneous system sketched here and in Figure 8.2. Let us survey the results in the order of the sets of equations, starting with Table 8.5's key results for equation (8.1) above.

There is one clear and important pattern in the responses of yields to soil-chemistry parameters. The statistically most significant influence is that of extreme soil pH—alkalinity in the north and acidity in the south. Alkalinity has a clearly negative effect on any measure of outputs in North China, be it grains or all main crops or all agricultural products. In the south, soil acidity also reduces agricultural productivity, primarily in nongrain products.

TABLE 8.6 Influences on soil chemistry in cultivated soils of China, circa 1985

	Elasticity of the Response of the Topsoil's . . .							
	Organic Matter		Total Nitrogen		Total Potassium		Alkalinity	
. . . to Percentage Changes in:	Elasticity	Standard Error	Elasticity	Standard Error	Elasticity	Standard Error	Elasticity	Standard Error
North China								
Main-crop output per cultivated hectare	0.191	-0.169	-0.139	-0.177			-0.872	-0.258
Total agricultural output/main-crop output	0.633	-0.2	0.272	-0.206			-0.398	-0.28
Multiple-cropping index	-0.163	-0.105	0.05	-0.105			0.782	-0.487
Fertilizer tons per cultivated area	-0.026	-1.347	-0.138	-0.609			1.894	-5.022
South China								
Main-crop output per cultivated hectare	-0.41	-0.259	-0.574	-0.245	0.326	-0.326	0.081	-0.447
Total agricultural output/main-crop output	0.419	-0.211	0.277	-0.2	0.266	-0.266	-0.2	-0.362
Multiple-cropping index	-0.299	-0.359	-0.322	-0.34	0.453	-0.453	0.827	-0.641
Fertilizer tons per cultivated area	-0.033	-0.105	-0.095	-0.099	0.132	-0.132	-0.575	-0.184

SOURCE: Lindert (1999).

NOTE: All outputs are priced in grain equivalents. The multiple-cropping index equals sown area divided by cultivated area. Each coefficient is an implied slope at the mean values of the independent variables. The equations omitted are those that failed the F-test, leaving the dependent variable exogenous for present purposes. In the case of North China, this applies for phosphorus and potassium; in the case of South China, this applies for phosphorus only. There is no equation for acidity in the north, or alkalinity in the south, because these conditions were too rare in the respective examples to warrant their being endogenous variables.

By contrast, soil organic matter and nitrogen are weaker in their effects on yields. They are both individually weak in the north and weak as a pair of variables in the south. In the north, they are not significant determinants of overall productivity, although higher organic matter, and a higher carbon/nitrogen ratio, reduce grain production, replacing it with non–main-crop production, presumably animal products on grasslands. In the south, organic matter and total nitrogen have opposing effects of similar magnitude. These two should be viewed together, since the organic-matter/nitrogen ratio tends to cycle around a long-run equilibrium level. The regression results imply that a sustained increase in both soil organic matter and soil nitrogen fails to have a significant impact on yields in the south, as well as in the north. Presumably, this lack of significance results from humans' ability to substitute quick-release nitrogen for soil nitrogen, with similar implicit substitution in organic matter.[13]

Total soil phosphorus tends to have weak negative effects on agricultural productivity throughout China. The negativity does not mean, of course, that greater phosphorus reduces plant growth. Rather, it seems to mean that soils in which total phosphorus was higher tended to be soils in which it was tied up in relatively fewer plant-available forms. One would have predicted a more positive role for phosphorus in the south.

Potassium was a significantly positive influence on productivity in the south but not in the north. This pattern makes sense, in that soil potassium (like phosphorus) is naturally lower in the humid south and is therefore more likely to constrain plant growth. An important pattern suggested here is that crop yields and the overall value of agricultural product depend mainly on those soil-chemistry parameters that in fact have *not* shown depletion since the 1930s. The most positive association is that between the rising soil-potassium trend and its positive importance for yields in the south. Similarly, agricultural output in South China clearly depends on acidity, a problem that was reduced between the 1930s and the 1950s (but may have worsened somewhat after the 1950s). Alkalinity assumes a similar but less prominent role in relating trends to productivity impacts: alkalinity showed no clear trend in the north, yet its level does matter to productivity.

By contrast, as we have seen, organic matter and nitrogen do not seem to matter much. How could this be, given the known dependence of plant growth on available nitrogen and on the various benefits of higher organic matter content? What makes it possible is that quick-release fertilizers can act as a substitute for soil organic matter and total nitrogen. Importantly, then, the nutrients that have been depleted over time in the Huang-Huai-Hai plain and the Chang Jiang plain (organic matter and nitrogen) are ones that can

---

13. The large implicit role of the carbon/nitrogen ratio, which equals the difference between the coefficients for (the logs of) organic mater and total nitrogen, remains a puzzle, however.

be replaced relatively easily. We return to this issue later when revisiting sustainability.

Continuing down Table 8.5, we find that the conventional agricultural inputs all raise output as we would have expected. The implied elasticities are usually positive and significant, as expected. On the other side of the causal circle, Table 8.6 explores the effects of crop yields, fertilizer, and cropping intensity back on the soil itself.

Raising the yields of the main crops (grains, oils, and cotton) does the soil few favors, according to cross-sectional patterns in the 1980s. True, in the north, the areas with greater main-crop yields also achieved lower soil alkalinity. This benefit is probably not just a mirage created by reverse causation, since the negative effect of alkalinity on yields was already addressed in the two-stage estimation. Yet cutting northern alkalinity is the only clear soil benefit from human interventions that raise yields of the main crops. Achieving higher main-crop yields in the 1980s did not seem to raise soil organic matter or nitrogen in the north. Nor did it alleviate soil acidity in South China. Worse, growing more of the main crops reduced soil organic matter and nitrogen in the south.

By contrast, raising the yields of agricultural products other than the main crops had clearly beneficial soil effects, as shown in the rows for "total agricultural output/main-crop output" in Table 8.6. Extra non–main-crop products, such as vegetables and animal products, significantly raised soil organic matter throughout China and tended to raise nitrogen and reduce alkalinity and acidity.[14] Any force that shifts land area and other inputs away from grains, oils, and cotton to other crops therefore may improve the soil characteristics measured here.

Will Development Mine the Soil?

With this view of the interactions of soil and agriculture in two developing countries, we can now suggest tentative new perspectives on the debate over the clash between agricultural development and sustainability in its effects on a particular environmental asset, the topsoil. Three perspectives deserve new attention, though the present chapter has offered only partial evidence on two of the three. Here "development" refers to a continued rise in living standards per capita, with the changes that usually accompany it, particularly shifts in demand away from staple foods, improvements in markets, and a shift in production away from agriculture. The effects of "development" on the soil, it

---

14. The favorable effect of non–main-crop yields on organic matter may be a hidden effect of organic fertilizers. Manures, green waste, and other organic fertilizers are not measured in the official fertilizer statistics and tend to be applied more intensively to specialty crops than to grains, oils, and cotton. On China's application of organic fertilizers since the 1930s, see Wen (1984) and Stone (1986).

is suggested, are quite different from the effects of additional population pressure at low income levels.

Shifting Food Demand

One aspect of human intervention, namely, the output mix, may have strong effects on soil chemistry. Raising cultivation of grains, oils, and cotton may fail to improve soil endowments (except for alkalinity reduction in the north), whereas shifting to other crops and to animal products may have beneficial effects.

The contrast between raising grains-oils-cotton production and producing other agricultural products implies a possible Engel effect that has gone unnoticed: Could it be that general economic development improves the soil by pulling food demand and input supplies away from producing staples, especially staple grains? It could do so even without anybody's having imagined such a pattern. This is not a certainty, however. Among the tasks needing further research is to sort out the complex implications of rising importance of animal products for the pattern of land use: Does it really shift land use toward soil conserving grasslands and legumes, or does it simply raise the nutrient uptake from the soil through conventional nonsoy grains as fodders?

Development and Soil-Investment Incentives

A second basic way in which economic progress is likely to improve agricultural soils has been implicit in many authors' writings and is independent of the new soil data presented in this chapter, so that it need be stated only briefly here.

A key ingredient to long-run economic development is that it reduces capital costs and clarifies property rights. To reap any gain that exists only in the future requires a present investment expense. The lower the real interest rate, and the less severe the rationing of capital, the more farmers and others can invest for the long term. Every behavior that can improve the land requires such waiting and would benefit from cheaper capital. So it is with investments in conservation and water control. Development makes them more profitable by cheapening capital. Development also makes them more profitable by giving the investor the clear title to the fruits of such investments in land.

Urban Encroachment

"One piece of good news the Chinese point to is that recent satellite surveys show that the nation has 132 million hectares of available crop land—38 percent more than previously believed. The bad news is that crop land is rapidly disappearing. More than 700,000 hectares of cultivated land were taken by construction during the past year" (Malthus goes east 1995).

Thus far we have been exploring trends in places with fixed soil attributes (soil class, parent material, and so on). One may ask, however: Didn't soil losses also take the form of replacing areas with better soil attributes with those having worse soil attributes? This conjecture may take many different forms. The most widely debated variant is the widespread concern about the loss of farmlands to cities, industries, and homes: Isn't it true that growing cities and towns are taking the best land away from agriculture and forcing farmers to use increasingly marginal lands? Doesn't that cut the total stock of soil nutrients, even aside from degradation on any one kind of land that stayed in agriculture?

A tentative answer can be given for China. The spread of cities and other nonagricultural land uses did indeed take land away from agriculture. According to a 1984 agricultural atlas, the stock of land taken by cities, towns, villages, and roads had reached 4.46 percent of the land in China (excluding the desert far west and the islands) in 1983. Assuming a fixed rate of nonagricultural land use per capita of nonagricultural population implies that agriculture lost 2.16 percent of its land area between about 1933 and 1983. That translates into a glacially slow rate of area loss for agriculture—something like 0.04 percent a year. Even the rate cited by the August 12, 1995, *Economist,* to show that "crop land is rapidly disappearing" in 1994–95 is only 0.53 percent a year. Although that may be considered a "rapid" rate in some perspectives, *The Economist* appears to have picked up the wrong number. It seems to be citing the 1994 figure of 708,700 hectares of total decrease in cultivated area. But the adjacent columns in the *China Statistical Yearbook* (China, State Statistical Bureau 1996) make it clear that the losses to construction totaled only 245,800—the rest were "lost" to orchards, ponds, temporary abandonment of flooded lands, and so on. D. Gale Johnson faults Lester Brown for the same switch of 1994 land areas (Johnson 1995).

The quality of the land thus lost was indeed somewhat above average. It is now possible to quantify, roughly, how much better the lost land is. According to the data in our present sample, that 50-year loss of 2.16 percent on the edge of cities and villages cost North China's agriculture 2.75 percent of its soil organic matter, 2.19 percent of its total soil nitrogen, 3.53 percent of its phosphorus, and 2.16 percent of its potassium. In an overall estimation of China's net investments in soil, these costs should be deducted from the change-in-quality investments just sketched.

To take proper account of the effects of nonfarm encroachments, however, one should give weight to other effects of the rise of nonagricultural population, effects that are already implicit in the historic-trend estimates given earlier. The buildup of nonagricultural population, especially around urban centers, tends to raise the levels of organic carbon and nitrogen in local agricultural soils. As observers have noted since the 1930s, China's urban-industrial expansion has raised the supply of manure, and to a lesser extent chemical fertilizers, for farms nearest to the cities and the industrial activity (Buck 1937; Wen Qi-xiao 1984). At the same time, the proximity of a greater nonfarm population also raises the marketability—or, under Chairman Mao,

FIGURE 8.3 A stylized picture of the effects of urbanization and nonagricultural population density on the total supply of soil nutrients for agriculture

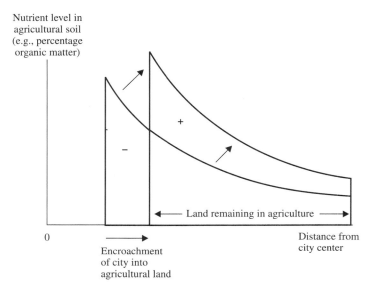

the planning urgency—of supplying that population with perishable foods at short distance.

The offsetting effects of urbanization-cum-industrialization on the nutrients of nearby soils are sketched in Figure 8.3 and quantified, very roughly, in Table 8.7. The negative effect is the more obvious: as cities and industries spread, farm land is lost (the negative area in Figure 8.3). On the other hand, having the city move outward brings product markets and farm input supplies closer to the remaining plots, causing a positive investment in the land (the positive area). The positive effect of a greater density of nonagricultural population could be either greater than or less than the loss of soil nutrients in the areas taken away from agriculture. Table 8.7 imagines how the magnitudes might have worked out for China over the half century ending in 1983, by borrowing regression coefficients for the effects of human employment density on soil chemistry (from Lindert, Lu, and Wu 1996a). For organic matter and nitrogen, the positive effect of growth in the nonagricultural population appears to have been strong enough to outweigh the direct losses of farmland. The effects of rising agricultural population were more negative. Overall, urbanization and industrialization seem to have augmented the stocks of soil organic matter and total nitrogen, though they may have depleted soil phosphorus and potassium.

TABLE 8.7 Offsetting effects of the rise of nonagricultural and agricultural human populations on the total soil-nutrient supplies for China's agriculture, 1933–1983

| | Percentage Gain or Loss in the Total Agricultural-Soil Stock of: | | | | | | | |
| | Organic Matter | | Nitrogen | | Phosphorus | | Potassium | |
Cause	North	South	North	South	North	South	North	South
Loss of agricultural land (a)	−2.75	−2.31	−2.19	−1.99	−3.53	−2.28	−2.16	−1.91
Rise in the density of (b)								
Nonagricultural employment (b1)	11.04	5.52	6.12	5.62	3.86	6.99	1.33	−0.27
Agricultural employment (b2)	−3.6	−1.92	2.99	−1.49	−1.33	0.31	0.12	−1.01
Net effect	4.1	1.1	6.9	1.98	−1.14	4.87	−1.19	−3.16

SOURCE: Lindert, Lu, and Wu (1995: app. U). The net percentage effects are not the sums of the component changes (a) (b1), and (b2), but rather the percentage changes implied by the products of (1 + component changes).

Changes in urbanization and industrialization thus may have offsetting effects on agriculture's land endowment. Future research should quantify these different effects more extensively than has been possible here and should add the changes at the outer, most rural land frontier.

Conclusion

The broadest outlines of the interaction of soil and agriculture are now somewhat clearer for two developing countries. We have some idea which dimensions of soil quality have improved and which have not. Soil organic matter and nitrogen appear to have declined on cultivated lands in both China and Indonesia. Total phosphorus and potassium have generally risen. Alkalinity and acidity have fluctuated, with no overall worsening. The topsoil layer has not gotten thinner. Some of the mixed trends revealed here have more effect on yields than others. China's patterns show that the decline in soil organic matter and nitrogen makes little difference, presumably because fertilizers can substitute for the soil endowment. More relevant are pH and total potassium, for which the trends are better.

While the growth of poor rural populations degrades the soil, economic development may improve the soil in three ways explored here:

1. Taking all soil-farming feedbacks into account, the shift in food demand away from staples toward legumes and animal products may replenish soil nutrients.
2. Development means cheaper capital and clearer property rights, which improve conservation.
3. Urbanization and industrialization raise the productivity of soils at the urban fringe. Data from China suggest that this effect is strong enough to cancel the loss of farm soil endowment from urban encroachment.

Such are the suggestions of the estimates presented here. It should be added, of course, that the data are not sharp enough to give a clear view of all regional soil dynamics. Like the Hubble telescope before its expensive repair, they can give only a blurry view from a superior vantage point. Fortunately, the current assertions about soil trends are so broad that the evidence is clear enough to be useful even without the sharpness of focus one would have wished for. There is the prospect that replicating such soil-history studies, even for just one or two other countries, could supplement what we are learning from the continuing official efforts to track soil trends into the twentieth-first century.

PART IV

Research for Genetic Improvement

9 The Role of Technology Spillovers and Economies of Size in the Efficient Design of Agricultural Research Systems

DEREK BYERLEE AND GREG TRAXLER

Following the Green Revolution beginning in the 1960s, investment in agricultural research in the developing world increased rapidly, exceeding that in industrialized countries by 1990 (Alston, Pardey, and Roseboom 1998). However, in recent years, investment in research has slowed in all regions and in many cases has declined. In the 1990s the emphasis shifted from growth of national agricultural research systems (NARSs) to more efficient use of the existing research infrastructure. "Rationalization" of research investments, downsizing, and formal approaches to setting research priorities are now the order of the day.

The design of efficient research systems in terms of location, size, number, and scope of research institutes depends on many factors. This chapter reviews two interrelated factors that critically influence the efficient design of research systems—technology spillover and economies of size and scope in research. When economies of size and scope in research are few, efficient design of a research system usually involves many small programs to generate technologies that are well adapted to local environments. On the other hand, when technology spill-ins can be captured and significant economies of size and scope exist, it is more efficient to have a smaller number of more centralized research programs.

The potential for research spillovers has been widely recognized in the literature on research and development (R&D) in general (Griliches 1992; Jaffe, Trajtenberg, and Henderson 1993) and in agriculture specifically (Evenson 1989, 1994). There are three types of spillovers. (1) Knowledge-related spillovers refer to new knowledge generated elsewhere (for example, a new research method or discovery) that is applied to a research process to enable more efficient generation of new technology.[1] (2) Technology-related spillovers come about when a technology itself is transferred or adapted to a new environment. (3) Price-related spillovers derive from price reductions in the same or related industries (sometimes referred to as pecuniary spillovers).

---

1. Evenson (1989) refers to these as pretechnology spillovers.

161

Research spillovers may occur across regions and across stages of research (that is, from basic to applied research). They may also occur across different commodities or even industries (Evenson 1989; Industry Commission 1995).

This chapter deals only with technology spillovers, focusing on inter-regional technology transfer. The conventional wisdom is that agricultural technology does not travel well because much technology is either agro-climatically specific, as in the case of biological technology, or sensitive to relative factor prices, as with mechanical technology. This belief originated from early, unsuccessful attempts to transfer technologies from industrialized countries with predominantly temperate, high-wage economies to develop-ing countries with mostly subtropical and tropical, low-wage economies. The experience with such transfers motivated a major expansion of capacity for technology generation within the developing world, both through rapid expan-sion of NARSs and through the creation of international agricultural research centers (IARCs) specifically designed to generate spillovers in the developing world. The key question now, given this large investment in research capacity in the developing world, is: What is the potential for "south-south" spillovers across developing countries? This question is especially relevant in today's world, where R&D, including agricultural research, is becoming increasingly globalized.

Although considerable literature exists on spillovers, little attention has been paid to the role of economies of size and scope in agricultural R&D. The presence of economies of size in research implies that the unit cost of produc-ing a given research product, such as a new plant variety, decreases as the size of the research effort increases. Economies of scope refer to a reduction in unit research costs as the breadth of the research institution expands, owing to sharing input and overhead costs across related research activities. Several authors, such as Ruttan (1982) and Pardey, Roseboom, and Anderson (1991), have noted the potential for economies of size and scope in agricultural re-search, but the empirical evidence is limited to date.

Although not strictly an economies-of-size effect, the "size of market" within the target area or mandate of the research program is another major determinant of the efficiency of research investments. Among research institu-tions with equal research costs per unit of research output, the institution that achieves the widest adoption of its research products will generate the largest social return on the investment. The fact that research programs have generally been established to conform to state or national political boundaries artificially truncates the natural target areas of many research institutions. The "small-country problem" is one manifestation of this type of fracturing of natural agroecological zones (AEZs). Research administrators who want to enhance systemwide efficiency face two critical challenges: identifying spill-in oppor-tunities for their small-market research institutions and designing institutional mechanisms for coordinating research responsibilities across traditional political boundaries.

Systems such as the United States Department of Agriculture (USDA), the Indian Council of Agricultural Research (ICAR) in India, and the Consultative Group on International Agricultural Research (CGIAR) have been established specifically to generate spillovers and to compensate for underinvestment in research by state programs (or national programs in the case of CGIAR) unable to capture the benefits from spillovers of their research products. In other words, although technologies frequently spill across political boundaries, states, or countries, the investments are made on the basis of benefits captured by producers and consumers within the political boundaries of a state or country (Ruttan 1982). Centralized research may enable efficiency gains through economies of size up to the point where such economies are offset by the location-specific advantages of technologies.[2]

The next section of this chapter provides a conceptual view of a research production function that incorporates economies of size, market size, and spill-ins to determine the optimal size of investment in research for a given market. The following two sections review recent empirical evidence on the various parameters of the research production function that relate to the chapter's central thesis. In particular, evidence is provided from developing countries on research spill-ins, effects of market size, and economies of size in crop-improvement research. The last section discusses policy implications with respect to research system design and the financing of research.

Conceptual Framework

A Research Production Function with Spill-ins

A research production function relating research output to a measure of research inputs can be conceived as a metafunction made up of research programs of increasing complexity and scope as the size of the research effort expands. The steps toward complexity can be categorized as follows:

1. Spontaneous diffusion of imported technologies without the benefit of local R&D.
2. Direct transfer of technologies after testing and screening by local R&D programs for adaptability to local environments.

---

2. While emphasis in this chapter is on interregional and international spillovers, the issues are equally important for determining the optimal number of research programs for a given region. Creation of research programs to target specific environments effectively narrows the range of spillover coefficients for each of the programs (Evenson 1989). The value added by these additional programs must be weighed against their cost.

3. "Adaptive" transfer of technologies whereby finished technologies from elsewhere are subject to local adaptation before local release (for example, the use of imported varieties as parents in local breeding programs).
4. Comprehensive applied research whereby imported knowledge from basic research conducted elsewhere is used in local applied research programs to produce home-grown technologies.
5. Comprehensive basic and applied research that uses imported knowledge and includes the ability to conduct basic or pretechnology research.

These research capacities often lead to discontinuities in the production function as each new step requires a minimum investment. For example, in a breeding program the transition from step 2 to step 3 involves the addition of a crossing program and early generation selection, which is considerably more expensive to undertake than testing (Brennan 1988).

The following discussion focuses on the direct and adaptive spillovers of technology (steps 1 to 3) (see Figure 9.1). Without research, some spontaneous diffusion may take place—this is represented by OA. With addition of local capacity to seek, screen, and test technologies from elsewhere for direct transfer, a new stage of the production function is reached—represented by AB'. The shift to adaptive transfer research requires the addition of specialized skills and facilities: a minimum threshold level of research effort, OO', is needed to produce research output. Additional research inputs allow movement along the research production function from A to B and then D.

Abstracting from differences in the timing of research costs and benefits, the economic surplus (ES) from investment in research is conventionally given by

$$ES = PQK_r(S_r) - CS_r,$$

where P is the price of output Q affected by the research. $K_r(S_r)$ is the research production function of Figure 9.1 that relates the proportional shift in the supply curve, K, to research input, S_r. S_r is measured here in scientific person years with unit cost C. The subscript $r = t, d$ represents research production functions for direct technology transfer and adaptive transfer.

ES is maximized at $dK/dS = C/PQ$. That is, the optimal size of the research program will depend on parameters of the research production function and the cost of research inputs in relation to the market size, PQ. Thus it may be profitable for a small region or country (a small PQ) to operate at X, with a direct transfer program, while a research program for a larger region or country (a large PQ) would operate at Y on the adaptive transfer function.

Adding fixed costs, the production function in Figure 9.1 allows for both economies and diseconomies of size as the size of the program expands. The shape of the cost function will be determined by three key parameters in Figure 9.1.

FIGURE 9.1 Research production function, allowing for spill-ins

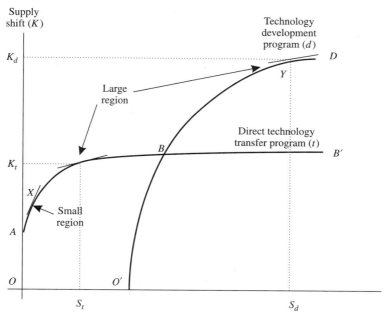

1. K_t/K_d represents the value added from adaptation of imported technologies. This ratio is directly related to the common definition of the spillover coefficient k_t/k_d, where $K = \alpha k$ with k representing the relative decline in production cost per unit area and α the adoption level.
2. S_t/S_d represents the additional cost of moving from direct transfer to adaptive transfer research.
3. PQ represents the market size targeted by the research program.

An additional dimension not included above is the difference in research lags for various types of research. Generally research lags become longer as one moves through the research steps listed above.

Spillover Potential

Applied studies of agricultural research have attempted to measure both spillover potential (for example, Davis, Oram, and Ryan 1987; Englander 1991; Maredia, Ward, and Byerlee 1996) and actual spillovers (for example, Brennan and Fox 1995; Traxler and Byerlee 2000). Spillover potential refers to the potential physical or biological performance of introduced technologies compared with local technologies. Actual spillovers are bounded by spillover potential but usually are smaller because of institutional and policy barriers that govern the transfer of technologies across political boundaries.

Several factors condition spillover potential:

1. *Agroecological similarity between the originating and receiving region.* Agroecological similarity is usually measured by climatic and soil data that are mapped into AEZs. However, these factors can be modified drastically by physical investments, especially in irrigation and water control.

2. *The degree of interaction between technology and the environment.* AEZs are best defined with respect to specific crops and types of technology (Chapman and Barreto 1994; Pardey and Wood 1994). Thus wheat research and rice research require different AEZs, but so does research on different aspects of each crop. An AEZ for wheat-improvement research will differ from an AEZ for wheat crop–management research. AEZ boundaries are dynamic and can be modified by the availability of new technologies that interact differently with environmental variables (Pardey and Wood 1994).[3]

3. *Local food tastes and preferences.* Even if there is perfect homogeneity of agroecological conditions, cultural differences in tastes modify the acceptance of new technologies, especially crop varieties. In many cases, these differences are expressed in local market prices and can be captured in a modified spillover coefficient that includes price effects.

4. *Relative factor prices.* Prices of labor and capital will be important determinants of the spillover potential of labor-saving technologies such as farm machinery and some types of chemicals. Rapid changes in labor prices relative to capital, as is currently occurring in much of Asia, may quickly alter the spillover potential of labor-saving technologies.

5. *Institutions.* Institutions such as land tenure or property rights condition potential applicability of some types of technologies, especially in natural resource management.

Actual Spillovers

Quantifying the benefits from agricultural research requires that actual spillovers of technology be measured. Several factors influence the realization of spillovers but are difficult to incorporate in ex ante assessment of spillover potential. These include historical, linguistic, and cultural links between re-

---

3. In the case of wheat, for example, the early semidwarf varieties developed and spread in irrigated areas were initially less successful in high-rainfall areas because of lack of resistance to the disease Septoria. However, with the incorporation of resistance to this disease, the distinction between irrigated and higher-rainfall AEZs for wheat-improvement research has blurred.

gions and countries (Eyzaguirre 1996), geographic proximity, and institutional and policy factors—some of which have been created to foster spillovers (such as research networks). Others, such as lack of systems of protection of intellectual property rights and rigid rules on testing and release of agricultural technologies, may reduce the degree and speed of spillovers (Gisselquist 1994).

Economies of Size and Scope

The effect of firm size and market structure on investment in R&D has generated a vast empirical literature in the field of industrial organization yet has virtually escaped notice in agricultural economics.[4] Various models of R&D have focused on both the size-input and size-output relationships. From the research-input perspective the question is whether the intensity of R&D investment increases with firm size. The question from the output perspective is whether the efficiency of R&D investment increases with firm size—that is, is the innovation-discovery process itself subject to size economies?

The context changes as the focus shifts from private R&D in manufacturing to public investment in agricultural research, but the importance of understanding the effects of size on research intensity and innovative efficiency persists. In agriculture, interest in research intensity is recast as the "small-country problem," which relates mainly to the issue of market size. If a commodity is produced in very small amounts, even a modest research effort will result in a high research intensity.

Economies of size, on the other hand, relate to the efficiency of producing a given research output, regardless of market size. Several factors may lead to economies of size and scope in agricultural research:

1. *Fixed cost of research.* Most research programs require certain minimum establishment costs in the form of research stations, laboratories and equipment, and administrative overhead that increase less than proportionally with the size and number of research programs.
2. *Specialization of scientific expertise and equipment.* Because of the specialized nature of much science, the addition of research capacity in a given field may be relatively "lumpy."
3. *Scientific synergism among a team of scientists.* For some types of research problems, researchers working in a team may be more productive than the sum of individual researchers working alone as a result of the intellectual stimulation provided by teamwork.

---

4. Reviews of the industrial innovation literature include Cohen and Levin (1989), Griliches (1990, 1994), Kamien and Schwartz (1982), and Scherer (1984). This literature focuses on the dynamic effects of size and market structure on innovation in the private sector, with little mention of public-sector research activity. The only empirical study found on size economies in agricultural research is by Branson and Foster (1987).

Several factors may result in diseconomies of size. In addition to diminishing marginal returns as one moves along the research production function, research for a larger and more dispersed area may entail higher transactions costs (for example, regional testing activities and meetings). For these reasons, research programs are likely to be most effective in their own "backyard." A larger, more centralized research program may also preclude the efficiency and innovation that would be generated by competition among smaller, rival programs. Finally, centralization of research into fewer, larger institutes may increase risks. These risks may include technological risk such as genetic uniformity as well as institutional risk from the natural cycles of research productivity in research institutions.

The design of a research program depends on the trade-offs between economies of size and the potential to capture spill-ins (Figure 9.2). Technological areas may fall into one of the four quadrants in Figure 9.2. Some types of research, such as molecular biology, are likely to be characterized by considerable size economies (because of high fixed costs) and high potential for spillovers, while others, such as agronomic research to develop crop management recommendations, are at the other extreme on both counts. In a few cases, an AEZ may be so specific to a given country or region within a country that there are few opportunities for spill-ins or spillovers (quadrant three of Figure 9.2). In other cases, an activity with scant economies of size may have high international applicability. The development of some types of broadly applicable research methods and certain types of social science research may fit this category.

Technology Spillovers in Practice

Estimating Coefficients of Potential Spillovers

Spillovers have long been recognized, but only recently have serious attempts been made to rigorously estimate potential spillover coefficients ex ante as a guide to decisions on the design of agricultural research systems. Most estimates are informed guesses by scientists based on environmental distance and knowledge of the technology.[5] The range of spillover coefficients in studies based on the method vary from almost 0 to 0.8–0.9.

A second, more objective approach, pioneered by Englander (1991) and modified by Maredia, Ward, and Byerlee (1996), uses the extensive data available on the performance of varietal technologies in national and international

---

5. This subjective method was first employed by Davis, Oram, and Ryan (1987) for developing a global spillover matrix for agricultural technologies, based on broad definitions of global AEZs defined by the Food and Agriculture Organization of the United Nations (FAO). Following Davis, Oram, and Ryan, similar methods have been used to estimate potential spillovers for agricultural technologies in South America (Evenson and da Cruz 1992) and to estimate potential spillover coefficients for rice technologies in Indonesia (Pardey and Wood 1994).

FIGURE 9.2 Illustrative categorization of research activities in terms of possible economies of size and spillover potential

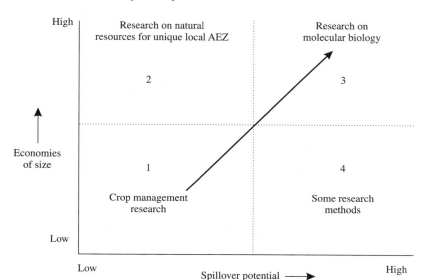

yield trials across sites and years. Spillover coefficients are econometrically estimated based on the performance of varieties of different origins in different environments. The general model employed by Maredia, Ward, and Byerlee (1996) is:[6]

$$Y_{ijt}^m = a + k\ VINT_i + \sum_{h=1}^{H} c_h\ DORIG_{hi} + \sum_{j=1}^{M} b_j\ DLOC_j + \sum_{t=1}^{T} u_t\ DYEAR_t + e_{ijt} \qquad (9.1)$$

where Y_{ijt}^m is the yield of technology i in location j in year t in environment m, $VINT_i$ is the vintage or year of release of technology i, $DORIG_{hi}$ is a set of dummies for environmental origin, h, of technology i, and $DLOC_j$ and $DYEAR_t$ are dummy variables to remove location and year effects in panel data. The key parameter estimated in this equation is c_h, the difference in yield in a given environment of technologies developed in other environments, relative to the yield of home-produced technologies. Converted to relative terms, this is a direct measure of the spillover coefficient, defined above.

This approach has been used to estimate spillover coefficients for wheat internationally (Englander 1991; Maredia, Ward, and Byerlee 1996) and for rice and wheat in India (Evenson, Pray, and Rosegrant 1998; Traxler and

6. Maredia, Ward, and Byerlee (1996) include the Mills ratio to remove effects on non-random entry and exit of varietal technologies in multiyear testing.

Byerlee 2000). A similar approach based on analysis of variance has been used by Henning and Eddleman (1986) for soybeans in the United States. In general, the results estimate higher potential spillovers than the subjective estimates; estimated spillover coefficients are often close to unity.

A second finding of these studies is that the estimated spillover matrices are not symmetric. This is to be expected because technological performance is governed by interactions that depend on both the genotype and the environment. For example, in the study by Maredia, Ward, and Byerlee (1996), two higher rainfall environments were distinguished—one with acid soils and one with normal soils. Varieties from the acid-soil environment performed well in the non–acid-soil environment because they had the required yield potential and disease resistance. However, varieties from the normal soil areas performed poorly in the acid-soil environment, because these varieties lacked acid-soil tolerance.

Finally, Maredia, Ward, and Byerlee (1996) found that for varieties developed by national research systems, all the spill-in coefficients were less than unity. However, their work also shows that varieties developed in the international system often had spill-in coefficients above unity, indicating that in many situations varieties developed in the international research system perform better than locally developed varieties. These results confirm that the IARCs are fulfilling their mandated role of providing widely adaptable germplasm.

Recent Evidence of Actual Spillovers

ECONOMETRIC STUDIES.   Several methods have been used to measure actual spillovers. One set of studies estimated spillovers on the basis of a production function that includes investment in research (or a proxy such as publications) both in the home environment and in other environments or regions. This approach provides an estimate of all spillovers: direct and adaptive transfers as well as research spillovers in the form of new knowledge. White and Havlicek (1981) and Evenson in various studies (Evenson 1989; Evenson and da Cruz 1992; Evenson and Kislev 1975) applied this approach to estimate interregional spillovers for the whole agricultural sector or for subsectors rather than for specific commodities and technology types.

The results of this work generally confirm large spillovers; spillover benefits usually exceed benefits in the home environment (Araji, White, and Guenthner 1995; Evenson 1989). Research on crops shows more site specificity than research on livestock, for which spillovers can be extremely high. Spillovers also tend to flow from larger regions with larger research investments to smaller regions. Some of this work has also examined international spillovers, especially Evenson (1974), Evenson and da Cruz (1992), and Thirtle et al. (1995). The results at the international level provide similar estimates of the magnitude and direction of research spillovers.

DIRECT OBSERVATION OF SPILLOVERS. A second approach to measuring actual spillovers is to trace actual technology flows across geographic regions within a country and across countries, for specific technology types and commodities. These studies, which have been primarily employed for tracking varietal technologies, have found surprisingly large interstate flows of technology. For example, for wheat in India and Australia the area sown to varieties developed in other environments or by central research programs often exceeds the area sown to home-produced varieties (Brennan 1999; Traxler and Byerlee 2000). There is also extensive evidence of international spillovers of varietal technologies. For example, wheats from the Ukraine were directly transferred to the United States in the early part of the twentieth century and widely grown until the 1930s. In the developing world, the major source of spillovers has been the international centers. Beginning with the Green Revolution, varieties from the Centro Internacional de Mejoramiento de Maíz y Trigo (CIMMYT) and the International Rice Research Institute (IRRI) have been widely transferred to the developing world. This pattern has been followed for almost all crops in the mandate of the IARCs (Evenson 2000).

Figure 9.3 shows the proportion of varieties of the three major cereal crops, rice, wheat, and maize, that are direct transfers from the IARCs.[7] For wheat and maize this proportion has been rising and now exceeds half of all varietal releases in the developing world outside of China. The proportion for rice is smaller and after peaking in the late 1970s has tended to fall. However, the rice data are dominated by India, which accounts for more than half of all releases. Without India, the situation for rice is similar to that of wheat. For example, even for a large country such as Indonesia, half or more of the rice area has consistently been sown to direct introductions from IRRI (Pardey et al. 1992).

It is likely that international spillovers are highest for a commodity like wheat, which is grown in relatively homogeneous production environments,[8] with little variability in local tastes and preferences for quality characteristics. Quality characteristics for other commodities are often quite location-specific (for example, see Unnevehr [1986] for rice). For some commodities, such as beans in Africa, consumer tastes may be so highly location-specific as to make it difficult even for country programs to develop widely accepted varieties (Sperling, Loevinsohn, and Ntambovura 1993). Direct-observation studies also confirm that, as expected, small NARSs with less resources to undertake comprehensive research programs depend more on direct transfers than do large NARSs. On the other hand, the large NARSs capture a high proportion

---

7. In addition, another 4 percent of varieties of wheat and 30 percent of rice were direct transfers from other NARSs.

8. The irrigated and high-rainfall environments together account for more than 70 percent of wheat production in the developing world.

FIGURE 9.3 Percentage of cereal varieties released in developing countries as direct transfers from IARCs, 1966–1990

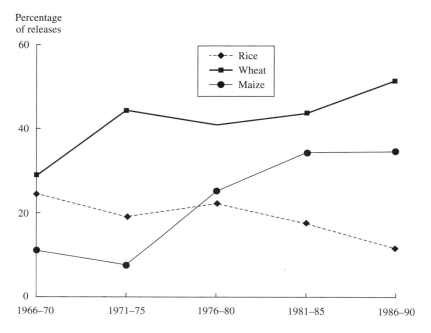

SOURCE: Unpublished CIMMYT and IRRI data files.

(59 percent) of the total spillover benefits of the international research system (Byerlee and Maredia 1999). It is important to note that, because the number of potential introductions is large and time is required to assess local perfor-mance, the screening and testing of imported technologies require considerable local research capacity and substantial resources. Byerlee and Maredia (1999) estimate that NARSs spend at least as much in testing and release of IARC-developed materials as IARCs spend in the development of those materials.

Technology generated elsewhere can also be adapted to the local environ-ment through further research. In practice, many research spillovers occur through this type of adaptive transfer. This has been most widely analyzed in the case of varietal technologies. Varieties developed elsewhere can be used directly after local testing or can be used as parents for development of new varieties. Figure 9.4 shows the adaptive transfer of rice, wheat, and maize varieties in the developing world. Adaptive transfers are important for all crops, but more so for rice. In general, large NARSs engage in adaptive transfers rather than direct transfers.

FIGURE 9.4 Percentage of cereal varieties released in developing countries as adaptive transfers with at least one IARC parent, 1966–1990

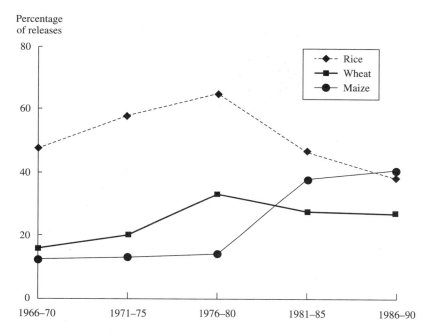

SOURCE: Unpublished CIMMYT and IRRI data files.

Indeed, no country can be an island with respect to technology transfer. Most industrialized countries depend on adaptive transfers with a significant percentage of varieties having at least one foreign parent. The United States, for example, has captured significant spillovers of wheat and rice varietal technologies from the IARCs (Pardey et al. 1996). Most of these spillovers have been adaptive transfers, but in the case of wheat in California, most varieties have originated directly from CIMMYT. The aggregate benefits of these spillovers have been valued in the billions of dollars.

There is less evidence on the direct transferability of other types of technologies. In the case of livestock, modern poultry technologies have proven to be highly transferable across countries, even without the input of local R&D (Narrod and Pray 2000). By contrast, the direct international transfer of natural resource management technologies appears to be limited. For example, despite considerable investment over three decades, IARCs have had limited success in transferring prototype technologies for resource management. The limited impact of this effort reflects the inadequate attention to the institutional and socioeconomic conditions in which the new technologies would be applied.

Farmers' socioeconomic circumstances, not just the agroecological circumstances, significantly determine location specificity of research on crop and resource management. In addition, the receiving NARSs have often lacked the capacity to undertake the extensive, adaptive research and extension required to use the prototype technologies.

Redefining the Conventional Wisdom on Spillovers

Conventional wisdom holds that the transferability of agricultural technologies decreases in order from chemical technologies, the most transferable, to varietal technologies, to agronomic crop management technologies. Indeed, chemical technologies appear to be highly transferable. Many of the same chemicals are used in the tropics and subtropics and in temperate areas. In addition, the expense of R&D for agrochemical technology has confined the development of these technologies to a few large laboratories, mostly in industrialized countries, with testing sites around the world. The development of pesticides is a classic example of a technology in quadrant three of Figure 9.2. In other words, there are considerable economies of size in agrochemical R&D, and the spillover potential is large. Other types of R&D that have been taken up by multinational firms, for example, research in molecular genetics and biotechnology, also conform to this model.

Biological technologies, such as varietal technologies, are assumed to be quite location-specific, with limited direct transferability (for example, Evenson and Binswanger 1978; Ruttan 1982). However, the accumulating evidence for the rice, maize, and wheat suggests that AEZs show considerable homogeneity across developing countries and that the potential for biological technology spillovers is large. The growing ability to describe AEZs through the new information technologies such as geographical information systems (GIS) should greatly increase the precision with which spillovers can be targeted across countries (Pardey and Wood 1994). At present, the major obstacles to realizing the spillover potential of biological technology appear to be institutional and policy barriers against technology transfer across national borders.

It is likely, moreover, that the spillover potential of varietal technologies has increased over time because environments have been "homogenized" owing to the widespread adoption of modern technology such as irrigation and fertilizer and because tastes and preferences have begun to converge. At the same time, the breeding approaches of the IARCs have produced broadly adapted varieties that interact less with the environment.

Crop and resource management technologies are the most site-specific and the least transferable. Fortunately, the fixed costs of crop and resource management research are often quite low, so that economies of size in conducting crop management research are limited. This type of technology increasingly is being transferred as principles and methods that can be applied by farmers themselves to suit their specific situations.

Economies of Size and Market Size in Practice

The second major determinant of efficient research design is economies of size in agricultural research. As noted, a large amount of research has analyzed economies of size in industrial R&D. Cohen and Levin (1989:1069) conclude that "the most notable feature of this considerable body of empirical research on the relationship between firm size and innovation is its inconclusiveness." Griliches (1990:1678) also finds that "the evidence is suggestive but not conclusive." These results reflect the inherently variable nature of the innovation-discovery process, as well as the broad array of time periods, industries, and empirical models used in the studies.

Almost no comparable studies of economies of size exist for the agricultural sector, although several authors have recognized the importance of the issue (Alston, Norton, and Pardey 1995; Evenson 1978; Pardey, Roseboom, and Anderson 1991; Ruttan 1978, 1982). This section uses regression techniques to analyze data from national and international crop-breeding research programs to (1) assess the effect of a country's size on research intensity, that is, the effect of market size on research efficiency, and (2) test for economies of size, that is, the relationship between the cost of developing new varieties and the size of the research program.

Three similar sets of data on crop-improvement research were analyzed (see Byerlee and Moya 1993 and Lopez-Pereira and Morris 1994 for the first two data sets, which come from CIMMYT, and Jain and Byerlee 1999 for the third from India):[9]

1. Country-level data on maize-breeding research (including private-sector research) in 44 developing countries.
2. Program-level data on wheat-breeding research at 63 research stations in 30 countries.
3. Program-level data on wheat-breeding research at 50 research stations in India.

Determinants of Research Intensity

Following Pardey, Roseboom, and Anderson (1991), the intensity of the agricultural research effort at the national level is hypothesized to be a function of the size of the agricultural sector, the opportunity to receive spill-ins, and agroclimatic diversity. This model is tested using the following logarithmic specification:

$$\ln(I_i) = \gamma_0 + \gamma_1 \ln(A_i) + \gamma_2 \ln(D_i) + \gamma_3 \ln(S_i) + \gamma_4 DAFRICA + \mu_i, \qquad (9.2)$$

---

9. Input data are approximated by information on human resources committed to crop improvement in 1992, measured in full-time-equivalent (FTE) scientist years. Crop-improvement scientists were defined to include breeders as well as scientists in supporting disciplines such as pathology and grain quality.

where I_i is the number of scientists per ton of production (a measure of research intensity), A_i is the crop area planted in 1990, D_i is a measure of environmental diversity using the average area per agroecological environment; S_i is the spill-in potential per million hectares, and *DAFRICA* is a dummy variable for African countries.

The coefficient of A is of primary interest. The diversity coefficient in the specification is expected to have a negative sign, since a larger area per environment implies less environmental diversity. The number of CIMMYT varieties released per million hectares in the country is used as a measure of spill-in potential for wheat, and the number of maize breeders employed in the private sector per million hectares in the country is used as a proxy for spill-in potential in the maize equation. The dummy variable for Africa is included in the maize equation to account for the fact that many research programs in this region are young and may not have reached an equilibrium with respect to size.

The results reported in Table 9.1 strongly support the idea that research intensity increases when research programs target smaller crop areas. The coefficient of A is significantly different from zero at the 1 percent level and indicates a negative elasticity of -0.4 to -0.6 of research intensity with respect to crop area. That is, the intensity of research declines by about 0.5 percent for

TABLE 9.1 Analysis of factors determining research intensity, international and national crop-improvement research

	International Wheat	International Maize	Indian Wheat
ln (Area)	-0.40	-0.58	-0.62
	$(4.28)^{***}$	$(6.80)^{***}$	$(9.21)^{***}$
ln (Spill-ins)	0.0002^a	-0.02^b	—
	(0.26)	(0.73)	
ln (Diversity)	-0.0002	0.0006	—
	(0.48)	(0.76)	
Dummy for Africa	—	-0.526	—
		(2.23)	
Constant	2.34	-0.042	6.30
	$(13.58)^{***}$	(0.064)	
R^2	0.60	0.56	0.83
n	31	44	20

SOURCE: Authors' estimates.

NOTE: Dependent variable is a log of full-time equivalents (FTEs) on production, 1990. Absolute value of t-ratios are given in parentheses. *** denotes significance at the 1 percent level.

[a]Number of CIMMYT varieties released per million hectares of wheat area.

[b]Number of private-sector maize researchers per million hectares of maize area.

each 1 percent increase in the area targeted for the crop. The estimated diversity and spill-in elasticities are very small and are not significant in either equation. This result is consistent with the idea that policymakers determine investment levels for reasons that are independent of the environmental complexity or the potential to free-ride on spill-ins.

The results of this analysis coincide with the findings of Byerlee and Maredia (1999), who also find a strong negative relationship between the unit cost of wheat-breeding research and the market size served by the research program. Largely for this reason, the cost of CIMMYT wheat research per hectare affected was lower than that in nearly all NARSs, with the exception of the largest NARS in Asia. These results also support those of Pardey, Roseboom, and Anderson (1991), who found that across some 130 countries research intensity for the research system as a whole is negatively related to country size.

Determinants of Research Productivity

To determine whether there are economies of size in research on varietal development, the rate of discovery of innovations is assumed to conform to a Poisson process, with the number of innovations in a period taking on non-negative, integer values, typically within a small range of observed values, and with a large number of zero observations.[10] For a discrete random variable Y, with observed frequencies y, $y \geq 0$, and for regressors X_i, the Poisson regression model is

$$\text{prob}(Y = y) = e^{-\lambda}\lambda_y/y! \qquad (9.3)$$

where the mean regression relationship is modeled as

$$\ln \lambda = \mathbf{X}\beta. \qquad (9.4)$$

Following the literature in the industrial sector, a Cobb-Douglas specification was used to estimate this mean relationship with the number of scientists as the measure of research input and number of varieties released as the measure of research productivity.[11] The results shown in Table 9.2 indicate significant

---

10. Poisson regression is more appropriate than the standard normal linear regression model for the analysis of count data such as patents, pharmaceutical discoveries, or varietal releases (Graves and Langowitz 1993; Hausman, Hall, and Griliches 1984; Jensen 1987; Winkelman 1994). The consequences of applying the normal linear regression model when the Poisson or the related negative binomial model applies are severe: estimators will be inconsistent and inefficient, and statistical inferences will be invalid. The Poisson specification also allows the counts, or the rate of arrival, to be aggregated over time as long as time independence can be assumed. "If the counting process is Poisson over time $t = 1$, T with parameter λ_{it}, then the aggregate data over period one to T are also Poisson with parameter $\lambda_i = \Sigma_t \lambda_{it}$." (Hausman, Hall, and Griliches 1984:911).

11. Significant cross-sectional variability exists, particularly in the international data sets, in the experience, training, and financial support of crop scientists and in the quality-adjusted output measure. It would be appropriate to weight the count of scientists by some proxy for talent, but no such measure is available. Likewise, varietal releases do not take account of differences in local release procedures.

TABLE 9.2 Analysis of the effects of program size on the number of varieties released, international and national crop-improvement research

	International[a]		India Wheat[a]	
	Wheat	Maize	All Varieties	Successful Varieties
ln (Public full-time equivalents)	0.46 (5.97)***	0.25 (5.98)***	1.13 (10.52)***	1.38 (6.80)***
ln (Private full-time equivalents)		0.03 (4.57)***		
ln (Area per environment)	−0.056 (1.19)			
Dummy for Africa		−0.23 (0.27)		
Dummy for Indian Council of Agricultural Research			0.86 (4.60)***	0.35 (0.38)
Constant	0.89 (2.44)**	2.26 (15.5)***	−0.84 (3.79)***	−2.40 (5.40)***
Log likelihood	−198.5	−219.2	−102.8	−54.2
n	63	44	50	50

SOURCE: Authors' estimates.

NOTE: ** and *** denote statistical significance at the 5 percent and 1 percent levels, respectively.

[a] Dependent variable is the logarithm of the number of varieties released.

diminishing returns to size in producing varieties in the international wheat and maize data sets, with elasticities of output response to additional researchers of 0.46 and 0.25.

In the case of India, an analysis of the number of commercially successful varieties as a measure of quality-adjusted output indicates that the elasticity of number of varieties with respect to size of program is 1.13 for released varieties and 1.38 for successful varieties. A Wald test fails to reject the null hypothesis of constant returns to size for either equation. The larger size elasticity in India than in the international wheat or maize data set is probably because many small programs in India have only one or two breeders. Fourteen of these 26 small programs had not released any varieties during the period of analysis. At the other extreme, two of the larger stations produced 33 percent of all varieties.

Although the results are preliminary and somewhat inconclusive, they are consistent with the conceptual framework described earlier, in which diminishing returns along the metaproduction function are expected. However, investment in crop-improvement research does tend to be lumpy. For example, Byerlee and Maredia (1999) estimate from an international survey of wheat-breeding programs that a program that only screens and tests imported technology employs one full-time scientist, compared with three for a program with full varietal-development capability. This finding justifies the presence of the significant discontinuities in the metaproduction function shown in Figure 9.1. Together the two analyses strongly indicate that the market size over which technologies are applied, rather than economies of size in producing those technologies, is the key determinant of research efficiency among programs, at least for crop breeding programs within the range of sizes analyzed.

Conclusions and Policy Implications

Returns to Investment in Research Revisited

Although spillovers have been widely recognized in the literature on agricultural R&D, they have rarely been incorporated into the economic analysis of investment in agricultural research. Benefits from research occurring in a given area have usually been attributed to the research conducted in that area. Given that spillovers are pervasive in agricultural R&D, this has resulted in biased estimates of returns to investment in research. Because spillovers tend to flow from large regions and from central research programs, the failure to include spillovers and spill-ins has inflated estimates of returns to research in the smaller regions and underestimated returns in the larger programs. (Two recent studies that highlight these biases are Thirtle et al. [1995] and Traxler and Byerlee [2000].)

It is also important to account for spillovers in the ex ante assessment of the efficiency of research programs. Maredia and Byerlee (2000) have developed point estimates of the research production function in Figure 9.1 to determine the optimal size of a wheat research program with different levels of spill-ins. Given the potential for spill-ins from the international system, Maredia and Byerlee asked what the value added was from establishing a full breeding program, compared with a testing program to screen imported materials. After evaluating 72 wheat-breeding programs in developing countries, they found that many wheat research programs were producing low or zero benefits at the margin (Table 9.3). Most of the inefficient programs were serving relatively small mandate areas, so economies of market size were a key determinant of efficiency. Many of the inefficient programs had a relatively high rate of return on investment; they were inefficient because they gave lower net present values than a smaller program to test and screen technologies. In other words, the rate of return for an individual program is an inappropriate guide for research investment decisions in the presence of spill-ins, because it does not measure the marginal return from changing the size of the program.

Research System Design: Number and Size of Research Programs

The efficient choice of number and size of research programs is a function of both the potential for spillovers and spill-ins, as well as economies of size and market size in research. Accumulating evidence shows that regions and countries can capture significant potential spill-ins of all types of technologies. An assessment of this potential should be part of any ex ante evaluation of research programs. Evidence on economies of size in research is still rudimentary and should be a topic of further research. Some fairly simple analysis using commonly available data, such as those reported in this chapter, would go a long way to informing research system design. Nonetheless, the empirical evidence at hand offers little support for economies of size as an important source of efficiency gains in varietal development research, particularly when compared with market-size effects. Even an efficient producer of varietal technologies such as CIMMYT finds that its cost per variety produced is only slightly less than the average of the 10 lowest-cost NARSs (Byerlee and Maredia 1999). Clearly, the reason that CIMMYT generates such a high return on its investment has more to do with the huge potential market for diffusion of its research products than its unit cost of producing those products.

It does seem that exploiting economies of market size is critical to enhancing the efficiency of research investments. The strong negative relationship observed between research intensity and market size is evidence that public-sector research systems have tended to establish individual programs with mandates that conform to political rather than agroecological boundaries, placing artificial limits on the diffusion of research outputs. Thus many public research programs serve markets of less than optimal size, and the ability to leverage the systemwide research budget is severely constrained by redun-

TABLE 9.3 Ex ante analysis of 71 wheat research programs in developing countries: Efficiency of varietal development (breeding) versus testing

Group	Net Present Value	Interpretation	Region	Number of Research Programs	Research Intensity (FTE/Mt)[a]
I	Less than zero	Inefficient Cannot justify current level of investment in wheat research (testing or breeding)	Sub-Saharan Africa	2	91
			West Asia and North Africa	4	
			South and East Asia	0	
			Latin America	6	
			Total	12	
II	0 < NPV (breeding) < NPV (testing)	Inefficient Current investment in breeding is earning positive NPV but less profitable than testing	Sub-Saharan Africa	4	8.1
			West Asia and North Africa	7	
			South and East Asia	1	
			Latin America	6	
			Total	19	
			Group I and II total	31	
III	NPV (breeding) > NPV (testing)	Efficient Current investments in breeding is most efficient	Sub-Saharan Africa	2	1.9
			West Asia and North Africa	11	
			South and East Asia	20	
			Latin America	9	
			Total	42	
			Group I, II, and III total	71	3.4

SOURCE: Maredia and Byerlee (2000).

[a] Full-time-equivalent scientists per million tons of wheat.

dancies and overlaps.[12] This failure of research system designers to take advantage of spill-in opportunities represents a more critical resource misallocation, or at least one that is more amenable to empirical rationalization than the ambiguous effects of economies of size per se.

The way that the private sector, which has strong incentives to improve efficiency in R&D, organizes research supports the key roles of market size and spillovers in efficient system design. The limited evidence suggests that the private sector is less concerned about political boundaries in establishing research facilities. For example, Pioneer Hi-bred International, Inc., invests nearly US$120 million per year in crop-improvement research, much of it to service the US$2 billion U.S. hybrid-maize seed market. In addition to its research headquarters in Iowa, Pioneer operates 23 satellite maize-breeding stations in the United States, each with essentially one full-time breeder. Pioneer makes intensive use of the new informational technologies to allow ready communication among breeding stations and access to specialists at headquarters. Emphasis is placed on systemwide testing of all advanced materials as a way of formalizing the search for agroecological spillovers. In effect, Pioneer operates a single "virtual research station" that is the sum of the abilities of all scientists in the system. The huge size of the U.S. maize seed market, combined with the highly developed system of communication and the apolitical criteria for establishing research mandates, has major influences on the organization of Pioneer's research.

The private sector also uses similar organizational approaches internationally, but institutional mechanisms for reducing the transaction costs of market entry across national borders have been slow to develop. The ability to market a variety in more than one country is important, because individually many countries may fall below the minimum market size needed for a company to recover its R&D investment. Market entry costs include not only R&D costs but also the costs and delays associated with overcoming policy barriers, many of which are supported or implemented by public-sector research administrators who often see the private sector as an unwelcome competitor. These barriers include excessive phytosanitary regulations on seed imports, rigid varietal-release procedures, local sourcing requirements for seeds, and inadequate legal protection of intellectual property or ineffective implementation of existing intellectual property laws (Ansaldo and Riley 1997). As a consequence of such regulatory barriers, Pioneer, for example, "restructured" its operations in Africa and the Middle East in 1993, closing or downsizing most operations in the region (Pioneer Hi-Bred International 1993). Regional efforts

---

12. As one example, in India 80 percent of the benefits from ICAR's national wheat-improvement program were generated within the mandate area of India's strongest state research program. Even though together these two programs produced 75 percent of all national wheat-improvement benefits and each earned a return above 60 percent, systemwide efficiency would be enhanced by refocusing the ICAR mandate (Traxler and Byerlee 2000).

to harmonize varietal release and seed certification policies have substantial potential to increase market size and attract private R&D especially in Africa, where country size is small. For example, countries in a region could agree that varieties released and seed certified in any country within a region could be used in all countries in the region without further local testing. Such a policy has the advantage not only of reducing costs but also of increasing the speed with which imported technologies are made available to farmers (Gisselquist 1994). The liberalization of trade and especially the growing prevalence of free-trade agreements regionally are already facilitating moves in this direction.

In the public sector, institutional mechanisms that encourage both two-way and one-way flows of technology have been developed to promote spillovers. Formal and informal research networks are the most common means of facilitating two-way flows of knowledge and technologies. In plant breeding these networks usually involve some type of national or international varietal performance trials that allow varietal technologies from different origins to be tested in many locations and that provide breeders with access to a wide range of new varieties for local screening. The large interstate spillovers of wheat varietal technologies in Australia reflect the effect of these trials. In some cases networks are more formal, involving not only trials but joint decisions on trial entries and coordination of research. The national coordinated programs for major crops that operate in many countries are an example of this type of network. Internationally, germplasm—testing nurseries run by the IARCs as well as a variety of specialized research networks perform a similar function. With the growing complexity of science and the reduced cost of international cooperation due to the Internet, a variety of other formal collaborative research mechanisms such as regional research consortia and biotechnology networks involving both the private and public sectors are being established to facilitate spill-ins and share research costs.

One-way flows of spillovers result from efforts by public research programs to solve the problem of market size and economies of size by creating centralized research facilities at the national, regional, or international level for the sole purpose of generating spillovers. Most large countries have a federal research system, and the IARCs perform a similar function internationally. In recent years, there has been a trend toward regional research associations among neighboring countries, beginning in Latin America (for example, Evenson and da Cruz 1992) and now expanding strongly in Africa and Asia.

Although conceptually appealing, centralized research institutes in practice have often had difficulty defining their comparative advantages. Federal research in the United States has moved toward more basic research; federal systems in the developing world, such as those in Brazil, India, and Pakistan, remain highly centralized, conducting much applied research even for major crops. In some types of research, especially varietal improvement, this centralized organization has been very successful, but for research on crop and resource management, payoffs appear to have been modest (Byerlee and Pingali 1995).

The international agricultural research system also has established a leading role in applied research in varietal improvement for most of the important food staples. A major explanation for the success of the IARCs is that they represent an institutional mechanism for transcending political boundaries. By organizing and financing international varietal testing nurseries, the centers greatly reduce NARSs' transaction costs in screening germplasm for spill-in potential. Equally important, finished varieties are made available to NARSs at no cost and without any intellectual-property—related restraints. Because diffusion of their varieties is not limited by political borders, they are able to exploit the full agroecological adaptability of their technologies, spreading technology generation costs over vast areas worldwide and generating extremely high returns on investment (for example, Byerlee and Traxler 1995).[13]

The success of the IARCs in varietal development indicates that they are low-cost producers of finished germplasm products and demonstrates their competitive advantage in applied plant-breeding research. However, this does not establish their comparative advantage in this type of applied research. Central research organizations designed to produce one-way spillovers have a comparative advantage in more basic and strategic research because of their unique access to international germplasm collections and advances in science. These organizations provide intermediate research products that shift upward the research production function for national programs that produce finished varieties. In practice the IARCs tend to invest a relatively small share of their resources in this type of prebreeding research (Pingali and Traxler 1997), even though the payoffs are potentially high (Evenson, Herdt, and Hossain 1996). Current strategies are likely to result in a yield plateau as researchers in both national and international programs experience diminishing marginal returns by moving further out on the same production function.

In a world without political boundaries and with centralized funding of agricultural research, an economic model could be developed to determine the optimum size of investment in research at different levels of centralization. But in practice the situation is much more complex. For example, in the common case of one IARC for a particular technology and many NARSs, the NARSs could take the IARC products as given for the purpose of making decisions on their research portfolios (for example, Maredia and Byerlee 2000). Alternatively, the IARC could take the NARS products as given for the purpose of

---

13. Some other types of research have also been shown to have high benefits that transcend national boundaries, especially biological control of cassava pests in Africa. However, the IARCs have yet to demonstrate a consistent track record in other technology types, such as crop and resource management, although a growing share of their resources are now devoted to this type of research.

its decisionmaking (for example, Chopra 1994). These alternatives could lead to very different outcomes, and neither is likely to lead to anything close to an optimum allocation of resources from a global viewpoint.[14] The marginal rate of return to additional research investments is likely to vary widely between the IARCs and the NARSs as a group and among individual NARSs, indicating suboptimal use of resources at the global level. Discussion between the IARCs and the NARSs to exploit complementarities can improve resource allocation. However, as long as resources are relatively immobile between the IARCs and the NARSs, and between individual NARSs, it is unlikely that globally optimal resource allocation will be reached.

Finally, there are a number of risk considerations that may influence the organization of research. A region or country that designs a research program to exploit spill-ins assumes a continuing and costless supply of spill-ins that exposes it to fluctuations in the productivity and priorities of the spillover-generating institutions. In addition, the free flow of technologies is at risk with increasing use of intellectual property rights to protect research products, even in the public sector and increasing country restrictions on exports of local germplasm. Finally, the dependence on a few centralized research programs may expose society to technological risks, such as those associated with genetic uniformity.

Research Funding in the Presence of Spillovers

The pervasiveness of spillovers has been one of the major explanations for the widely observed underfunding of research as shown by the high rate of return on research (Ruttan 1982). Theoretically it is possible to estimate an optimal subsidy for research based on expected spillovers (Schweikhardt and Bonnen 1992), but in practice it is difficult to administer such a scheme. Centrally funded programs that might be justified on the basis of spillovers are usually based on "political" criteria such as population and agricultural production. The generation of spillovers is often concentrated in only a few underfunded programs, despite high returns. At the same time, those programs that are, or potentially are, primarily spill-in recipients appear to overinvest in technology development for widely adaptable technologies (Maredia and Byerlee 2000).

These anomalies reflect the political economy of research funding. Whereas spillovers are based primarily on agroclimatic similarity and technology characteristics, funding for public research is based on political constituencies defined by political boundaries. For this reason regional and international research has been difficult to fund over the long term. This dilemma is manifested in the recent funding shortfalls to the IARCs, especially in germplasm improvement, despite the fact that IARC programs in some crops, especially

---

14. In addition, the wide diversity of NARSs considerably complicates IARC decisionmaking in this case.

rice and wheat, are probably the most successful research programs in history in terms of the size of benefits generated.

Logic suggests that one solution to this dilemma would be to shift the burden of research funding at the regional and international levels to the main beneficiaries. The recent establishment of a regional fund for research in Latin America, through contributions of national governments, represents a step in this direction. This fund, which is carefully identifying research priorities on the basis of potential spillovers in the region, is providing research grants on a competitive basis to NARSs, IARCs, and other research organizations. Another interesting example of innovative funding of regional research is provided by the Latin American Fund for Irrigated Rice, whereby public and private research organizations and farmers themselves are funding a regional rice research program at the Centro Internacional de Agricultura Tropical (CIAT). Similarly Australian farmers through the Grains Research and Development Corporation (GRDC) have provided small contributions to CIMMYT in recognition of the substantial spillover benefits to Australia. At the international level, a growing number of developing countries are contributing to the budgets of the IARCs, although the total contribution of these various efforts still accounts for only a small share of IARC budgets.

In sum, the trend toward more efficient research designs for research systems is already well under way. Where research is shifting to the private sector, and where barriers to technology transfer across political boundaries are no longer significant, private-sector R&D based on "natural" research boundaries will promote efficient research designs. In the case of public-sector research, innovative funding mechanisms are being developed to provide the basis for efficient organization of central, regional, and international research. The increasing importance of the new biotechnologies is leading to a variety of new institutional mechanisms to share costs and benefits of research across national boundaries and between the private and public sectors. However, these same recent technologies are also increasingly being protected under intellectual property rights laws that may slow technology flows across countries. It is still too early to say whether these various influences will positively or negatively affect the significant benefits that the international research system has provided over the past three decades, but there is much scope to improve research system design through further analysis of the interrelated issues of spillovers and economies of size.

10 The Value of Plant Biodiversity for Agriculture

ROBERT EVENSON AND BRIAN WRIGHT

Agricultural genetic diversity has received increasing attention over the past several decades. Facilities for ex situ conservation have proliferated, and in situ conservation has been the focus of much discussion. As property rights for commercial seeds are being strengthened in many countries, and as claims for compensation for use of landraces (varieties collected from farmers' fields) and wild varieties (varieties from related uncultivated species) are being asserted more and more forcefully, it is important that all parties develop a reasoned view of the value of the resources at issue and agree on the means to derive that value. This chapter is a contribution to that end.

Historical Sketch

Of the approximately 250,000 species of higher plants identified to date, approximately 30,000 are edible, and about 7,000 have been cultivated or collected systematically by human populations. Of these, only 120 are of significant economic importance. Thirty cultivated species account for roughly 90 percent of dietary energy and protein consumption.

Among the important cultivated species, farmers have created diversity over and above the natural diversity created by Darwinian processes. They did so through the normal process of harvesting and planting, in which high-yielding plants contribute a greater share of what is sown the next year, and through the systematic selection of superior new cultivated varieties (cultivars) from existing stands of cultivars (aided by mutations) as they migrated to new areas.

Over centuries many new biotypes, usually termed "landraces" or "farmers' varieties" were created within the major cultivated species. Until the early twentieth century, genetic improvement consisted largely of identifying a superior landrace from a crop's geographic center of diversity and obtaining it by fair means or foul. (Thomas Jefferson reportedly smuggled rice out of Italy in his clothing, risking a penalty of death [Fowler 1994:14].)

In what are now developed economies, private actions and national policies for the acquisition and conservation of agricultural and genetic resources

187

have passed through several phases in the past two centuries. In the nineteenth century ex situ conservation took place in botanical gardens, the original form of the national field genebank. If it proved superior against existing cultivars in trials, it was distributed in the nation or its colonies and adopted for production. Good cultivars were national resources—even state secrets—as in the case of tea traded by the Dutch (Juma 1989). Protection of genetic resources in large part consisted of efforts to prevent acquisition by potential competitors. Problems of extinction were generally not viewed as pressing.

In the twentieth century, formal plant breeding came to dominate cultivar selection as the means of genetic crop improvement. Most collections of genetic resources for breeding have been ex situ collections (that is, collections in which the cultivar is conserved away from its natural habitat). In the first decades of modern plant breeding, these collections consisted chiefly of landraces of the cultivated species.

Modern Crop Breeding and Its Breeding Materials

As breeding has progressed, the practice of screening and selecting parent varieties from landraces (or wild or weedy varieties) has become less attractive because improved varieties produced by plant-breeding techniques dominate in terms of yield. Checking landrace yield potential in a cross-breeding program is a long and expensive process with unpromising outcomes relative to the use of improved cultivars for further breeding. Screening for pest and disease resistance is usually much faster and cheaper, so for some crops (notably rice, wheat, and cotton) landraces continue to be used. In general single genes are sources of pest and disease resistance. However, they have also been important for yield improvement. The progress of wheat and rice breeding accelerated in the 1950s when the potential contribution of dwarfing genes to yield enhancement was identified. These cultivars were subsequently used to breed further generations of semidwarf cultivars, which have been widely adopted in developing and developed countries.

In general, in the early part of this century, breeders kept only the cultivars they thought they needed, and they favored materials capable of producing competitive cultivars after a generation or two of crosses. The survival of landraces depended on survival in situ (that is, in their natural habitat) in botanical gardens or in university researchers' collections. The only systematic collection of a wide variety of landraces of a variety of crops was located at the Vavilov Institute in Leningrad (St. Petersburg), Russia.

Over the past century, public (including international, nonprofit) breeders have played the dominant role in providing farmers with new cultivars for the major crops. This is now changing for some major crops. Public and international breeders have been even more dominant in the collection and storage of genetic resources, in basic research, and in back-crossing to produce enhanced germplasm (breeding materials, including seeds, roots, and cells conserved in vitro) for use by breeders. The typically public provision of new genetic material is complemented by private reproduction. Most of the annual supply of nonhybrid seed for most major crops comes from farmers' own fields. Private efforts to assay and incorporate landraces and wild materials from genebanks via conventional breeding appear to be beyond the scope of even the large private firms.

The Vulnerability Shock of the 1970s

In the 1970s, international attitudes toward germplasm conservation changed because of potentially catastrophic problems with modern high-yielding varieties (HYVs) of two major crops. In the United States an epidemic of corn-leaf blight in the southern United States caused a 15 percent drop in national corn yield in 1970, highlighting the genetic vulnerability of the corn crop. "Texas" male-sterile cytoplasm, widely used to reduce the cost of hybrid breeding by eliminating the need for physically "detasseling" the maternal cultivar to prevent self-fertilization, made the crop susceptible to corn-leaf blight. This experience demonstrated the potential hazards of relying on a narrow genetic pool for breeding popular crop cultivars. In an influential study, the National Academy of Science found the principal U.S. crops to be "impressively uniform and impressively vulnerable" (National Research Council 1972). Around the same time, the first high-yielding rice cultivar produced by International Rice Research Institute (IRRI)—the widely adopted IR-8—began to experience serious problems with pests and diseases.

Germplasm Conservation

In response to the genetic vulnerability identified in HYVs in the early 1970s, many medium- and long-term germplasm storage facilities were established, and some existing breeders' collections were expanded. The national and international nonprofit sector managed most of these genebanks, on the principle of free acquisition and distribution of genebank resources. But decentralized private efforts to collect stocks of "heirloom" fruit and vegetable cultivars also increased (Vellvé 1992: chap. 4 and annex 2).

Size and Scope of Germplasm Conservation

By 1984 there were 133 agricultural genebanks (Hanson, Williams, and Freund 1984), and by 1992 there were 58 facilities with long-term, subfreezing storage capacity, including 7 at international agricultural research centers (IARCs) and 21 in developing countries (see Chang 1992; Wright 1997). Table 10.1 reports data compiled by the Food and Agriculture Organization of the United Nations (FAO) on estimates of the number of landraces within the major cultivated species for each crop. (There are in total about 1 million distinct landraces.) Estimates of the proportion held in ex situ (that is, in genebanks) collections are

TABLE 10.1 Genetic resource diversity collection and utilization of commodities

Commodity	1997 Area	Landraces		Wild Species		In Situ Collections	Ex Situ Collections		
		Number	In Collections	Number	In Collections		Major Collections	Accession	CGIAR
	(mha)	(× 1,000)	(percentage)	(units)	(percentage)		(units)	(× 1,000)	(percentage)
Cereals									
Bread wheat	—	—	95	24	60	Few	24	784	16
Durum wheat	—	150	95	24	60	Few	7	20	14
Triticale	—	—	40	—	—	—	5	40	38
Rice	152	140	90	20	10	Few	20	420	26
Maize	143	65	90	—	15	Few	22	277	5
Sorghum	44	45	80	20	0	Few	19	169	21
Millet	37	30	80	—	10	None	18	90	21
Barley	65	30	—	—	—	—	16	484	5
Oats	16	—	—	—	—	—	20	222	0
Rye	11	—	—	—	—	—	8	287	0
Food legumes									
Beans	27	—	50	—	70	Few	15	268	15
Soybeans	6,667	30	60	—	—	None	23	174	0

Chickpeas	11	—	—	—	75	—	13	67	41
Lentils	3	—	—	—	95	—	5	26	30
Fava beans	3	—	—	—	25	—	10	29	33
Peas	7	—	—	—	0	—	18	72	0
Groundnuts	23	—	—	15	28	—	16	81	18
Cowpeas	7	—	—	—	30	—	12	86	19
Pigeon peas	4	—	—	—	22	—	4	25	52
Lupin	1	—	—	—	—	—	10	28	0
Root crops									
Potato	19	—	95	—	30	Few	16	31	20
Sweet potato	10	5	50	—	—	Few	7	32	21
Cassava	16	—	35	—	29	—	5	28	30
Yam	3	3	—	—	—	—	2	12	25
Other									
Sugarcane	19	20	70						

SOURCE: Evenson, Gollin, and Santaniello (1998).

NOTE: CGIAR—Consultative Group on International Agricultural Research; mha—million hectares.

also presented. Globally the number of landraces in a cultivated species is roughly proportional to planted area. For most cereals 80 to 90 percent of the original landraces are now held in collections. For food legumes and root crops the proportions collected are lower.

With the advent of wide-crossing techniques that enabled crossing of cultivated and related wild (and weedy) species in the same genus, genebank collections were expanded to include wild species and related weedy materials. The numbers of wild relatives tend to be unrelated to the planted area of the domestic relative. Individual wild varieties tend to exhibit far less genetic diversity than cultivated species, which often have many landraces in their pedigrees.

Table 10.1 also summarizes the very limited data on in situ collections for crops. For some important crops no in situ collections exist. No breeding programs in any established crop report significant current utilization of in situ collections for breeding purposes. In contrast, all important crops have ex situ collections. There are roughly 6 million accessions (samples of conserved varieties) for all crops in these collections.

Research centers that are part of the Consultative Group on International Agricultural Research (CGIAR) hold substantial proportions of the accessions for most crops. The CGIAR accessions are not fully duplicated in national agricultural research system (NARS) collections. The proportions of accessions that are landraces are quite low, reflecting the proliferation of improved cultivars and their dominance as breeding material. For major commercial crops the proportions of wild-relative accessions are very low.

In sum, although most of the accessions in any genebank are duplicated elsewhere, and although most are not landraces or wild cultivars, the scope and magnitude of the conservation effort since 1970 have been impressive.

Problems with Germplasm Conservation

The quality of the conservation effort does not necessarily match its scope. Sustained successful conservation of genetic resources requires reliable climate control, protection from pests, and the "growing out" (replanting) of materials before they lose the capacity to regenerate. Successful conservation of the full range of genetic diversity (including intracultivar diversity) in open-pollinated plants requires large samples and careful control of regeneration to maintain the genetic characteristics of the accession. It is difficult to meet all these conditions within typically scant operating budgets.

A continuing problem from the breeders' viewpoint has been inadequate documentation and evaluation of genebank accessions. Nearly half of all accessions worldwide lack passport data (description of the sample's origin and history) or information on the sample's characteristics, rendering such accessions more difficult and costly for breeders to use effectively.

Recently the assertion of property rights over plant genetic resources (PGRs) and complementary biotechnologies has introduced new challenges (see the section "Intellectual Property Rights and the Private Sector," later in this chapter). The continued viability of a system built around the principle of free acquisition and distribution of genebank resources is open to question unless satisfactory institutional responses to intellectual property claims can be developed.

The long-term viability of in situ conservation may be even more problematic in many locations. As development proceeds and the value of farmers' time and the nature of their consumption patterns evolve, it will be difficult to maintain the historical level of farmer involvement in in situ conservation (Wright 1996a.) And even where long-term, in situ conservation can be successful, ex situ conservation is necessary to support the needs of breeders.

The typical place of seed collections in the production of new crop varieties by conventional breeding is shown in Figure 10.1. The production chain begins with varieties in situ, in farmers' fields (for landraces), in and around their fields (for weedy varieties), or in natural settings (for wild varieties). Many advocates of preserving biodiversity favor in situ or on-farm collections on the grounds that they are "dynamic" and "natural." But most major food crops are grasses dependent on farming activities for their continued propagation, often at locations far removed from the crop's "center of origin." Some breeders are designing on-farm or in situ collections to foster dynamic change in diversity.

When collected, varieties in situ are placed in genebanks, after quarantine and cleaning if necessary. Their origin and history are recorded on "passport data" in a databank. Typically, they are deposited in both a base collection (that is, the long-term conservation facility) and a working collection, which holds germplasm for use by breeders and others as needed.

Even the working collection in a genebank is not extensively used by breeders. Prebreeding is increasingly becoming an essential activity for converting new genetic sources into ones that breeders find useful. The output of prebreeding is "enhanced germplasm," which is held in "breeders' collections," public or private deposits typically at a different location than the genebank and conveniently accessible to breeders. Enhanced germplasm or "elite cultivars" are in turn used to produce cultivars that are evaluated as candidates for release to farmers. Cultivars selected as new releases are first planted on public or private farms for multiplication to build up the available quantities to the levels needed for distribution to farmers.

After release to farmers, a cultivar is typically adopted in a diffusion pattern that starts slowly, speeds up, and then slows as maximum adoption is approached. Within five years or a decade, use of a popular cultivar often declines as a new, more attractive successor is developed and diffused in turn.

Developments in Biotechnology Relevant to Conservation

In recent years biotechnology has enabled breeders to use genebanks more efficiently and enlarged the scope of genebank materials available for breeding

FIGURE 10.1 The chain of seed collections in conventional crop breeding

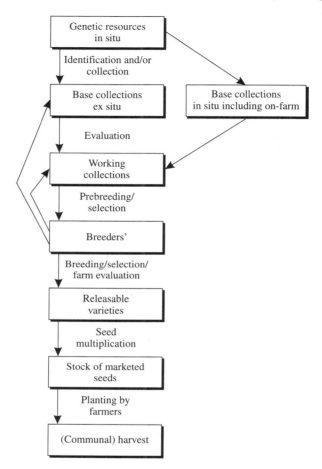

purposes. New advances have also furnished novel means of genetic progress that are independent of, and often substitutes for, genebanks. These developments are discussed in this section.

Wide-Crossing Techniques

The advent of wide-crossing techniques (such as embryo rescue methods) has enabled the crossing of cultivated and related wild (and weedy) species in the same genus. The development of resistance to "grassy stunt" disease in modern rice cultivars using a gene from a related species is one example of this technique.

Markers for Identification of Genetic Material

With varying degrees of precision, it is now possible to distinguish many differences between cultivars using genetic markers. This technology helps facilitate the introduction of new traits into enhanced germplasm. It has also been used to identify and remove excessive numbers of duplicate accessions from genebanks. Molecular-marker technology can also be used to help police intellectual property rights over a proprietary cultivar against illegal appropriation for breeding by a competitor. Finally, since identification of single genes is now possible, patents are obtainable and enforceable for genes—not just for the life form containing that gene.

Gene Transfer Technology

Over the past two decades genetic-engineering techniques have enabled transgenic plants—plants containing an alien gene from another species that may not be closely related—to be developed. Although transgenic plant collections are not yet extensive, these biotechnology developments have important implications for the collection and evaluation of genetic resources to support plant improvements.

For example, the current ability to transfer genes between cultivars and species, or even between plants, animals, and microorganisms, has complex implications for agricultural genetic resources. First, it is bound to make breeding for a given goal cheaper. It can reduce the time taken to introduce useful genes from otherwise inferior cultivars by eliminating years of back-crossing. It can also expand the set of genetic resources available for crop improvement far beyond the species at hand. For example, genes from *Bacillus thuringiensis* (Bt) have been used widely to produce pest-resistant commercial cultivars of many types of crops, including corn, cotton, canola, and potatoes, and fish genes have been introduced into potatoes in an attempt to induce tolerance to cold.

Genetic Modification

Several approaches have been used to modify the genetic characteristics of the plants themselves. These include (following Orton 1988)

1. somatic cell variation, including "somaclonal variation" associated with in vitro ("test-tube") propagation;
2. transposable elements, which have the potential to move genes and sets of genes as well as alter their expression and are being investigated as a means of generating cultivars with novel characteristics;
3. irradiation, which has induced mutations that generate new germplasm such as new barley cultivars; and
4. chemical-induced mutations, including the use of some prominent carcinogens.

Implications for Germplasm Conservation

The implications of biotechnology for genebanks are ambiguous. As discussed in greater detail in Wright (1996a), biotechnology makes screening and use of crop germplasm faster and cheaper. On the other hand, gene-transfer technology is expanding the sources of crop improvement far beyond crop germplasm to include the universe of plants, animals, and other life forms. Artificially induced mutations are another source of improvement.

Biotechnology's effects can also be felt through the continuing improvement in technology for conservation of germplasm. Cryogenic techniques can greatly increase the intervals between regeneration and so reduce the problem of genetic drift. If genetic conservation becomes sufficiently cheap, it will be easier to continue to support it with realistic user fees.

Use of PGRs for Breeding: Evidence

The extent to which genetic resources are used in crop breeding varies by crop. Several major crops for which landraces have been used extensively in breeding are considered below.

Rice

Gollin and Evenson (1996) studied rice varietal releases of *Indica* type and *Japonica* type over the 1962–91 period. A total of 1,709 varietal releases were classified by releasing country and release date. The genealogies of each release were analyzed, and this enabled further characterization of breeding strategies and of the landrace complexities (see Hargrove et al. 1990). IRRI made a number of the crosses from which these varieties were selected, but it officially released only a few varieties. India, with 26 different rice-breeding programs, led all countries with 643 releases over the period. Releases were made from more than 100 breeding programs around the world. Annual releases were approximately 20 per year in the early Green Revolution period, nearly 80 per year during 1976–80, and around 75 per year since.

Table 10.2 summarizes the source of these releases. Panel I of Table 10.2 shows the location of the breeding program where rice crosses were made. IRRI was an important producer of these crosses. In the early Green Revolution period, 1966–70, IRRI made 25 percent of all crosses leading to varieties. This percentage has declined somewhat (to 12 percent in the most recent period), but IRRI's plant-breeding program remains a potent contributor to varietal development.

Panel II of Table 10.2 summarizes parental data. IRRI produced crosses from which 24 percent of varietal parents were selected. NARSs produced 18 percent of such crosses. The most frequent (successful) breeding strategy over this period has been the "one parent from IRRI, one from a NARS" strategy.

TABLE 10.2 Flows of international genetic resources for rice, pre-1965 to 1991

	Pre-1965	1966–70	1971–75	1976–80	1981–85	1986–91	Total
				(percentage)			
I. Release varieties based on:							
IRRI cross	3	25	19	22	18	12	17
(through INGER)	(0)	(0)	(2)	(13)	(14)	(11)	(8)
Other NARS cross	16	7	6	6	6	5	6
(through INGER)	(0)	(0)	(0)	(2)	(4)	(3)	(3)
Own NARS cross	81	68	75	72	76	83	77
II. Parents of released varieties (one or more parents):							
IRRI cross	0	24	29	33	23	19	24
(through INGER)	(0)	(0)	(0)	(9)	(20)	(15)	(10)
Other NARS cross	27	25	21	15	18	20	18
(through INGER)	(7)	(2)	(5)	(9)	(15)	(15)	(10)
Own NARS cross	73	51	50	52	59	6	58
III. Frequency of parental/cross with no foreign genetic resource:							
All NARS parents	24	11	8	6	7	10	8
IV. Landrace content of released varieties, parent greater than:							
4	10	31	47	67	62	56	55
9	0	3	13	39	34	32	27
15	8	0	3	21	18	18	14
Percentage from IRRI	3	3	59	79	74	71	68
Average number of landraces	2.55	4.01	5.29	8.15	7.49	7.23	—
V. Landrace introduction							
Number from IRRI	0	16	14	21	11	13	80
Number from NARS	21	87	126	146	171	180	758

SOURCE: Evenson, Gollin, and Santaniello (1998).

NOTE: IRRI—International Rice Research Institute; INGER—International Network for the Genetic Evaluation of Rice; NARS—National agricultural research system.

The international exchange dimension of rice breeding is evident from the relatively low percentage of varietal releases for which all parental material comes from national sources. (Most of these releases were made in India.)

Panel IV of Table 10.2 shows the increase in landrace content of released varieties. The average number of landraces has risen from under 3 to around 8, with some recently released varieties having more than 25 landraces in their genealogies. More than 70 percent of these landraces were brought into the genealogies through the pedigree of an IRRI ancestor.

Panel V shows that an impressive number of new landraces (and one or two wild species) have been introduced into the pool of successful international varieties. The fact that the 1,709 releases included 838 landraces that were not in the pre-1965 varietal landrace pool shows that genetic-resource collections have been valuable. But which genetic-resource sources have been valuable? The data in panel V show that IRRI crosses have actually introduced few landraces into the pool. Only 80 of 838 new landraces were introduced via IRRI crosses. By contrast all the landraces in released varieties—roughly 70 percent—came through an IRRI cross. Two factors account for the latter situation. First, IRRI's powerful breeding lines incorporate many landraces first incorporated (outside of their source in situ) in a NARS cross. Second, the widespread use of IRRI crosses as breeding lines means the landrace content in them is widely disseminated.

Gollin and Evenson (1996) have noted that a small set of landraces has been built into the IRRI breeding lines based on the original semidwarf plant design that has served as the basis for much of the varietal development described here. Although IRRI has had excellent access to genetic resources, it did not invest heavily in efforts to exploit more landrace materials and was not highly successful in such exploitation. This was in part because the "narrowness" of the original Green Revolution plant design limited the combinability and usefulness of new landrace materials. NARSs, even though they had poorer access to genetic-resource collections, had somewhat broader plant design bases and were somewhat more diligent in searching for landrace-based traits. Thus, though landraces have been incorporated extensively in modern rice cultivars, the large IRRI genebank has not been a major source of landraces as breeding material. This is true more generally. Indeed, breeders have used genetic resources in other crops far less extensively than they have in the case of rice.

Maize (Corn)

Maize is of particular interest in this discussion for two reasons. First, because of the success of hybrids and the size of the market, maize is the most attractive major crop to private breeders. In 1986, 92 percent of U.S. maize hybrids had at least one proprietary parent (Darrah and Zuber 1986). Second, maize breeders in the United States continue to produce impressive yield increases decade after decade. For example, hybrid maize yields in central Iowa (United States) increased at about 74 kilograms per hectare per year for the past 70 years (Duvick 1996). Yet "production of this major crop is based on a combined breeding effort that probably uses less than three percent of the available germplasm" (Salhuana, Pollak, and Tiffany n.d.). The major hybrids all trace back to six pure-line ancestors in the United States. Smith (1988) and Cox et al. (1988) conclude that less than 1 percent of U.S. hybrid maize had non–North American exotic germplasm.

In developing countries, HYVs of maize constitute only around half of the total plantings. Centro Internacional de Mejoramiento de Maíz y Trigo (CIM-MYT), the international agricultural research center responsible for maize (as well as wheat), apparently has not incorporated a wide base of germplasm for disease resistance into their (open-pollinated) maize releases.

The lack of adaptive breeding capacity in developing economies has created vulnerability problems, as suggested by the National Research Council (1993:75):

> Maize hybrids developed in both private and public sectors have spread to developing countries where they were previously absent and, for the present, have brought novel germplasm to these countries. Dominance by just a few hybrids may now be of concern in some of these countries. Those countries with a high proportion of area sown to HYVs face a dilemma. They probably cannot return to cultivating the indigenous maize varieties without reducing yields, yet they cannot continue to plant the same high-yielding varieties indefinitely because new pest races likely will appear, causing disastrous epidemics. The vulnerability is particularly acute in tropical and subtropical areas that lack a cold season.

By the early 1980s, "perhaps only five percent of the over 260 races of maize accessions in germplasm banks had been tapped thus far for use in genetic improvement programs" (Salhuana, Jones, and Sevilla 1991:40–42). In response to this situation, the Latin American Maize Project (LAMP) was initiated as a public-private multinational collaboration to "evaluate for future use the agronomic characteristics of maize accessions in Latin American and U.S. germplasm banks" (Salhuana, Jones and Sevilla, 1991:40). This project is discussed later in this chapter.

Wheat

In modern wheat breeding, the search for pest and disease resistance is highly important. A recent survey of wheat breeders (Rejesus, Smale, and van Ginkel 1996) indicates wide use of advanced lines and CIMMYT cultivars in breeders' "crossing blocks," the nurseries that furnish the parental stocks for breeding. But landraces constitute only around 8 percent of the breeding material, and generally the landraces are not replaced as frequently as other materials. The use of genebanks in breeding new cultivars is disproportionately low.

Soybeans

Sprecht and Williams (1984:65) found that of 136 successful soybean cultivars released by U.S. breeders during 1939–81, 121 had cytoplasm from just five introductions. Only six ancestral strains accounted for nearly 60 percent of the germplasm in these 136 releases and for a similar percentage in cultivars released during 1971–81.

> More recently, Gizlice, Carter, and Burton (1994) concluded that "nearly 75 percent of the genes in modern soybean cultivars are present in 16 cultivars and a breeding line released before 1960. Breeders have remained dependent on this early genetic core of breeding material and have rarely introduced new germplasm."

Edible Beans

The National Research Council (1972) reported that "a dangerously small germplasm base" supports much of the edible dry-bean production in the United States. Adams (1977) concluded that pinto beans faced the highest risk owing to their extreme homogeneity. In 1982 this warning was vindicated by a rust epidemic in pinto beans that caused yield losses of 25 to 50 percent in Colorado and Wyoming and cost US$15–20 million (National Research Council 1993). Silbernagel and Hannan (1992:2) comment that "the need for genetic diversity and enactment of PVPA (Plant Variety Protection Act) have not stimulated the utilization of the *Phaseolus* collection of more than 11,000 accessions."

Valuation of Genetic Resources

A key distinction should be made between use value (essentially, value derived from use) and nonuse or existence value for PGRs. Many organizations, both governmental and nongovernmental, have expressed increased concern regarding existence values—in particular, the need to prevent species extinction and loss of habitats associated with species. This focus on increased biodiversity value has emerged independently of the breeding valuation expressed by agriculturalists, and its proponents often do not clearly distinguish between the crosses that dominate accessions in genebanks and the landraces and wild and weedy varieties collected in situ.

One might expect that use value and existence value would naturally complement each other, providing a basis for mutual support for policy actions that conserve biodiversity. This is not always the case. Agricultural interests are often seen as the enemies of biodiversity conservation by the biodiversity community, which takes the conversion of uncultivated land to cropland to be a threat to species. Increased intensity of agricultural production (via increased fertilizer and chemical use) is also seen as a threat to biodiversity.

Use value ultimately derives from consumer valuation of final products. Risk-averse farmers also find use value in crop varieties with "stability" under changing weather conditions. But stability and diversity may have public-good value as well because of reduced danger of pest outbreaks and other hazards. Plant and animal breeders can incorporate these features into breeding programs, but some regulation (or subsidy) may be required to optimize the desired effects in farmers' fields.

The next sections list methods of assessing use value, review empirical studies using these methods, and summarize policy implications.

Contingent Valuation or Willingness-to-Pay Assessments

These assessments entail asking respondents "willingness-to-pay" questions. This method is suitable for existence valuation by consumers. In fact, it may be the only feasible method, but it is not suited to use value of PGRs. The complexity of plant and animal breeding effectively limits the application of subjective (willingness-to-pay) methods for agricultural biodiversity because only specialists are competent to understand the breeding processes, and they are not the major beneficiaries. No subjective studies of this type are available.

Travel Cost Methods

Travel cost methods can be used to infer values from the willingness of people to travel and incur expenditures in order to enjoy biodiversity goods. These methods have been used to value recreational sites, but they appear quite inappropriate for PGRs in general, and no known studies of this type value genetic resources per se.

Asset Value Studies

In some cases, assets, including the PGR stocks of breeders, are sold. In other cases the actual value of PGR stocks may be observed. A number of such sales have taken place, but no systematic effort to value PGRs on this basis has been made.

Field Diversity Studies of Crop Variability and Vulnerability

Field diversity methods relate measures of yield variability to genetic content. The crop-yield variability literature has examined at least some dimensions of the diversity-vulnerability association. In particular, there is little evidence that "modern" crop varieties are more vulnerable to yield disturbances than traditional varieties (or incur higher crop insurance premiums). If there is a pattern, it is that modern varieties have less yield variability than older, early modern varieties or farmers' varieties. This is hardly surprising given the emphasis that plant breeders have placed on host-plant resistance (HPR) to insect pests and diseases and on host-plant tolerance (HPT) of abiotic stresses through qualitative trait breeding. Even when a few modern varieties dominate production (as in rice and wheat), those varieties actually contain a greater variety of valuable landrace genetic resources than the cultivars they replaced.

Hedonic Trait Value Studies

These studies attempt to identify "PGR content" values from hedonic regression techniques and have been applied to breeding values. Three studies for rice in India have used varietal data where qualitative trait content could be valued in a hedonic specification (a specification that can directly estimate qualitative trait values). In the first study, reported in Gollin and Evenson (1998a), data on actual varieties planted in farmers' fields were used to construct measures of the proportions of area planted to varieties with particular sets of traits. District rice yields (with some control for prices and input use) were regressed on these proportions for the years for which data were available. The study found that when varieties with abiotic stress tolerance and certain agronomic characteristics were made available to farmers, yields rose. Gollin and Evenson (1998a) also found that the number of landraces from both national and international origins had a strong, positive impact or yield.

A study for India (Evenson and Rao 1998) was based on farmers' yield data by variety. The Indian Council of Agricultural Research (ICAR) compiled the data for one study by selected districts and years. ICAR reported yields for the three highest-yielding varieties in trials on sample farms in each district-year combination for irrigated and unirrigated rice. Each variety was assigned trait characteristics (rated by breeders), and yields were related to these characteristics. Fertilizer use was measured as well. The data set covered the years 1977 to 1989 and some 45 districts. A second Indian varietal data set contained data reported by five State Departments of Agriculture. For each state-year combination, all important varieties planted were included in the data set. Yield and area planted data came from farmers' yield crop-cutting estimates. The estimation equation used the standard productivity relationship including research, extension, and infrastructure.

The estimates from the two databases reinforced each other. Varieties with insect resistance showed better performance in the field in both data sets (although neither data set showed that resistance to brown plant hopper has value). The estimated yield consequences of disease resistance, on the other hand, were much weaker. Both data sets showed yield effects for sheath blight resistance. The state data set showed a blast resistance effect and a positive, nonsignificant rice Tungro virus effect. Economic calculations indicated that conventional breeding for disease resistance produced a 7–10 percent yield gain in India. Conventional breeding for insect resistance produced a 10–14 percent yield gain. Future conventional breeding efforts are likely to increase yields further—perhaps doubling them in another 20 years.

An Indonesian study (Evenson 1998a) used crop-loss and pesticide-use data in a trait-value study. It also used total-factor productivity (TFP) at the crop level. Crop losses by type (insect and disease) were measured by province and year by the Ministry of Agriculture. Data on varieties planted and trait ratings by variety were also available by province and year. Thus it was possible to compute the percentage of area planted to crops with specific traits in each region and period.

The study concluded that conventional plant breeding had reduced crop losses from insects by 3–5 percent (of crop value) in the 1980s. The potential exists for another reduction of 3–5 percent if biotechnology methods enable a more complete incorporation of insect resistance traits. The evidence was less clear for disease resistance traits. Only rice Tungro resistance showed loss reduction. The pesticide-use estimates indicated that the total set of HPR traits reduced pesticide use by 20 percent.

Another Indian study (Evenson 1998b) examined the effects of prebreeding and breeding particular traits into wheat and rice varieties. The availability of HPR and HPT traits and the number of landraces in Indian rice varieties essentially extended HYV acreage from roughly 40 percent of Indian rice production to more than 70 percent. The economic value of these traits was estimated to be 10 percent of the value of rice in India. (Note that breeding, prebreeding, and collection activities as well as the collections themselves are jointly responsible for this value.)

A Breeding Production Function Study

In production function studies, breeding output is estimated as a function of breeding inputs. The chain of genetic resources (Figure 10.1) used in production of new cultivars is taken into account. One such study (Gollin and Evenson 1998b) reports a breeding production-function study for rice for 1965–90. The dependent variable in the study was the NARS rice varieties that met official release standards in the locations for which they were produced. Varietal releases were categorized by the route, or pathway, from origin to release. The explanatory variables included measures of the activities of the International Rice Germplasm Collection (IRGC) and the International Network for the Genetic Evaluation of Rice (INGER), national demand, and national plant breeding activities.

Estimates implied that the INGER nurseries stimulated more international search for genetic resources. INGER's stimulus is partly due to the fact that the network's nurseries actually include parent and grandparent cultivars that were not initially introduced through the network.

Each landrace added from IRRI sources causes approximately 0.68 added varieties to be released in each future year. (This coefficient is based on an assumption of replication in 15 countries.) IRGC also has an impact on released varieties because it induces INGER to add nurseries. The addition of one accession to IRGC produces 0.0052 more varieties. Thus, adding 1,000 accessions to IRGC causes 5.2 additional varieties to be released in each future year.

Gollin and Evenson computed the present value of adding 1,000 cataloged accessions to IRGC. Using the estimated coefficient for the impact on INGER nurseries, they computed the value of adding the accessions to be roughly US$100 million discounted at 10 percent ($350 million discounted at 5 percent), assuming a 10-year lag between accessions and economic impact. The present value of a landrace added to varieties by IRRI is US$86 million discounted at 10 percent (US$272 million if discounted at 5 percent). For a landrace added by a NARSs, the value drops to US$33 million (US$104 million if discounted at 5 percent).

Public-Private Cooperation in Evaluation of PGRs: An Example

The empirical studies reviewed earlier are for rice, a crop for which genetic resource collections are most heavily used. These studies suggest that genebanks for rice should be expanded to include as many landraces, wild species, and weedy relatives as possible. Further investment in evaluation is justified, as discussed later.

However, for other crops we do not observe extensive use of the landraces and wild and weedy varieties held in genebank collections. This may be due to market failures or may reflect the low social use value. So how should genebank collections be evaluated? This is a crucial question for policymakers.

LAMP (see Salhuana, Jones, and Sevilla 1991) illustrates the nature of the task involved in evaluating a more substantial portion of conserved genetic resources. The project, supported by Pioneer Hi-Bred International, with administrative support from the U.S. Department of Agriculture, involved the collaboration of 30 to 40 scientists in more than 70 locations. Fourteen thousand accessions were evaluated for yield potential in different environments. If Pioneer, the largest corn breeder, prefers to support a project that treats results as public knowledge rather than finance an entirely private venture, then it is unlikely that private efforts of this magnitude will be feasible for other crops with smaller market size or without protection against appropriation via replanting. LAMP could be emulated by joint public-private efforts to use the germplasm of other major crops more efficiently.

Intellectual Property Rights and the Private Sector

Plant genetic resources obviously have social value. But they have private value only if their benefits can be appropriated by the private sector. For nonhybrids (and hybrid parents), legal protection is necessary. Means of protecting agricultural genetic resources differ widely across countries. In many cases, products related to health have been exempt from protection; foodstuffs can also come under this classification. Resistance to granting protection (patents) for life forms, especially for animals, also exists.

Types of Legal Protection of Genetic Resources

SEED AND BREED CERTIFICATION.   Certification guarantees the nature and genetic background of the seed or breed. In general, it does not prevent the sale of similar uncertified products by competitors. Thus it is more like a trademark than a patent, and it requires protection against counterfeit products. If, however, the government prohibits the sale of uncertified materials for breeding purposes, the market power of oligopolistic, certified seed suppliers could be enhanced and genetic diversity reduced. Vellvé (1992) claims that European Union legislation designed to construct a common catalog of varieties approved for sale in the European Union has had this narrowing effect.

TRADE SECRETS.   Trade-secret protection can protect the proprietary information useful to a firm from disclosure to competitors. Such protection is available in various forms in different countries. A general requirement is that firms make an effort to protect secrets.

Obviously information embodied in seeds or other genetic material that is sold cannot be protected by secrecy. But materials used in the production process of the secret holder can be protected. Thus in 1987 the "genetic message" of an inbred line of corn used to breed commercial hybrids for sale was found to be protected by Iowa state trade-secret law, in *Pioneer Hi-Bred International v. Holden Foundation Seed* (Seay 1993). If the parent genetic material could be reverse-engineered from the hybrid seed and duplicated in a new plant, such protection presumably would be ineffective for hybrid breeding.

PLANT PATENTS.   In the United States, asexually reproduced plants excluding tubers may be patented by the inventor or discoverer under the Plant Patent Act of 1930, subsequently amended. Plants found in an uncultivated state are excluded. The plant patent in general complies with provisions of the 1978 Act of the International Union for the Protection of New Varieties of Plants (the UPOV Convention). (For more on plant patents, see Fowler 1994 and Seay 1993. For a discussion of UPOV, see Greengrass 1993.)

PLANT VARIETY PROTECTION CERTIFICATES.   These means protect varieties that are genetically uniform and distinct from other known varieties and breed true. The U.S. Plant Variety Protection Act, which is generally consistent with the UPOV Convention, provides narrow protection: protected plants may be freely used for breeding. And in a much quoted example, a different flower color in a soybean plant satisfied the distinctiveness criterion. The revised act mentions the protection of "essentially derived varieties," but the category is not defined. Finally, farmers are allowed to replant their cropped land with the seeds they produce, and despite recent revision of the 1970 act, the leakage to other farmers is claimed to be difficult to police. On the other hand, Monsanto has successfully policed replanting of transgenic soybean and cotton by U.S. farmers using licenses related to planted acreage rather than seed use per se.

UTILITY PATENTS.   In the landmark *Diamond v. Chakravarty* decision of 1980, the U.S. Supreme Court ruled that the patent system covered living things, microorganisms in particular. In *Ex parte Hibberd,* the Board of Appeals and Interference confirmed in 1982 that seeds, plants, and tissue culture could be patented. Genes could also be patented. The deposit of stable materials such as seeds at an International Depository Authority meets the requirements for an enabling patent description. (Such a deposit substitutes for a written description enabling a person skilled in the art to reproduce the invention.)

The TRIPS Agreement and Its Implementation

At the insistence of the United States, the agreement entitled Trade-Related Aspects of Intellectual Property Rights, Including Trade in Counterfeit Goods (TRIPS) was adopted in the recent General Agreement on Tariffs and Trade (GATT). Article 27, 3(b), includes the provision that "members shall provide for the protection of plant varieties either by patents or by an effective *sui generis* system or by any combination thereof," and Article 27, 1, includes a novelty requirement. Exactly how binding this requirement for plant variety protection shall be may well depend on the interpretation of Article 27, 2, which provides for exclusions necessary to protect "human, animal, or plant life or health, or to avoid serious prejudice to the environment" (Contracting Parties to the GATT Uruguay Round, including GATT 1994).

Materials to be patented must be placed in a recognized depository and made available to the public. (Under U.S. law, this is required only after the patent is granted.) For example, the American Type Culture Collection has been reported to have 107 patented plant-variety seeds available, including alfalfa, beans, cabbage, coffee, corn, cress, lettuce, pepper, rape, safflower, soybean, spruce, tobacco, tomato, and wheat (Jong and Birmingham 1996). Clearly breeders are no longer relying only on trade secrecy to protect these varieties. Depositories are also available for patenting bacteria and fungi. Many other nations appear to be implementing patent protection for plants, either in response to the TRIPS agreement or in anticipation of revenues from the sale of biodiversity products to pharmaceutical companies and others including plant breeders.

The Trend to Expand Proprietary Rights

At present, an alignment of disparate forces is encouraging nations north and south to establish and expand proprietary rights over agricultural genetic resources. The Biodiversity Convention (United Nations Conference on Environment and Development 1992) called for the recognition of farmers' rights with respect to the farmers' varieties used widely in plant breeding programs. In a parallel development, intellectual property rights over genetic resources have become increasingly important as incentives for plant breeders and as the focus of fierce and complex legal disputes in the developed economies.

There is no doubt that genetic resources of all types increasingly will be subjected to proprietary controls ranging from some kind of enforcement of farmers' rights in response to political pressure in the south to increased adoption of regular patent policy for genetic resources. This trend is fueled by nationalism and perception of natural biodiversity as a significant source of great wealth in the south and by the recognition in the north of a comparative advantage in production of intellectual property via biotechnology.

Understandably, nations that have provided plant germplasm at no charge to seed breeders worldwide are not happy with a system in which the improved variety is sold by the breeders under a patent or other effective means of protection. Ironically, the United States, in its efforts to globalize recognition of intellectual property rights, has actually encouraged developing countries, under the rubric of farmers' rights, to enforce property rights over germplasm formerly freely available to breeders in the United States and elsewhere (see Wright 1996b).

Implications of Proprietary Rights for Plant Breeding

How will the trend to establish and expand proprietary rights over agricultural genetic resources affect the structure of plant breeding? First, it is clear that private breeders currently do not have a strong enough demand for genebank services to cover the cost of genebank operations. Furthermore, much of the service a genebank provides is in the nature of an international public good, in that it supports the conservation of cultivars that have existence value (and perhaps information value) to societies beyond their private value to present breeder clientele. Therefore the operation of genebanks must remain public, or at least heavily subsidized, if they are to survive at their present scope as proprietary rights expand.

Second, increased legal protection of genebank resources may jeopardize the free acquisition and distribution of these resources. The implications of patenting germplasm are complex. For major crops, patenting a cultivar is unlikely in and of itself to be a good substitute for hybridization that protects against unauthorized use and creates new private markets. In a decentralized, competitive farming sector, policing of replanting by farmers is difficult. Private wheat-seed markets appear to thrive only in parts of the United States where farmers have no on-farm storage. In England a flat-rate royalty on proprietary cultivars is collected via seed-cleaning services. More generally, if a farmer's own seed production (or that of a friend or neighbor) constitutes competition for the proprietary seed originally planted and that competition is difficult enough to monitor, the Coase conjecture applies: monopoly rents cannot continue to be collected even under a patent. For crops with lower (but still substantial) sales volume, such as edible beans, it is possible that rents appropriable for patented seed might not support a serious private breeding industry that does much more than repackage public cultivars.

Less direct effects of patents might be more important in the near future. If parent lines become subject to reverse engineering of hybrids (re-creation of parent lines from the genetic information in the hybrid seeds), patents of the parent lines should continue to afford the protection provided by hybridization alone. (A concentrated breeding industry should be much easier to monitor than multitudes of commercial farms.)

The patenting of genes, as distinct from plant cultivars, is already making it possible for large corporations to produce herbicide-tolerant and transgenic, pest-resistant plants. Violations of proprietary rights to a gene may well be simpler to detect than violation of cultivar patents, because the latter violation encompasses hard-to-detect acts such as reuse of a seed. For herbicide-tolerant genes, the question arises whether patent protection should be extended to the gene as well as the herbicide. Can greater profits be leveraged from a monopoly in both? Or is the patented gene a means of extending the exploitation of herbicide innovation beyond the expiration of the herbicide patent? The legality of contractual stipulations that require users of the herbicide-tolerant gene to use the proprietary (former patent) version of a herbicide is apparently questionable.

Producers of both semiconductors and biotechnology products have recently discovered that patent protection cuts two ways. Ceteris paribus, it boosts production incentives by eliminating competition. But in crop breeding, patents will also protect the rights of producers of the inputs into breeding. Payment of upstream royalties for germplasm and the costs of checking for prior patents and of registering patents in relevant countries will all increase the cost of production.

Currently, U.S. patenting of biotechnology is somewhat unpredictable and inconsistent. At times the novelty and workability requirements seem to be violated, and the initial scope of claims is sometimes ridiculously large, as in the broad patent claims of Agricetus to genetically engineered cotton and genetically transformed soybeans (see Rural Advancement Foundation International 1994). Mistakes are often eliminated on appeal, but the process is uncertain and costly. Many patent attorneys believe that in the United States, patenting in biotechnology and other high-technology industries is currently excessive and wasteful.

If, as seems likely, agreement on farmers' rights policy will continue the "grandfathering" of current ex situ deposits, the agreement will have scant effect on plant breeding in the medium term, given the low current intensity of landrace use. For new deposits, though such an agreement might well hinder exchange of germplasm and information, it might have some positive effects as well. Breeders might be more willing to invest in screening germplasm of farmers' landraces for selection in commercial releases if they can, by acquisition of an exclusive license, preclude free riding on their screening results by competitors.

Patenting has the potential to increase the rate of biotechnical change by encouraging the development of efficient means of identification and transfer of relevant genes, speeding up the breeding process, and expanding the scope for genetic improvements far beyond the genetic potential of a given species. It will also affect aspects of genetic research and development policy.

How will the increasing importance of proprietary rights affect the public-private balance? In competitive agricultural sectors, all but perhaps the most applied breeding operations will continue, in the near future, to be predominantly public for crops that are not hybrids and do not have patented genes. Patenting might have a greater effect on the operation of public breeders than on the privatization of crop-breeding research. In general, crop-breeding research will require continued public support or financing by levies or producer groups. Patenting by public-sector enterprises can change incentives for cooperation and reduce information exchanges within and between organizations. On the other hand, it can bring market incentives to bear on researchers and can be an indicator of general performance.

If advances in biotechnology can provide new and more efficient means of preventing free riding via replanting, then much more of the applied breeding function will be privatized. Such an advance could also make open-pollinated varieties more interesting for private breeders and eliminate some of the deadweight loss of more costly hybrid breeding undertaken to enforce property rights.

Transgenic products that incorporate patented genes are currently being produced and marketed privately with patent protection, often by large corporations with the collaboration of privately funded public research institutions. Exactly how the organization of transgenic production will evolve is unclear. It may be more efficient to have transgenic plant production that is specialized and separate from applied breeding, if adequate contractual forms can feasibly facilitate the necessary flows of information and genes between plant breeders and biotechnologists. Efficient patent protection could help bring about such specialization. But recently, contracting problems and other forces appear to be moving the private seed-breeding industry rapidly toward a vertically integrated oligopoly for major commercial crops such as corn and cotton.

The traditions of public-sector investment in plant breeding and free exchange of genetic resources between research centers should, and probably will, change as incentives for private-sector plant breeding and even for genetic resource collection change. Private firms have increased plant-breeding activity both because of changes in intellectual property rights and because of the development of biotechnology (genetic engineering) tools. But despite this trend the public-sector role in plant breeding has not disappeared or even decreased in many countries.

The changes in private-sector incentives have not been uniform across countries. For many developing countries, little or no expansion in private-sector research has taken place. Nor is this likely to change in the near future.

The fundamental problem of underinvestment in genetic-resource evaluation and in prebreeding activities has not been resolved by changes in the private sector. Public-sector investment in collection, maintenance, and evaluation of genetic resources will continue to be appropriate worldwide. For countries with limited technological infrastructure, public-sector plant-breeding programs supported by the international research centers will continue to be the dominant—in many cases the only—providers of improved crop technology.

New policy interfaces and new mechanisms for providing public-sector research services in the presence of changed incentives for the private sector and increased private-sector plant breeding will have to be developed. These are institutional challenges, and they are not insurmountable. If badly handled, they can reduce the effectiveness of agricultural research programs. If they are handled creatively, the agricultural sector in most countries will be better served by a new mix of public- and private-sector research programs

11 The Evaluation of the Economic and External Health Benefits from Canola Research

RICHARD GRAY AND STAVROULA MALLA

In producing many crops there is an inherent trade-off between quantity and quality. This holds true for genetic selection. Yield will be maximized only when it is the criterion for selection, so the economics of quality selection is important for designing and evaluating research programs.

The most successful crop-development project in Canadian history involved an explicit decision to improve product quality. When erucic acid in rapeseed oil was shown to be a threat to human health and glucosinolates in rapeseed meal were shown to be a threat to animal nutrition, the newly formed Rapeseed Council of Canada embarked on an ambitious research and development program virtually to eliminate these harmful components, even at the expense of reducing the genetic potential for yield. The research and development program, which also had large agronomic, extension, and market-development components, was so successful that the genetically altered crop "canola" became the second-largest crop in Canada. Health information resulting from medical and nutritional research also played a role in the crop's success. The price of canola oil increased in the late 1980s, when medical evidence showed that substituting canola oil for other vegetable oils reduced coronary heart disease. The ability of canola oil to reduce heart disease created an unanticipated benefit for consumers and taxpayers. The research and development of the crop increased consumption, which led to less heart disease and reduced public health care costs.

This chapter describes the economic impact of improved genetic quality and health information on the rapeseed/canola industry. First, the chapter describes how the research and development program allowed an infant industry to overcome significant obstacles and eventually become a large, important industry. Next, an economic model and historical data are used to illustrate the economic trade-off involved in quality improvement. The same model is then used to estimate the economic effects of recent health information that has increased demand for canola oil. The chapter concludes with estimates of how increased canola consumption reduced the incidence of coronary heart disease

211

and related public-health costs in Canada, arguing that these significant costs should be incorporated into the economic evaluation of research.

The Development of the Canola Industry

Rapeseed was used to produce lamp oil at least a thousand years ago in China, India, and Europe (White 1974). It was not until the early nineteenth century that rapeseed was cultivated in Canada. Rapeseed oil was used initially as a marine lubricant because of its ability to adhere strongly to steam-washed metals. During World War II the rapid increase in steam-powered naval and shipping activity created a strong industrial demand for rapeseed (White 1974). In the same period, because of a serious shortage of edible fat and oil in Canada, a small portion of the black, pungent rapeseed oil was further refined for human consumption. Both forms of demand fell in the postwar period, so the production and use of rapeseed dramatically declined.

During the late 1940s and early 1950s, Agriculture Canada researchers initiated a systematic research program for rapeseed, focusing on innovations in processing and on agronomic improvement (Downey and Robbelen 1989). These scientists were looking for import replacements, since soybean production was increasing in the United States while Canada had no secure domestic supply of edible vegetable oils. In addition, by 1954, a depressed wheat economy created an incentive to find an alternative crop for prairie wheat farmers.

The commercial sale of rapeseed oil as an edible product began in the mid-1950s. Almost immediately, the nutritional aspects of rapeseed oil were questioned. In 1956, K. K. Carroll of the University of Western Ontario found that consumption of rapeseed oil by rats resulted in reduced weight gains, fatty hearts, and increased weight of adrenal glands (Sauer and Kramer 1983). On July 23, 1956, the Canadian Food and Drug Directorate of the Department of National Health and Welfare ruled that "rapeseed oil was not an approved edible oil in Canada and that, in view of literature reports of abnormalities arising from feeding rapeseed oil to experimental animals, sale of this oil for edible purposes was to cease immediately and all stocks currently on retail shelves were to be withdrawn" (Youngs 1974). The ban did not last long. The Department of Health and Welfare was persuaded to withdraw its objection after a thorough review at the Canadian Committee on Fats and Oils meeting in October 1956. The committee concluded that, because of the lack of evidence regarding the effects of human consumption of rapeseed oil and its limited use in the Canadian diet, there was no indication that rapeseed oil represented a hazard to Canadian human health (Youngs 1974).

It was also shown that when rapeseed meal was used as animal feed its high levels of glucosinolates could cause metabolic upset, lowering the efficiency of feed-to-weight-gain ratios in the case of nonruminant animals (Bell 1955; Bell and Wetter 1974; Blakely and Anderson 1948; Bowland et al. 1965;

Nordfeldt et al. 1954). Based on these findings, Bell (1955) suggested limiting rapeseed meal to 10 percent or less of the total feed ration for animals.

In response to the human health and animal nutrition concerns, the rapeseed breeding program started to focus on quality characteristics. By the early 1960s, plant breeders had isolated rapeseed plants that were low in erucic acid and others that were low in glucosinolate content (Kneen 1992). The first low–erucic-acid rapeseed variety was released for production in Canada in 1968. By this time there were also many other low–erucic-acid varieties under development (Stefansson 1990).

Until 1967, the development of rapeseed was almost fully in the public domain. Agriculture Canada played a key role in providing the resources as well as choosing the research and development agenda. Its scientists' early focus on processing and agronomics gave them a holistic view of industry needs. The research efforts were successful, as shown in Figure 11.1, resulting in more than a million acres planted each year by the late 1960s and 586,000 metric tons of rapeseed production by 1966.

In 1967 the Rapeseed Association of Canada was established in recognition of the potential of the crop and of the need for some central body to develop and improve the rapeseed industry. The association represented 12 groups, including the commercial crushing industry, exporting companies, provincial departments of agriculture, and the university research community, as well as Agriculture Canada (Kneen 1992). This broad representation of the industry and research community allowed the association to identify research objectives and to develop a coordinated approach to research and development. The activities included market promotion, product development, genetic improvement, and agronomic research and extension.

The Rapeseed Association was a nonprofit organization largely funded by the industry. Seventy percent of its budget came from a voluntary 50-cents-per-metric-ton levy on rapeseed exports and seed crushed domestically; the other 30 percent came from government sources. The industry participated well in the voluntary scheme, and the levy acted as a general tax on production, which, as Alston and Pardey (1996) point out, resulted in consumers and producers sharing the cost of research in approximate proportion to gains from increased output. The ability to raise funds and provide research resources gave the association a great deal of control over the research agenda.

The greatest challenge facing the newly formed association was the human health issue. This issue became a focus in 1970 at the International Rapeseed Conference at Ste. Adele, Quebec, where presentations showed that consumption of high–erucic-acid oils caused myocardial lesions in the heart tissue of animals (for example, Abdellatif and Vles 1970; Beare-Rogers 1970; Salmon 1970; Walker et al. 1970). At the same conference, plant breeders reported that new low–erucic-acid rapeseed varieties had been developed in many countries. After some deliberation a resolution was passed that all coun-

FIGURE 11.1 Canadian rapeseed/canola acreage and production, 1942–1993

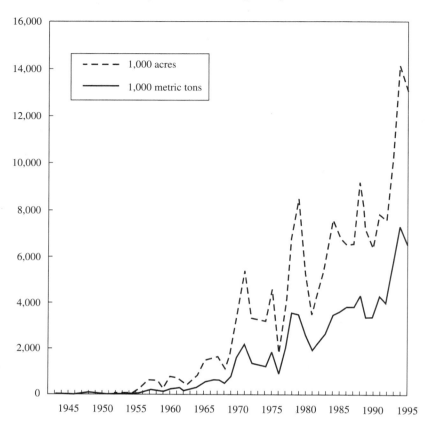

SOURCE: Statistics Canada, *Cereal and Oilseeds Review.*

tries should gradually switch to low–erucic-rapeseed varieties (Rapeseed Association of Canada 1970).

At this point the Rapeseed Association of Canada was clearly committed to converting the industry to low–erucic-acid rapeseed varieties. The goal was accomplished very rapidly. By 1974, just six years after Agriculture Canada registered "Oro," the first low–erucic-acid variety, 95 percent of rapeseed acreage in western Canada was planted to low–erucic-acid varieties. The secondary objective, reducing the glucosinolate content of the meal, was also realized. In 1977 Agriculture Canada registered "Candle," the first Polish rapeseed variety with low erucic acid and low glucosinolates (double-low). By 1984 farmers had converted to the double-low varieties (Kneen 1992). By 1985, the first double-low Argentine varieties were registered, and 70 varieties were registered by 1995.

As part of its market development strategy the Rapeseed Association saw a need to differentiate the new varieties from the older varieties in the marketplace. In 1978 the name "Canola" was initially registered by the Western Canadian Oilseed Crushers Association to designate "double-low" rapeseed varieties with 5 percent or less erucic acid in the oil and 3 milligrams per gram or less glucosinolate in the meal. In 1980, to complete the process, the Rapeseed Association of Canada changed its name to the Canola Council and assumed the canola trademark. In 1985, the Canola Council of Canada and Agriculture Canada presented data to the Food and Drug Administration of the United States Department of Health and Human Services, which granted canola oil the status of "Generally Regarded as Safe" (GRAS) (FDA: Act. 21 CFR Part 184, 1555c). This designation developed a new marketplace for canola oil. In the following year, the Trade Marks Branch of Consumer and Corporate Affairs further tightened the quality restrictions on the canola trademark.[1]

From 1967 to 1985 the Rapeseed Association (Canola Council after 1980) was clearly in charge of the industry's research and development strategy. The council emphasized quality and exceeded its goals while agronomic research and extension continued to improve farm management of the crop. The overall impact was a significant growth in production, from 511,000 metric tons in 1967 to 3.5 million metric tons in 1985 (see Figure 11.1).

By 1985, canola was established as the third most important crop in western Canada and no longer faced the erucic acid and glucosinolate issue that had threatened the very existence of the industry. Canola farming increased further, from 6.9 million acres in 1985 to a peak of 14.2 million acres in 1994. This growth was in part fueled by strong canola-oil prices, which, as examined later, can be attributed to some extent to information that canola oil could reduce the risk of coronary heart disease. During much of this period canola became the most profitable crop in the rotation for many producers, and the area of canola became constrained only by climate and rotational considerations to control disease. The high relative prices also expanded canola plantings well into the semi-arid and arid areas of the prairies.

An Economic Model to Measure Research Effects

A simple economic model can be used to illustrate the overall economic trade-off involved in a decision to improve quality. (For examples, see Lemieux and

---

1. The new canola trademark designated rapeseed varieties with erucic acid less than 2 percent and glucosinolate less than 30 micromoles per gram (Kneen 1992 and Dupont et al. 1989). This restriction continues in effect.

FIGURE 11.2 The effects of quality improvement on prices and quantities

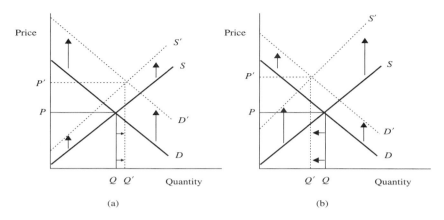

(a)

(b)

Wohlgenant 1989; Ulrich et al. 1987; Unnevehr 1986; Voon 1991; Voon and Edwards 1992.) An improvement in quality must come at some resource cost. In genetic selection, higher quality usually comes at some expense to yield, which is no longer the sole consideration of research. (A variety that was both higher yielding and higher quality would clearly dominate. Choices, then, are among varieties that are not superior in all attributes.) If yield is reduced or costs increase, the supply curve for the product shifts up, as shown in Figure 11.2a. This means less of the higher-quality product will be produced for any given price. The quality improvement will also increase the willingness to pay for a product, which is reflected in an upward shift in the demand curve; that is, consumers are willing to pay more for any given quantity of product. The upward shift in both the supply and the demand curves results in a higher market price for the higher-quality product.

The economics of the decision are interesting because the quantity can either increase or decrease with quality improvement. If willingness to pay increased by more than the increase in cost, the quantity demanded would increase, and both producers and consumers generally would benefit from the change (Figure 11.2a). The opposite can also occur: if cost increased by more than willingness to pay, the quality improvement would result in a smaller quantity being produced and consumed, which could leave both producers and consumers worse off (Figure 11.2b).[2] Since there is no economic incentive for adopting uneconomic changes, they are far less likely to occur than welfare-

---

2. If both supply and demand shifted in a parallel fashion, then there would be a one-to-one correspondence between the direction of the quantity effect and the direction of the welfare impacts.

enhancing improvements. Nevertheless, mistakes can be made in a volatile economic environment.

The effects of a consumption externality can be incorporated into this framework by introducing a social demand curve, which represents the private demand plus the external costs or savings. In the case of canola, in which consumption may reduce the public cost of health care, the social demand curve lies above the private demand curve, with the difference between the two curves representing the per-unit, external health cost savings. In this case the total social benefit is measured using the area under the social demand curve.

The effects of health information on the canola market can be modeled as an increase in the private demand or willingness to pay for any given quality and quantity of canola oil. This demand shift will increase the quantity demanded and the price that will leave canola producers better off. As discussed later, the effect on consumers is theoretically somewhat ambiguous.

Incorporating Vertical Linkages and Trade

A more complex economic model is needed to examine the effects of quality improvement on sectors within the Canadian canola industry. The decision of the Rapeseed Association to pursue quality improvement had economic effects on canola producers, canola crushers, meal users, canola-oil consumers, and taxpayers. These effects have not been restricted to Canada, since seed, meal, and oil are all traded internationally. Canada cannot be considered a small country in terms of canola production, given that Canadian canola seed, oil, and meal exports made up 74 percent, 18 percent, and 28 percent of total world exports, respectively (Oils World Annual 1993), from 1988 to 1992. To show how a change in quality affects Canadian producers, crushers, meal users, oil consumers, and taxpayers requires a disaggregated economic model that recognizes the vertical linkages among these sectors, as well as trade linkages with the rest of the world.

Because of Japan's size and policy differences the Japanese canola sector is modeled separately from the rest of the world (ROW). Japan imported about 80 percent of Canadian canola-seed exports in 1988, but this figure shrank to 59 percent in 1994. Japanese imports of canola seed and meal are free of duties and restrictions (Peters 1995), while imported canola oil is subject to an import tariff. The flat-rate fixed tariff of 17,000 yen per metric ton ($162.35 per metric ton Canadian in 1992) represented 28 percent of the price of crude canola oil (Kneen 1992). With this tariff regime, the Japanese crushers have been protected enough that Japan has produced virtually all its own canola oil from crushing imported seed, while the private import of oil has remained uneconomic. Modeling Japan separately from the ROW allowed the incorporation of the effect of Japan's policy of discouraging the importation of canola oil in favor of seed and meal.

The three-region, four-sector market is modeled mathematically using linear demand curves for oil and meal and linear-supply (or marginal-cost) curves for seed and processing inputs. The mathematical model as described in the Appendix is solved by imposing market-clearing conditions for the horizontal and vertical relationships, as well as Japanese policy decisions.

A slightly simplified form of the mathematical model is depicted graphically in Figure 11.3. In this illustration the meal sector is excluded from the model, with the remaining sectors modeled as if meal had zero value. The model is a set of linear supply and demand functions representing a static (single-period) model with competitive market-clearing conditions.[3] Panel (a) represents the canola-oil market. The demand curves are denoted as D_o^C, D_o^J, and D_o^R for Canada, Japan, and the ROW, respectively. The total demand curve for canola oil is labeled D_o^T, which is the horizontal sum of Canadian, Japanese, and ROW demand. Panel (b) presents the market for canola processing inputs. S_p^C, S_p^J, S_p^R, and S_p^T are the corresponding supply curves for processing inputs in Canada, Japan, the ROW, and the total supply. Finally, the canola seed market is depicted in panel (c): S_s^C, S_s^J, S_s^R, and S_s^T are the supply curves for Canada, Japan, the ROW, and the total, respectively.

The vertical relationship in the industry represents canola seed being crushed (processed) to produce oil. We were able to simplify modeling this vertical structure by adopting a fixed-proportions model, since an analysis of the data suggested that canola seed produced 40 percent of its weight in canola oil and 58 percent of its weight in canola meal, over a number of years, despite large swings in the relative price of oil to meal. Accordingly, the quantity axis for oil is scaled to units of 40 metric tons of oil, which is consistent with a 100-metric-ton unit for seed because canola oil makes up 40 percent of the total volume of canola-seed units for processing inputs. Units are chosen so they match as well.[4]

Since the oil is produced in fixed proportions, it is straightforward to develop the appropriate derived demand or derived supply for each market. The total supply function S_o^T for canola oil is the vertical sum of the processing inputs S_p^T and seed S_s^T supply (marginal-cost) curves. The total derived demand for processing inputs D_p^T is equal to the vertical difference between the demand for oil and the marginal cost of seed S_s^T. The total derived curve D_s^T for canola seed is the total demand for canola oil D_o^T minus the marginal cost of processing S_p^T.

---

3. In this simplified form of the model the meal sector is not included, and the Japanese restriction on oil imports is not modeled. Nevertheless, it does serve to illustrate how simultaneous vertical and horizontal relationships can be modeled in a graphical framework.

4. To include the meal sector in a graphical framework would require a fourth panel denominated in 0.58-metric-ton units. The demand for meal would be added to the oil demand to derive the demand curve for seed and processing services. In this case the derived supply of oil would include seed production and processing marginal costs minus the price of meal.

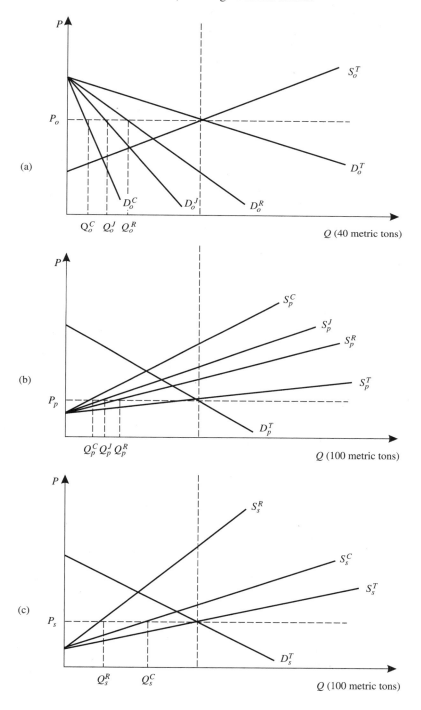

FIGURE 11.3 The three-sector, three-region canola market

Traded quantities can easily be derived from the figure. For instance, at the price P_s for canola seed, the quantity of seed supplied in Canada is Q_S^C. The supply of processing inputs in Canada (equal to the quantity of seed processed) equals Q_P^C, which is less than Q_S^C, so the remainder $Q_S^C - Q_P^C$ is exported at price P_s. Japan, on the other hand, does not produce seed (only 1 percent of the total consumption between 1988 and 1992), so the quantity for processing equals Q_P^J, the amount of seed it imports.

This economic model can be used as a tool for comparative static analysis. The shift of a single supply or demand curve in one country will have implications for all nine markets. In addition to estimating the impacts on prices and quantities, changes in consumer surplus can be measured easily, as changes in the area above the price line and below the demand curves, and changes in producer surplus as the area above the supply curve and below the price line.

The Effect of Selecting for Quality on Rapeseed Yields

The Rapeseed Association explicitly decided to pursue the goal of producing rapeseed that was low in both erucic acid and glucosinolates. Selecting varieties for quality at the expense of yield shifts the marginal-cost curve for seed upward, which tends to reduce profitability. An accompanying upward shift in demand tends to increase profitability. Given the two effects—one positive and one negative—it is important to determine their size and whether they are temporary or permanent.

We use data from Saskatchewan to estimate both the short-run and long-run reductions in yield resulting from the decision to switch to canola. To measure the effect of a quality change on yield, genetic influences must be separated from weather, input use, and other exogenous factors. For this purpose, the best measure of the relative yield of different canola varieties was plot data from research-station yield trials at a number of locations across Saskatchewan (Saskatchewan Agriculture and Food, various issues). The experiment is designed to minimize the effect on potential yield of nongenetic variables (for example, weeds and moisture). The yield of each variety is reported relative to a base variety. These relative yield indexes for each canola variety were converted to the same variety base, especially the variety Torch, whose base yield was indexed to 100 by 1976. To reflect the pattern of adoption, the yield index for each variety grown was weighted by its seeded acreage (Prairie Pools, Inc.) and summed to produce an annual yield index for the mix of varieties grown each year.

Plotting the annual, weighted-average yield index over time (Figure 11.4) reveals a steady growth in rapeseed yields until 1978, followed by a marked reduction in yields from 1978 to 1982 and continued growth after that period. This pattern is consistent with the adoption of a higher-quality, lower-yielding crop: the drop in yields almost exactly corresponds to the period when the first

FIGURE 11.4 Saskatchewan yield index rapeseed/canola, 1960–1992

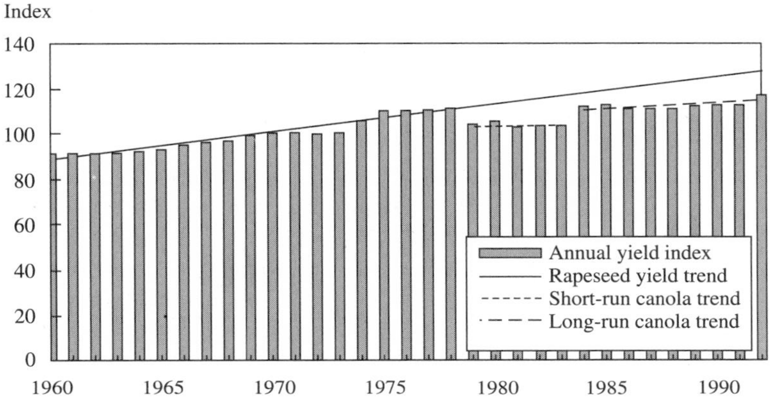

SOURCE: Authors' calculation.

canola variety was introduced, and yields increased after the process of adoption was complete.

To estimate the change in yield resulting from the preference for quality, the following regression was estimated:

$$Y_t = \alpha_1 + \beta_1 T_t + \alpha_2 D_{2t} + \beta_2 D_{2t} T_t + \alpha_3 D_{3t} + \beta_3 D_{3t} T_t + \varepsilon_t, \quad (11.1)$$

where Y_t is the annual weighted average yield index for each year; T is an annual time-trend variable, $1960 = 1$; D_{2t} is a dummy variable, which is zero before 1979 and one from 1979 to 1983; and D_{3t} is a dummy variable, which is zero before 1984 and one from 1984 to 1992. The yield regression included two slope-shifting dummy variables and two intercept-shifting dummy variables, resulting in estimation of three separate regression lines. The first regression segment, representing the pre-canola period (1960–78), has an intercept equal to α_1 and a slope equal to β_1. The second regression segment, representing the adoption period (1979 to 1983), has an intercept equal to $\alpha_1 + \alpha_2$ and a slope equal to $\beta_1 + \beta_2$. The third regression segment, representing the postadoption period (1984–92), has an intercept equal to $\alpha_1 + \alpha_3$ and a slope equal to $\beta_1 + \beta_3$. This segment represents the yield potential in the period following the introduction of canola.

The regression yielded the following equation (with the student t-values for each coefficient reported in parentheses):

$$Y_t = 86.16 + 1.27T_t + 12.31D_{2t} - 1.054D_{2t}T_t + 8.93\ D_{3t} - 0.658D_{3t}T_t + \varepsilon_t$$

$$\quad\ (89.6)^* \quad (15.3)^* \quad (1.12) \qquad (-2.04) \qquad\quad (1.19) \qquad (-2.54)^* \qquad\qquad (11.2)$$

$R^2 = 0.978, \qquad\qquad\qquad \bar{R}^2 = 0.974 \qquad\qquad\qquad$ 27 degrees of freedom

The regression was corrected for second-order autocorrelation, which still resulted in inconclusive evidence about the presence or absence of positive first-order autocorrelation (D-W = 1.4975). For a two-tailed test at the 95 percent confidence level, with 27 degrees of freedom, parameter estimates having a *t*-ratio of less than −2.05 or more than 2.05 are statistically significantly different from zero. Significant parameters are marked with an asterisk.

As a baseline we projected the regression line from the rapeseed period through the canola adoption period and the postadoption canola period, arguing that the yield growth would have continued on trend if growers had not decided to switch to canola. As can be seen in Figure 11.4, the canola trends are well below the trend established for rapeseed. The yields for the canola adoption period (1979–83) are on average 9.4 percent below the trend for rapeseed yields. Using the postadoption 1984–92 trend the predicted 1990 yields were 9.1 percent below the trend for rapeseed.

To examine whether yield changes occurred during the adoption period, we tested the joint restriction that both α_2 and β_2 are equal to zero. The computed F-value for this test was 36.7, far in excess of the 5 percent critical value of 4.28, leading to the conclusion that introducing canola varieties reduced yield in 1979–83. The second hypothesis is that after a period of adjustment canola yields still lag behind the projected yields of rapeseed varieties. To examine this hypothesis we tested the joint restriction such that α_3 and α_3 are equal to zero. This test resulted in an F-value of 33.61, far in excess of the 5 percent critical value of 4.28, providing strong statistical evidence of a substantial difference between postadoption canola yields and the trend established by rapeseed. Thus, there is statistical evidence that the adoption of canola quality resulted in a reduction in genetic yield potential, which has persisted many years after adoption.

The Shift in Demand as a Result of Positive Health Information

The strong linkage between blood cholesterol and coronary heart disease has led to much research on how consumption of different types of fats affects serum cholesterol levels. This issue first gained attention in the late 1950s when research showed evidence of a relationship between fat intake, high blood cholesterol levels, and coronary heart disease (Ahrens et al. 1957). Subsequent research showed that the consumption of saturated fatty acids increased blood cholesterol levels whereas polyunsaturated vegetable oils reduced cholesterol levels (Hegsted et al. 1965; Keys 1970; Keys et al. 1965). These findings are thought to have precipitated the trend away from animal fat consumption and an increase in the demand for vegetable oils.[5] During the late

---

5. For a related discussion of the effects of health information on demand, see Yen and Chern (1992).

1970s and early 1980s medical research discovered that some vegetable oils that were high in saturated fatty acids, particularly coconut and palm oil, were as harmful as animal products (Reiser et al. 1985).

In the mid-1980s, a continued concern about nutrition and fat intake brought about research that highlighted the nutritional differences between two more categories of vegetable oil: those high in polyunsaturated fatty acids (for example, soybean oil and corn oil) and those high in monounsaturated fatty acids (for example, canola oil and palm oil). Until then, it was believed that polyunsaturated fatty acids lowered serum cholesterol levels while monounsaturated fatty acids had no effect. In 1984, for the first time, it was shown that consumption of monounsaturated fatty acids also lowered cholesterol and that these fatty acids were in fact preferable to polyunsaturated fatty acids because the monounsaturated fatty acids lowered LDL (harmful) cholesterol levels but not HDL (beneficial) cholesterol levels (for example, Ferro-Luzzi et al. 1984). This research made canola oil preferable, from a health perspective, over oils high in polyunsaturated fatty acids.

Canola oil competes with other vegetable oils, primarily soybean oil. Figure 11.5 illustrates that before the late 1980s canola oil generally sold at a discount to soybean oil and has often been at a premium since.

To quantify how health information affected demand for canola oil, we estimated a demand curve for canola oil using the using the following equation:

$$P_{ct} = 419.8 + 0.210\ P_{st} + 32.2\ D_t - 4.08\ Q_t + \varepsilon_t \qquad (11.3)$$
$$\phantom{P_{ct} = }(5.13)^* \ (4.37)^* \qquad (1.59) \qquad (-0.381)$$

where P_{ct} is the Canadian monthly average canola oil price (CA\$ per metric ton) between April 1983 and December 1992 (Statistics Canada, Cereals and Oilseed Review, various issues), deflated by the consumer price index (Statistics Canada 1990 = 100); P_{st} is the U.S. soybean oil price (CA\$ per metric ton) (USDA, Agricultural Outlook, various issues), deflated by the consumer price index (Statistics Canada 1990 = 100); D_t is an intercept-shifting dummy variable, which is zero before the 1988 crop year and one after the 1987 crop year, reflecting the influence of health information published in 1986 and 1987; Q_t is the world quantity of canola oil consumed (million metric tons) (USDA, Production, Supply and Disposition Data Base, 1994), and ε_t is an error term that is assumed to be normally distributed. The terms in parentheses are student *t*-values with 111 degrees of freedom. An asterisk denotes a coefficient that is different from zero with 95 percent probability.

The equation was estimated using single-equation ordinary least squares (OLS) corrected for second-order autocorrelation with a standard Cochrane-Orcutt type of procedure in Shazam 6.0.[6] The adjusted R^2 for the regression

---

6. The computed Durbin-Watson coefficient, after the correction for second-order autocorrelation (D-W = 1.645), lies between the lower and the upper limit; hence, there is inclusive evidence regarding the presence or absence of positive higher-order autocorrelation.

FIGURE 11.5 Canola oil–soybean oil premium, 1983–1994

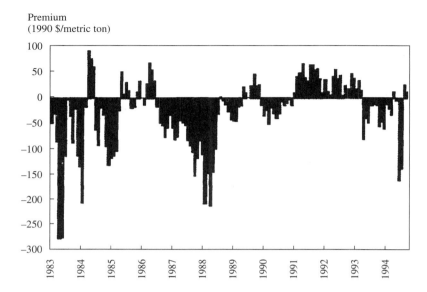

SOURCE: Authors' calculations.

was 0.96. The sign of each estimated coefficient was consistent with prior beliefs. The coefficient on the intercept-shifting dummy variable is greater than zero with a probability of 94 percent, which indicates an upward shift in the demand curve as a result of the positive health information. The regression results show the best-point estimate of the vertical shift in the demand curve to be +CA\$32.2 per metric ton.

The Market Effects of Quality Improvement

This section considers the economic effects of the quality improvement associated with the switch from rapeseed to canola varieties. We assume that, given the earlier problems with erucic acid, the creation of canola quality characteristics was a necessary condition for nutritionists to consider canola a healthy oil and therefore the shift in demand from health information was made possible by the quality improvement. Restricting the quality-induced demand shift to be equal to the observed shift in demand of CA\$32 per metric ton associated with health information provides a clear counterfactual—albeit conservative— illustration of the economics of quality improvement.[7] The 9.1 percent reduc-

---

7. A case could also be made that in the absence of the quality improvement the demand for rapeseed would have contracted because of erucic acid concerns. However, the amount demand would have contracted is difficult to estimate.

tion in genetic yield potential reported earlier is used to determine the cost of improving quality. Combining the yield reduction with the demand increase allows an overall assessment of the economic effects of the quality improvement.

A mathematical version of the graphic model discussed earlier was used to measure the market effects of the shift in the supply of canola seed and the shift in demand for canola oil. The parameters of each demand and supply curve were constructed according to the average prices and quantities that existed in the 1988–92 (1990) period and to reflect specific elasticity estimates obtained from the literature. The model is static and contains no stockpiles, so that quantities at each level sum in direct proportion to the quantity of seed produced. The price of canola seed plus the processing margin just equal the price of meal and canola oil. The prices, quantities, and elasticities for the base case are reported in Table 11.1. The 1990 base case reflects the canola market as it existed with higher (canola) quality in place.

To measure the market effect of quality improvement, in the counterfactual simulation, the 1990 base case was altered to reflect the lower quality (rapeseed) situation with higher yield but reduced demand for oil (that is, as though canola had not been adopted). It was assumed that the supply curve for seed in Canada would have been 9.1 percent greater (pivoting from the quantity intercept), and the demand curve for canola oil in Canada and the ROW was shifted downward by CA$32.2 per metric ton (parallel shift).[8] The demand curve in Japan was not shifted, reflecting the low rate of coronary heart disease in that country and general lack of concern with the disease.

The model is then re-solved to find the price and quantity equilibrium for rapeseed that would have existed in 1990 if canola had not been adopted. The linear structure of the model lends itself to a solution using matrix inversion. We chose to solve the model using the Solver routine in Microsoft Excel 5.0 by searching for the set of prices where the vertical relationships held and all markets cleared.

A comparison of the base case to the rapeseed situation, as reported in Table 11.1, shows how the decision to adopt canola quality affected the quantities demanded and supplied, and the prices, in the various sectors. As expected, the price effect of adopting canola quality was positive for canola oil (CA$26.0 per metric ton) and canola seed (CA$8.3 per metric ton). In Canada, the quantity of canola seed supply fell (−0.243 million metric tons) as the yield reduction more than offset the positive price effect. In the ROW production

---

8. The choice of a pivotal supply shift from the quantity axis allows the price intercept to shift but by a smaller amount than the drop in marginal cost at greater quantities providing an intermediate to the case to the standard pivotal or parallel shift. The parallel demand shift also represents an intermediate case where it is assumed the willingness to pay increases by the same per-unit amount regardless of the quantity.

TABLE 11.1 The effects of quality change on the canola industry given an upward shift in demand and a proportional reduction in supply

		The Base Case (Canola Qualities 1990)			Changes Due to Quality Increase		
	Elasticity	Price	Quantity	Surplus	Price	Quantity	Surplus
		(Can$/metric ton)	(mmt)	(Can$)	(Can$/metric ton)	(mmt)	(Can$)
Canada							
Supply of canola seed	1.31	261.2	3.343	333.3	8.3	−0.243	0.6
Supply of processing inputs	5	56.8	1.51	8.6	0.3	0.035	0.4
Demand for canola oil	−2.44	552.7	0.385	43.6	26.0	0.011	2.4
Demand for canola meal	−0.71	167.2	0.339	39.9	−3.2	0.005	1.1
Japan							
Supply of canola seed	0	261.2	0	0	8.3	0.000	0.0
Supply of processing inputs	5	56.8	1.82	10.3	0.4	−0.060	−0.7
Demand for canola oil	−0.74	552.7	0.728	371.9	24.5	−0.024	−18.1
Demand for canola meal	−0.46	167.2	1.2416	225.6	−3.2	0.011	4.0
Rest of the world							
Supply of canola seed	1.09	261.2	19.297	2312.5	8.3	0.667	157.0
Supply of processing inputs	5	56.8	19.31	109.7	0.3	0.448	5.0
Demand for canola oil	−2.05	552.7	7.943	1070.8	26.0	0.183	48.7
Demand for canola meal	−1.03	167.2	11.5506	937.3	−3.2	0.230	37.0

SOURCE: Authors' calculations.

increased in response to higher prices. The quantity of canola consumed increased in Canada and the ROW, where the demand shifted, but was reduced in Japan, where no demand shift took place. Overall, there was a small increase in the world quantities of seed produced and products consumed. This increased the quantity crushed and increased the crushing margin ($0.3 per metric ton). It also increased the quantity of meal produced, and the price of canola meal fell by CA$3.2 per metric ton.

The welfare implications of the switch to canola quality are also reported in Table 11.1. For the elasticities and the supply and demand shifts assumed in the base case, the quality improvement resulted in an overall gain in economic surplus. Consumer and producer surplus increased in all markets except Japan, where higher prices reduced quantity demanded because there was no offsetting demand shift. Because Japan processes only for the domestic market, the reduction in domestic consumption of oil also reduced processing producer surplus.

If the recent $32 per metric ton increase in demand can be attributed to the switch to canola that was associated with a 9.1 percent reduction in yield, the decision produced at least modest gains for the Canadian producer and the industry as a whole. A detailed sensitivity analysis was done by Malla (1996) on the elasticities used in the model as well as the size of the supply and demand shifts. Changes in elasticities changed the distribution among participants but had a very modest effect on the overall economic gain. Benefits increased with the size of the demand shift and decreased with increases in the size of the supply shift. It should be noted again that these estimates of benefits are very conservative, and we assume that the human health concern about erucic acid would not have reduced the demand for rapeseed in the absence of the switch to canola. Otherwise, a demand shift much greater than the one observed in 1988 might be attributable to the decision to pursue canola quality.

The Economic Impact of Health Information

This section examines the market and welfare effects of health information. Consumer information can alter the demand for products and thus have a direct impact on an industry and the returns to a particular research program. In addition, many private and public agencies must decide how to allocate budgets between advertising and research. The welfare effect of information has not been resolved in the economics literature, so we compare alternative measures.

One of the analytical mainstays of neoclassical welfare analysis is the use of "willingness to pay" as a measure of consumer surplus or welfare. Consumer surplus is measured as the change in area above the price line and below a Marshallian demand curve. This calculation gives a measurement of compensating variation from a change in price.[9] This conventional approach relies heavily on an assumption that preferences or tastes remain stable before and after a price change. By convention, economists have often adopted the policy of assuming that the demand curves before and after the introduction of information can be used to calculate the change in consumer surplus. However, using this conventional approach to measure the welfare impacts of information can produce some very curious results: information that increases the willingness to pay for a product enhances welfare, whereas information that reduces demand reduces welfare.

This approach is illustrated in Figure 11.6a, which assumes no price effects, and in Figure 11.6b, which assumes an upward-sloping supply for the good. The ex ante demand curve, represented by the curve D, refers to the situation before new information is provided. The curve D'' represents an enhanced ex post demand curve, as a result of introduction of favorable information, and D' represents a reduced ex post demand curve that would result, alternatively, from the introduction of unfavorable information. Using the conventional measure, the information shifting the demand curve to D'' results in an increase in economic surplus of *acfd* in both figures. When the information reduces the willingness to pay to D', there is a loss in economic surplus of *dfhg*, illustrating the possibility of a loss in welfare from information.[10]

An alternative that uses only the ex post demand curve to measure welfare effects also has merit. Consumers maximize expected utility, which includes welfare, in this and future time periods. If consumption today has future effects on utility, these costs and benefits will be incorporated into the present demand curve to the extent that they are anticipated. Ignorance of a future effect in general will not eliminate its existence. Thus, an uninformed consumer will pay future costs or receive future benefits related to present consumption whether he or she is aware of the effects or not. Information about future health effects will improve the individual's ability to assess future costs related to present consumption. The informed demand curve will better reflect these future costs (or benefits) and therefore may be a more appropriate measure of economic surplus than the uninformed curve. This approach is similar to the one proposed by Dixit and Norman (1978), who propose using either ex ante or ex post curves to measure the welfare impacts of advertising.

---

9. Exact measurement of compensating variation requires the measurement below a Hicksian demand curve. Marshallian measurement is a close approximation when price changes are small, income elasticities are close to one, or the expenditure on the good in question is a small budget share.

10. This paradox is only partially addressed by extending the analysis to a multimarket framework using expenditure functions and indirect utility functions. If information suggests that a product is less desirable, then the individual will receive less utility for the same amount of expenditure as before. In the absence of a perfect substitute, individuals receiving this information must now take measures or expend more money to reach the same level of utility.

FIGURE 11.6 The conventional and ex post measures of the welfare effects of information

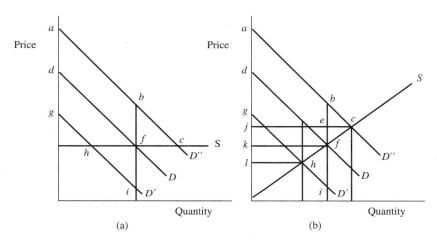

(a)   (b)

Applying the ex post measure of consumer surplus change results in an unambiguous gain in economic surplus from information. This is illustrated in Figure 11.6 (a and b). When the ex post demand curve D'' is used to measure the surplus change, the gain is equal to area *bcf.* When demand shifts to D', there is also a gain in economic surplus equal to area *fih.* Interestingly, as illustrated in Figure 11.6b, with demand enhancement there is a transfer from consumers to producers equal to area *jefk,* which leaves producers un-ambiguously better off but can leave consumers worse off. With demand-reducing information producers are unambiguously worse off and consumers are unambiguously better off. These effects are very different from those derived using the conventional welfare measures.

As a means of contrasting the conventional to the ex post consumer surplus approach, we employ both to measure the welfare effects of the demand-shifting health information on the participants in the canola industry. The mathematical model described in the Appendix was solved for the base case as described in Table 11.1. To measure the impact of health information, it was assumed that the health information alone was responsible for the upward shift in the demand curve of $32 per metric ton for canola oil in Canada and the ROW.

The results of the simulation are reported in Table 11.2. As expected, health information had a positive effect on the quantities produced and con-sumed in Canada and the ROW, which was accompanied by an increase in the price of oil, seed, and processing. The higher price for seed reduced the quan-tity of oil for processing in Japan. The increase in world production of seed

TABLE 11.2 The effects of health information change on the canola industry

	Price Change	Quality Change	Ex Post Surplus Change	Conventional Surplus Change
	(dollars per tonne)	(million tonnes)	(million dollars)	(million dollars)
Canada				
Production of canola seed	6.35	0.107	20.9	20.9
Production of processing inputs	0.37	0.049	0.54	0.54
Consumption of canola oil	23.64	0.015	-8.69	3.25
Consumption of canola meal	-4.71	0.007	1.58	1.58
Total Canada	—	—	14.34	26.28
Japan				
Production of canola seed	6.35	0	0	0
Production of processing inputs	-0.33	-0.053	-0.61	-0.61
Consumption of canola oil	21.89	-0.021	-16.17	-16.17
Consumption of canola meal	-4.71	0.016	5.82	5.82
Total Japan	—	—	-10.97	-10.97
Rest of the world				
Production of canola seed	6.35	0.512	120.98	120.98
Production of processing inputs	0.37	0.623	6.96	6.96
Consumption of canola oil	23.64	0.254	-180.64	67.36
Consumption of canola meal	-4.71	0.336	53.67	53.67
Total ROW	—	—	0.96	248.96
World total	—	—	4.33	264.28

SOURCE: Authors' calculations.

increased the quantity of meal produced, which resulted in lower world meal price.

Using the conventional approach to measure the change in consumer surplus, the information produced positive gains for canola oil consumers in Canada ($3.25 million) and the ROW ($67.36 million) as well as modest gains to meal consumers and processors. The largest gain was created for seed producers in Canada ($20.9 million) and the ROW ($121 million). Japanese consumers of canola oil experienced a loss because their demand curve did not shift, even though prices increased. The reduced Japanese quantity of oil demanded also reduced returns to Japanese processors.

Using the ex post demand curve to measure welfare effects, the overall gains are much more limited, suggesting a modest gain in world total economic surplus of $4.33 million. Although canola oil consumers in Canada and the ROW could increase consumption to take advantage of the health information, this was more than offset by the loss in welfare created by the price increase on preexisting units, resulting in a net loss of $8.69 million for Canadian oil consumers and a $180 million loss for ROW oil consumers. Stated another way, endowed with health information, consumers would pay these amounts to revert to the pre-information price and quantities.

Using either measure of consumer surplus, canola seed producers are the largest beneficiaries of health information. A sensitivity analysis suggested that this relationship held true over a wide range of supply and demand elasticities.

Incorporating Health Cost Externalities into Welfare Analysis

In the late 1980s, studies in Canada, the United States, and Finland showed that diets that substituted canola oil for other fat sources resulted in significant decreases in serum cholesterol (for example, Rudel et al. 1990; Wardlaw et al. 1992). In 1984 it was shown that consumption of monounsaturated fatty acids lowered LDL (harmful) cholesterol levels with no effect on HDL (beneficial) cholesterol (Ferro-Luzzi et al. 1984). As a result of this health information, canola oil became the oil of choice to reduce the risk of coronary heart disease.

Despite the recognition of a link between fat consumption and heart disease by the medical community and the public at large, there has been very little study of the economic effect of dietary change. An extensive review of the economics and health economics literature revealed only two related studies. Oster and Epstein (1986) and Oster and Thompson (1996) examine the role of saturated fat consumption in U.S. health care costs. With the exception of Malla (1996), we did not find any studies that examined nutrition and disease costs in Canada, and none dealt with canola oil consumption.

To estimate the health and economic effects of changes in canola oil consumption in Canada required an examination of three relationships: (1) the linkage between canola consumption and blood cholesterol levels; (2) the relationship between cholesterol reduction and coronary heart disease reduction; and (3) the relationship between the reduction in coronary heart disease and the disease costs in Canada.

The Linkage between Canola Oil Consumption and Blood Cholesterol

A review of the clinical evidence began with a search for all dietary studies in which canola oil replaced a portion of the saturated fat sources in the regular diet and the change in serum cholesterol was measured. Studies were located through a Medline search for entries related to canola intake and serum cholesterol and through discussion with investigators in the field to discover further publications (as reported in Malla 1996 and Malla et al. 1995). Studies were chosen that kept the total fat, as a percentage of energy, constant during the trial. The six studies that met these requirements were reviewed. Four studies were of controlled diets. In the other two, subjects consumed their regular diets except for the change in oil type. The study populations ranged from 8 to 59 people. The baseline total serum cholesterol ranged from 4.4 to 7.1 mmol/L, which covers the whole range from light-risk to high-risk individuals (Reeder et al. 1995). On average, the substitution of 10 grams of monounsaturated fatty acids for saturated fatty acids resulted in a reduction in total serum cholesterol of 3.9 percent. The substitution of 10 grams per day of canola oil, which is high in monounsaturated fatty acids, for fat sources high in saturated acids will lower total blood cholesterol by an average of 2.3 percent.

The Relationship between Blood Cholesterol and Coronary Heart Disease

A second set of medical studies has drawn a very strong linkage between total blood cholesterol and coronary heart disease. Evidence from both epidemiological and clinical studies led the National Cholesterol Education Program's Expert Panel on the Detection, Evaluation, and Treatment of High Blood Cholesterol in Adults (Expert Panel 1988:37) to conclude that "epidemiological studies and clinical trials are remarkably consistent in supporting the projection that for individuals with serum cholesterol levels initially in the 250 to 300 mg/dl range, each one percent reduction in serum cholesterol level yields approximately a two percent reduction in coronary heart disease." Moreover, in the long term, epidemiological studies suggest that a 1 percent reduction in serum cholesterol levels may result in a 3 percent reduction in coronary heart disease rates (Davis et al. 1990).

Combining the relationship between diet and serum cholesterol and that between serum cholesterol and coronary heat disease allows a calculation of the expected reduction in heart disease given a dietary change. The medical and nutritional studies would suggest that substituting 10 grams per day (3.65 kilograms per year) of canola oil for saturated fats in the diet would result, on average, in a 2.3 percent reduction in total blood cholesterol and, on average, a 4.6 percent reduction in the incidence of coronary heart disease.

The Relationship between Coronary Heart Disease and Health Costs

In 1993, the total cost of coronary heart disease in Canada was estimated by Moore et al. (1996) to be $7.4 billion per year. This makes coronary heart disease the most expensive subcategory of disease.[11] The high cost of coronary heart disease is not surprising given that it is still the leading cause of death in Canada—accounting for 22 percent of all deaths and 5 percent of both hospital admissions and hospital days in Canada in 1991–92 (Reeder et al. 1995). The per capita costs of coronary heart disease are $265 per year for Canada's population of 28 million. To calculate the impact on health costs we assumed that a 1 percent reduction in the incidence of coronary heart disease would be accompanied by a 1 percent reduction in the costs of coronary heart disease.[12] Given the hundreds of hospitals involved, there are no apparent economies of scale in the treatment of coronary heart disease. The calculation implicitly assumes that the costs associated with premature death could be prevented in the absence of coronary heart disease. It also assumes that the survivors of the coronary heart disease go on to incur similar (at least not reduced) costs for other diseases. If we apply this one-to-one ratio, a 4.6 percent reduction in coronary heart disease is accompanied by a 4.6 percent reduction in the cost of the disease, which represents a 1993 annual cost savings of $12.20 per capita.

Per-Unit Health Externalities

The linkage between consumption and health costs allows a per-unit cost saving from consuming canola oil to be estimated. Given the annual per capita dietary change of 3.65 kilograms, the savings average $3.34 per kilogram of canola in the diet. Given that approximately one-half of the canola oil purchased is actually consumed (the rest being discarded), this works out to $1.67 per kilogram of disappearance.

The magnitude of these numbers is very large relative to the price of canola oil, which has a wholesale price of about $0.60 per kilogram. A sensitivity analysis on key assumptions revealed that this externality can vary over a large range but remains economically important, even when very conservative estimates are made.

---

11. These estimates are almost certainly conservative because, out of a total of $71.7 billion in direct costs, $27.6 billion, or 39 percent, was unclassifiable by disease category. In addition, the indirect costs due to short-term disability from CHD could not be calculated and thus are not included in these figures.

12. Oster and Thompson (1996) use a more complex approach examining the probability of various disease outcomes for a group of high-risk males. These results are consistent with those obtained using the simple proportional approach.

To illustrate how important the externality is, consider the effect of health information that increased canola consumption in Canada by an estimated 15 million kilograms. Given a $1.67 per kilogram externality, such a demand shift would reduce health costs by an estimated $25 million per year in Canada. This welfare effect is the same magnitude as the total private effects of the health information. To the extent that canola research has led to the substitution of this oil for saturated fats in the Canadian diet, a large taxpayer externality was generated through agronomic and genetic research in canola.

The large estimates also suggest that harmful fats have large negative health costs associated with their consumption. Because these costs are largely borne in the public sector, they are external to the marketplace. Per-unit externalities of such a magnitude merit further economic study because they may have implications for the economics of research and food policy in general.

Summary and Conclusions

This chapter has outlined some economics of canola research in Canada. As World War II ended, the industrial marine-lubricant market for rapeseed oil shrank, and research was reoriented toward creating an edible oil and meal suitable for livestock rations. When problems were identified with erucic acid in the oil and glucosinolates in the meal, the research community began to develop a breeding program to address these problems. This effort became focused in 1970 when the Rapeseed Association of Canada created an industry and research community driven toward a common goal of eliminating erucic acid and glucosinolates from rapeseed. The Rapeseed Association created the resources as well as means for coordinating the efforts in genetic research, agronomic research, processing research, and market development activities. They were very successful in their endeavor and were soon able to overcome the quality problem by commercializing low glucosinolate and erucic acid (double-low) varieties of rapeseed. The association named the new, higher-quality crop canola.

In making the switch to canola some genetic yield potential was given up. During the process of adoption of canola varieties, genetic yield potential fell 9.4 percent below the long-run trend established by rapeseed. There is some evidence that this reduction in yield, resulting from quality improvement, was permanent. Even in the postadoption period yields remain 9.1 percent below the trend established by rapeseed. Despite the loss in genetic yield potential, the crop remained profitable as a result of agronomic research that continued to increase yields at the farm level and a price premium.

When health information increased the demand for canola oil, the effect on demand more than offset the reduced genetic potential. More important, the quality improvement removed the health concerns relating to eurcic acid, which had the potential to result in a ban on human consumption of rapeseed oil. If the quality issue had not been addressed, the demand for oil would have been much smaller, resulting in lower prices and a much smaller industry. Thus, not only did the quality improvement result in an increase in producer surplus, but it obviated a potential loss of markets and severe contraction of the industry.

In the late 1980s, nutritional research created positive health information about canola that increased demand and raised the price of canola oil relative to soybean oil by an estimated \$32 per metric ton. This health information provided additional benefits for seed producers and processors, resulting in a crop that now has an area constrained only by rotation frequency and climate. How to measure the effect of information on consumer welfare is somewhat unclear. Consumers are willing to pay more for canola oil than before the information became available, but they now face higher prices for canola oil and would clearly prefer pre-information prices and quantities to the postinformation market quantities and prices. Regardless of how consumer surplus is measured, there was an overall gain to the canola industry from health information.

Preliminary research suggests that canola has also provided substantial benefits to taxpayers through reduced incidence and cost of coronary heart disease. These external cost savings are as large as the market value of the crop. This suggests that the health care costs associated with nutrition may be an important but largely neglected aspect of the economics of agricultural and research policy.

Appendix—Mathematical Form of the Model

Mathematically, the four-sector, three-country model can be represented by the linear supply and demand equations outlined in Appendix Table 11.1, where P is price; QS and QD are quantity supplied and demanded; $b, d, \ldots, x$ are demand and supply price slopes; $a, c, \ldots, w$ are the intercept terms; the subscripts s, p, o, m denote the seed, processing, oil, and meal sectors; and the superscripts C, R, J, T refer to Canada, the ROW, Japan, and the total. Six additional market clearing conditions are reflected in a market equilibrium:

$$QS_s^T = QS_s^P$$
$$0.4W_p^T = QD_o^T$$
$$0.58QS_p^T = QD_m^T$$
$$0.4P_o + 0.58P_m - P_s = P_p$$
$$0.4P_o^J + 0.58P_m - P_s = P_p^J$$
$$0.4Q_p^J = QD_o^J$$

(11.4)

For the base case the slope and intercept of each supply and demand curve are calculated to pass through the price and quantity that reflect the market in 1990 and to have point elasticities that correspond to those estimated in the literature. These prices, quantities, and elasticities are reported in Table 11.1.

APPENDIX TABLE 11.1 Linear supply and demand equations for the economic model

Region	Seed Sector Supply	Processing Sector Supply	Canola Oil Demand	Canola Meal Demand
Canada	$QS_s^C = a + bP_s$	$QS_p^C = g + hP_p$	$QD_o^C = m - nP_o$	$QD_m^C = s - tP_m$
Japan		$QS_p^R = i + jP_p$	$QD_o^R = o - pP_o$	$QD_m^R = u - vP_m$
ROW	$QS_s^R = c + dP_s$	$QD_p^J = k + lP_p^J$	$QD_o^J = q - rP_o^J$	$QD_m^J = w - xP_m$
Total	$QS_s^T = QS_s^C + QS_s^R$	$S_p^T = QS_p^C + QS_p^R + QS$	$D_o^T = QD_o^C + QD_o^R + QD$	$D_m^T = QD_m^C + QD_m^R + QD$

To examine the effect of quality improvement, the supply curve was modified for Canada along with the demand curves for Canada and the ROW:

$$QS_s^{C'} = a + b(1 - x)P_s$$
$$QD_o^{C'} = m + nk - nP_o \qquad (11.5)$$
$$QD_o^{R'} = o + pk - pP_o$$

The constant x reflects the yield reduction, and k equals CA\$32 per metric ton and represents the shift in demand due to higher quality (9.1 percent).

To estimate the effect of health information on the sector, only the demand curves for Canada and the ROW were shifted upward:

$$QD_o^{C'} = m + nk - nP_o$$
$$QD_o^{R'} = o + pk - pP_o \qquad (11.6)$$

Again, here the shift in demand, k, is equal to \$32 per metric ton.

To speed up the process of calculating the effects of the reduction in yield and the increase in demand due to health information, the equilibrium prices and quantities for any given set of supply and demand curves were found in a spreadsheet (Microsoft Excel 5.0) using the "Solver" routine by searching for the set of prices and quantities where all markets cleared simultaneously while maintaining the vertical price and quantity relationships. Prices, quantities, and elasticities used for each supply and demand curve are provided in Table 11.1.

PART V

Conclusion

12 Directions for Agricultural Research and Development Policy

WALTER J. ARMBRUSTER AND PETER J. BARRY

This volume reviews past and present policies and emerging issues related to agricultural productivity, agricultural research and development (R&D), and natural resource management. One of its purposes was to document what was known about long-standing issues; another was to lay out some new or emerging issues. The intention was not necessarily to resolve these issues or to draw definitive policy conclusions. Rather, the aim was more modest: to develop a sense of which issues were likely to be enduring, rather than transitory; to document progress in providing economic tools and evidence as an aid to decisionmakers; and to identify knowledge gaps. In this concluding chapter we present the key points from the previous chapters and synthesize the findings.

Changing Contexts and Agendas

In Chapter 1, Julian Alston, Philip Pardey, and Michael Taylor sketch out the contemporary, changing context for agricultural science policy, including an overview of investment patterns, the private sector, and key policy developments. In chapter 2, Ismail Serageldin revisits some of these contextual issues and adds his further perspectives on the changing global agenda for agricultural R&D. As Chapter 1 describes, over the past half century, technological advances created through R&D have supplied a growing world population with more and better feed, food, and fiber. At the start of the the twenty-first century, however, important science-policy questions remain. What public policies should be adopted both to ensure that the expanding world population will have adequate food supplies and, simultaneously, to protect the natural resource base appropriately for future generations? How much should be spent on R&D related to the conservation and management of natural resources used in or affected by agriculture versus other types of agricultural R&D? What are the benefits from R&D? Who receives them? How can the benefits be measured? And how should research be evaluated and prioritized? These and other related questions must be addressed in the context of a changing, complex global economic order, with changing trade and international technology generation and transfer regimes. Institutional barriers or inertia and shifts in the sources of funds and the agencies conducting R&D raise new policy questions and pose major challenges to both private- and public-sector decisionmakers.

In Chapter 2, Ismail Serageldin argues for a comprehensive perspective and a holistic approach to R&D policy, emphasizing the issues in developing countries—places where perhaps the policies will have more impact on individual lives. He argues that it is imperative to reduce poverty, ensure food security, and manage natural resources simultaneously; that rural well-being must include a prosperous agriculture sector for smaller and medium-sized farms; and that agricultural research must take a systems view and interdisciplinary approaches to deal with the complex issues involved.

Serageldin sets out an agenda and some provocative policy prescriptions, drawn from his experience as vice president of the World Bank and chairman of the Consultative Group on International Agricultural Research (CGIAR). He argues that publicly funded research should focus on national and international public goods, leaving private-goods research to the private sector; that developing new agricultural technology will increasingly be a responsibility shared by the private and public sectors, perhaps through partnering or other collaborative arrangements. He identifies the challenge of having to identify truly public research goods and then find ways to fund them and disseminate the results. Serageldin raises the concern that the poorest countries may be increasingly locked out of the benefits of science in a kind of "scientific apartheid." In this context, the future looks bleaker if patenting of processes and products of research increases markedly, especially in the area of biotechnology and transgenic plants. Beyond agricultural science, he points to a host of issues that will constrain the benefits from agricultural science—investing in agricultural R&D is necessary, as a key element of promoting development, but only a part of the answer.

Productivity Measures and Measurement Challenges

In Chapter 3, Zvi Griliches, the senior expert in the field, provides a unique perspective after 40 years of working on developing methods for measuring productivity, the effects of R&D, and the adoption of new technology. Within all of economics, this line of work epitomizes the combination of economic thinking and careful use of economic statistics to address questions about the world. Nevertheless, in his broad-ranging and insightful assessment of the state of the art Griliches identifies a number of unresolved conceptual and statistical problems. Included are the meaning and measurement of the depreciation of "knowledge," the implications of imperfect markets for knowledge-based products, and the need to consider simultaneously how research affects output and how output affects research. The resolution of these problems will lead to greater precision and enhanced usefulness of the research payoff measures.

In Chapter 4, Barbara Craig and Philip Pardey address some of the productivity measurement issues highlighted by Griliches, with an application to U.S. agriculture. Specifically, they show the benefits from dealing explicitly with changes in the quality of inputs and outputs using state-specific data for the United States. Although their more careful approach to (dis)aggregation does not, as it happens, in this instance change the findings for overall national rates of productivity growth, there are important implications for productivity patterns among states and for certain states in particular. The main benefit from their approach is a richer understanding of the sources of productivity growth, as promised by Griliches when he first suggested these ideas in the 1960s.

Chapter 5, by Prabhu Pingali and Paul Heisey, involves a shift of focus, to look at agricultural productivity in a range of developing countries, as measured mostly by crop yields. This yield evidence is complemented by tabulation and discussion of published evidence on productivity patterns in developing countries. Pingali and Heisey report that cereal crop productivity—as indicated by yield growth rates for rice, wheat, and maize—grew markedly during the 40 years 1956–95. Significant productivity growth has occurred for rice in Asia, wheat in irrigated and other favorable production environments worldwide, and maize (corn) in Mesoamerica and other selected locations in Africa and Asia. The most widespread indication has been a striking increase in land productivity in areas with growing land scarcity. Labor productivity has also grown outside of Sub-Saharan Africa. In general, the phases of technology change in cereal crop production include land augmentation, followed by labor substitution and then by intensification of knowledge and management. In the authors' view, the major contributions to this growth process have come from research-induced developments of new technology, investment in infrastructure and education, and policy reform. Research and education have had the greatest and most sustained successes; policy reforms, while important, tend to yield one-time benefits.

Pingali and Heisey find that despite these significant accomplishments, and similar to the case of the developed countries, recent signs indicate a slowdown in productivity growth of the primary cereals, rice and wheat, especially in the intensively cultivated lowlands of Asia. Degradation of the land base due to intensive cultivation, along with slower growth of investments in research and infrastructure and the increasing opportunity cost of labor, caused the slowdowns in productivity growth. The authors argue that restoration and revitalization of support for research and education are urgently needed in order to accelerate technology-induced growth in agricultural productivity in the future and to meet the demands from an increasingly knowledge-intensive agricultural sector.

Research, Productivity, and Natural Resources

Can new research and technology solve problems of water, soil, and air degradation caused by past research and technology along with other factors? Preliminary analyses suggest mixed results, with positive yet limited potential for new R&D to solve these problems. More direct yet politically and administratively difficult policy instruments may be needed in some cases. The three chapters in this section explore different elements of the emerging concerns with sustainability and the implications for agricultural R&D in conjunction with other policies.

In Chapter 6 Wilfred Beckerman throws down the gauntlet to the proponents of sustainable development. He challenges various popular ideas about the nature and extent of resource scarcity and the obligations of the current generation to future generations. To some, these arguments may seem simply polemical, but Beckerman provides a mixture of data, anecdotes, and economic argument that together ought to make us all rethink (or at least consider rethinking) a number of widely held ideas about natural resources and policies to protect them. Specifically, he shows that there is nothing particularly intergenerationally equitable about the objective of sustainable development. He also points out, however, that this does not relieve us of any need to consider our moral obligations to future generations. But he suggests that shifting the policy focus with a view to providing just institutions and a decent society now will achieve more currently, perhaps without doing any harm to the cause of intergenerational equity.

These arguments have important implications for those who would argue that agricultural technology, or agricultural science, ought to meet some constraint of sustainability. In contrast, productivity growth and technological change may be constrained inadvertently when a common-property, open-access resource is subject to government regulations intended to meet environmental and resource conservation goals.

In Chapter 7, James Wilen and Frances Homans document a decline in productivity in the North Pacific Halibut Fishery over the 1935–78 period. The decline came in response to tightly regulated fishing seasons intended to preserve fish populations and their natural habitats. Often natural resources are used in commercial production on a basis of common property or open access, and in such instances a firm's profit motivations may lead them to overexploit and underconserve such poorly priced resources. Policies aiming to correct this type of distortion can have unintended implications for productivity and technological change. Stringent regulations by one government agency could even induce production inefficiencies that counter another agency's attempts to promote technological change. As Wilen and Homans demonstrate with their application to the North Pacific Halibut Fishery, to develop informed policy in such circumstances requires an understanding of regulatory mechanisms and behavior and their interplay with the production technologies and industry behavior.

In Chapter 8, Peter Lindert provides new insight on the relationship between soil degradation, economic development, and agricultural research, using unique, historical data reaching back to the 1930s. Soil organic matter and nitrogen appear to have declined on cultivated lands in both China and Indonesia during this time. Total phosphorous and potassium on rural lands in these countries have generally risen. Alkalinity and acidity have fluctuated with no overall worsening. The topsoil layer has become thinner.

Lindert observes that some of these mixed trends have greater effects on crop yields than others. China's patterns show that the decline in soil organic matter and nitrogen makes little difference, because fertilizer can substitute for the soil endowment. Lindert further concludes that, while the growth of poor populations may degrade the soil, economic development may correspondingly improve the soil in three ways. First, taking all soil-farming feedback effects into account, the shift in food demand away from staples toward legumes and animal products can replenish soil nutrients. Second, development means cheaper capital and clearer property rights, which improve conservation. And, finally, urbanization and industrialization raise the productivity of soils at the urban fringe—data from China suggest that this effect is strong enough to cancel the loss of farm soil endowment from urban encroachment. On balance, the research-induced payoffs of economic development can more than offset the research-induced costs from resource degradation.

Research for Genetic Improvement

Much of the past work on the economics of agricultural R&D has focused on genetic improvement, especially crop improvement, partly because of the central role of crop improvement in the agricultural technological revolution in this century, in rich and poor countries alike, and partly because the economics is easier for evaluating this type of technological change. But the economics of genetic improvement is becoming harder with changes in institutional arrangements and the nature of the relevant science. The genetic research environment in agriculture is being transformed by innovation and biotechnology and intellectual property protection. This transformation involves several issues relevant to agricultural research and development policy, including plant breeding, conservation of germplasm, legal protection, advances in biotechnology, shifting patterns of demand, and privatization.

One set of important emerging issues relates to the changing location specificity of technologies, spillover effects, cost economies, and the optimal institutional configuration. In Chapter 9, Derek Byerlee and Greg Traxler review the literature on economies of size, scale, and scope in agricultural research and provide empirical evidence on wheat-breeding research using

Indian data and some international cross-sectional data. Their results show that it is important to allow for technology spillovers in evaluating individual programs. When spillovers are taken into account, the true nature of economies of size, scale, and scope is revealed, and the indication is that a much smaller number of wheat-breeding programs is economically efficient. For instance, 2 of 20 programs evaluated in India accounted for more than 75 percent of the total benefits from wheat research in that country.

Issues of biodiversity and intellectual property regimes surrounding agricultural genetic resources are increasingly controversial and likely to have far-reaching consequences for agricultural policies, including effects through trade negotiations. In Chapter 10, Robert Evenson and Brian Wright discuss the value of plant biodiversity in agriculture. They begin with a brief historical overview of the conservation of crop germplasm and its use in modern crop-breeding programs. The issue of valuing agricultural biodiversity is contentious. The authors point out that biodiversity has long been central to agriculture and the improvement of plants and animals. Originally, farmers cultivated plants and in the process performed a type of plant breeding by selecting seeds for each new crop. As human populations grew and migrated, they created more landraces or "farmers' varieties." This creation of within-species diversity produced the basic raw materials for the formal plant-breeding programs that began in the twentieth century. Evenson and Wright go on to outline several economic approaches to valuing crop genetic resources. And they conclude with a review of intellectual property regimes as they affect genetic resources in agriculture, highlighting some implications of these property rights for plant breeding, in particular. The authors suggest that most agricultural genetic resources remain underused. Joint public and private efforts to use germplasm of major crops more effectively may be a useful and beneficial strategy.

Genetically modified organisms raise concerns that are seen by some as food-safety issues. Technological changes can confer benefits through changes in actual or perceived food safety as well. In Chapter 11, Richard Gray and Stavroula Malla illustrate the importance of health benefits from the genetically modified crop canola and from canola research. The innovation in this study is to allow for the health effects of a healthier diet when canola oil replaces saturated fats and its effects on the incidence of coronary heart disease. In addition to measuring the conventional economic welfare measures of benefits from R&D-induced productivity gains, the authors allow for the effects on health care costs, taking into consideration the difference between private and social costs of health care, given the public health system in Canada. Their careful and comprehensive analysis leads to some striking results. The external health savings attributable to canola consumption are as large as the gross value of the crop, much greater than the conventionally measured benefits to producers and consumers, calculated without considering health effects.

In Closing

Taken together, the chapters of this book tell a compelling story about the past accomplishments, emerging issues, and future potential for agricultural R&D. The breadth of issues and the linkages among them are important highlights. Agricultural R&D will continue to address the productivity of farms and farm inputs, but the current and future agendas are much broader. The scope encompasses rich and poor countries alike, it addresses issues up and down the food chain (including consumers), it reflects both public and private support of research, and it considers the linkages between national and international research and research policies. Important research questions and concerns now include the environment and natural resource conservation, food safety and human health, poverty and hunger, and the costs and benefits of biotechnology and genetic diversity. Agriculture interacts with each of these.

At the same time, we must recognize that many of the current issues will not be resolved based on research results alone. For example, current issues in biotechnology are being addressed in the political arena, which is heavily influenced by forces other than agricultural research. Environmental interests and consumer and food safety organizations have substantial influence on decisions being made in the public sector and in private firms. Nonetheless, agricultural research findings will continue to provide a basis for better-informed policy dialogue and public policy and private sector decisions on the issues crucial to the future productivity of the agricultural sector and the food system in a global context.

These issues are not confined by geographic or national boundaries. They are global in nature, transcending borders within and between countries and continents. They bring new, multicultural interests to the R&D table. They call for a strategic international perspective, involving greater degrees of cooperation, collaboration, and coordination across scientists, disciplines, policymakers, and stakeholder groups. Such a perspective is essential to mobilizing the scientific expertise, leveraging available resources, and building upon the high social rates of return on public investments in agricultural research achieved during the past century.

References

Abdellatif, A. M. M., and R. O. Vles. 1970. *Physiopathological effects of rapeseed oil and canbra oil in rats.* In *Proceedings of the International Conference on the Science, Technology, and Marketing of Rapeseed and Rapeseed Products.* Ottawa: Rapeseed Association of Canada in cooperation with the Department of Industry, Trade, and Commerce.

Adams, M. W. 1977. An estimation of homogeneity in crop plants, with special reference to genetic vulnerability in the dry bean, *Phaseolus vulgaris L. Euphytica* 26:665–679.

Ahmed, Y. J., S. E. Serafy, and E. Lutz, eds. 1989. *Environmental accounting for sustainable development.* A United Nations Environment Programme (UNEP)/ World Bank Symposium. Washington, D.C.: World Bank.

Ahrens, E. H., J. Hirsch, W. J. Insull, R. Blomstrand, T. T. Tsaltas, and M. L. Petersen. 1957. The influence of dietary fats on serum lipid levels in men. *Lancet* 1:943–954.

Ali, M. 1998. Technological changes and resource productivity in Pakistan's agriculture. Draft paper. Washington, D.C.: World Bank.

Ali, M., and D. Byerlee. 1991. Economic efficiency of small farmers in a changing world: A survey of recent evidence. *Journal of International Development* 3 (1):1–12.

Ali, M., and L. E. Velasco. 1993. Intensification and induced resource degradation: The crop production sector in Pakistan. Los Baños, the Philippines: International Rice Research Institute. Mimeo.

Allard, R. W. 1992. Predictive methods for germplasm identification. In *Plant breeding in the 1990s,* ed. H. T. Stalker and J. P. Murphy. Wallingford, U.K.: CAB International.

Alston, J. M., G. W. Norton, and P. G. Pardey. 1995. *Science under scarcity: Principles and practice for agricultural research evaluation and priority setting.* Ithaca, N.Y.: Cornell University Press.

Alston, J. M., and P. G. Pardey. 1996. *Making science pay: The economics of agricultural R&D policy.* Washington, D.C.: American Enterprise Institute Press (AEI Press).

Alston, J. M., P. G. Pardey, and J. Roseboom. 1998. Financing agricultural research:

International investment patterns and policy perspectives. *World Development* 26 (2):1057–1072.

Ansaldo, R. W., and R Riley. 1997. Prospects and constraints for hybrid maize in developing countries. In *Easing barriers to movement of plant varieties for agricultural development,* ed. D. Gisselquist and J. P. Srivastava. World Bank Discussion Paper 367. Washington, D.C.: World Bank.

Araji, A. A., F. C. White, and J. F. Guenthner. 1995. Spillovers and the returns to agricultural research for potatoes. *Journal of Agricultural and Resource Economics* 20 (2):236–276.

Arnade, C. A. 1992. *Productivity of Brazilian agriculture: Measurement and uses.* Washington, D.C.: United States Department of Agriculture, Economic Research Service, Agriculture and Trade Analysis Division.

———. 1994. *Using data envelopment analysis to measure international agricultural efficiency and productivity.* Washington, D.C.: United States Department of Agriculture, Economic Research Service, Agriculture and Trade Analysis Division.

Arrow, K. J. 1962. Economic welfare and the allocation of resources for invention. In *The rate and direction of inventive activity: Economic and social factors.* Princeton: Princeton University Press.

Artuso, A. 1995. Economic analysis of biodiversity as a source of pharmaceuticals. In *Emerging connections: Biotechnology, biodiversity and sustainable development.* Washington, D.C.: Pan American Health Organization and International Institute for Cooperation in Agriculture.

Asian Productivity Organization (APO). 1987. *Productivity measurement and analysis: Asian agriculture.* Tokyo: APO.

Australian Industry Commission. 1995. *Research and development.* Canberra: Australian Government Printing Service.

Bachrach, C. 1990. *Essays on research and development and competitiveness.* Cambridge: Massachusetts Institute of Technology.

Ball, V. E. 1985. Output, input, and productivity measurement in U.S. agriculture, 1948–79. *American Journal of Agricultural Economics* 3:475–486.

Ball, V. E., J. Bureau, R. Nehring, and A. Somwaru. 1997. Agricultural productivity revisited. *American Journal of Agricultural Economics* 79 (4):1045–1063.

Ball, V. E., F. M. Gallop, A. Kelly-Hawke, and G. P. Swinand. 1999. Patterns of state productivity growth in the U.S. farm sector: Linking state and aggregate models. *American Journal of Agricultural Economics* 81 (1):164–179.

Bardhan, P. K. 1970. Green Revolution and agricultural laborers. *Economic and Political Weekly* 5 (29–31) (Special number, July): 1239–1246.

Barker, R., and V. Cordova. 1978. Labor utilization in rice production. In *Economic consequences of the new rice technology.* Los Baños, the Philippines: International Rice Research Institute.

Barker, R., and R. W. Herdt. 1985. *The rice economy of Asia.* Washington, D.C.: Resources for the Future.

Barker, R., and R. W. Herdt, with B. Rose. 1985. *The rice economy of Asia.* Los Baños, Laguna, Philippines, and Washington, D.C.: International Rice Research Institute and Resources for the Future.

Barton, G. T., and M. R. Cooper. 1948. Relation of agricultural production to inputs. *Review of Economics and Statistics* 2:117–126.

Beare-Rogers, J. L. 1970. *Nutritional aspects of long-chain fatty acids.* In *Proceedings of the International Conference on the Science, Technology, and Marketing of Rapeseed and Rapeseed Products.* Ottawa: Rapeseed Association of Canada in cooperation with the Department of Industry, Trade, and Commerce.

Beckerman, W. 1972. Economists, scientists and environmental castastrophe. *Oxford Economic Papers* 24 (3):327–344.

———. 1974. *In defence of economic growth.* London: Duckworth.

———. 1979. Does slow growth matter?: Egalitarianism versus humanitarianism. In *Slow growth in Britain: Causes and consequences,* ed. W. Beckerman. Oxford: Clarendon Press.

———. 1994. "Sustainable development": Is it a useful concept?. *Environmental Values* 3:191–210.

———. 1995a. *Small is stupid.* London: Duckworth. (Published in the United States as *Through green-colored glasses.* 1996. Washington, D.C.: Cato Institute.)

———. 1995b. How would you like your sustainability sir?: Weak or strong? A reply to my critics. *Environmental Values* 4:169–179.

———. 1997. Intergenerational equity and the environment. *Journal of Political Philosophy* 5 (4):391–405.

———. 1999. Sustainable development and our obligations to future generations. In *Fairness of Futurity,* ed. A. Dobson. Oxford: Oxford University Press.

Beckerman, W., and J. Pasek. 2001. *What price posterity? Environmental ethics for a new millennium.* Oxford: Oxford University Press.

Bell, F. H. 1981. *The Pacific halibut: The resource and the fishery.* Anchorage: Northwest Publishing Co.

Bell, J. M. 1955. The nutritional value of rapeseed meal: A review. *Canadian Journal of Agricultural Economics* 35:242–251.

———. 1981. From rapeseed to canola: A brief history of research for superior meal and edible oil. Paper presented at the 70th Anual Meeting of the Poultry Science Association, Vancouver, British Columbia, Canada.

Bell, J. M., and L. R. Wetter. 1974. Utilization of rapeseed meal. In *The story of rapeseed in Western Canada.* Regina, Saskatchewan: Saskatchewan Wheat Pool.

Berndt, E. 1991. *The practice of econometrics: Classic and contemporary.* Reading, Mass.: Addison-Wesley.

Beverton, R. J. H., and S. Holt. 1957. *On the dynamics of exploited fish populations.* Fisheries Investigations Series 2 (19). London: Ministry of Agriculture, Fisheries and Food.

Bhalla, S. A. 1988. Does land quality matter?: Theory and measurement. *Journal of Development Economics* 29 (1):45–62.

Bierenbaum, M. L., R. P Reichstein, T. R. Watkins, W. P. Maginnis, and M. Geller. 1991. Effects of canola oil in serum lipids in humans. *Journal of the American College of Nutrition* 10:228–233.

Binswanger, H. P., S. R. Khandker, and M. R. Rosenzweig. 1993. How infrastructure and financial institutions affect agricultural output and investment in India. *Journal of Development Economics* 41 (2):337–366.

Binswanger, H. P., and P. L. Pingali. 1988. Technological priorities for farming in Sub-Saharan Africa. *World Bank Research Observer* 3:81–98.

Bishop of Kingston. 1971. Man's hope of survival. *Observer* (London), December 19.

Blakely, R. M., and W. R. Anderson. 1948. The effects of various levels of rapeseed oilcake meal intake diet on the weight of the thyroid glands in turkey poults. *Scientific Agriculture* 28:393–397.

Block, S. A. 1993. Agricultural productivity in Sub-Saharan Africa. Ph.D. diss., Harvard University.

Blundell, R. S., and S. Bond. 1995. Initial conditions and moment restrictions in dynamic panel data. Working Paper W95/17. Institute of Fiscal Studies, London.

Bohn, A., and D. Byerlee. 1993. The wheat breeding industry in developing countries: An analysis of investments and its impacts. Part I of *1992/93 CIMMYT world wheat facts and trends.* Mexico City: Centro Internacional de Mejoramiento de Maiz y Trigo (CIMMYT).

Boserup, E. 1965. *Conditions of agricultural growth: The economics of agrarian change under population pressure.* Chicago: Aldine.

Bowland, J. P., D. R. Clandinin, and L. R. Wetter. 1965. *Rapeseed meal for livestock and poultry: A review.* Ottawa: Canadian Department of Agriculture.

Branson, I., and P. Foster. 1987. Economies of size of USDA agricultural research stations. *IEEE Transactions on Engineering Management* 34 (3):156–160.

Bray, F. 1986. *The rice economies: Technology and development in Asian societies.* Oxford: Blackwell.

Brennan, J. P. 1988. *An economic investigation of wheat breeding programs.* Agricultural Economics Bulletin No. 35. Armidale, Australia: University of New England, Department of Agricultural Economics and Business Management.

———. 1999. Efficiency in wheat improvement research: A case study of Australia. In *The global wheat improvement system: Prospects for enhancing efficiency in the presence of spillovers,* ed. M. K. Maredia and D. Byerlee. Research Report No. 5. Mexico City: Centro Internacional de Mejoramiento de Maiz y Trigo (CIMMYT).

Brennan, J. P., and P. N. Fox. 1995. *Impact of CIMMYT wheats in Australia: Evidence of international research spillovers.* Economic Research Report No. 1-95, Wagga Wagga, Australia: New South Wales Agriculture.

Brown, L. 1994. *The state of the world.* New York: Norton.

———. 1995. *Who will feed China?: Wake-up call for a small planet.* New York: Norton.

Brush, S. B. 1995. Valuing the commons: The worth of crop genetic resources. Paper presented at the Symposium on Genetic Resources—IRP and Ownership, 87th Annual Meeting of the American Society of Agronomy, St. Louis, Mo., October 30.

Buck, J. L. 1937. *Land utilization in China.* Chicago: Chicago University Press.

Budhaka, B. 1987. Thailand. In Asian Productivity Organization (APO), *Productivity measurement and analysis: Asian agriculture,* 439–484. Tokyo: Asian Productivity Organization.

Byerlee, D. 1987. *Maintaining the momentum in post–Green Revolution agriculture: A micro-level perspective for Asia.* International Development Paper No. 10. East Lansing: Michigan State University.

Byerlee, D., P. R. Hobbs, B. R. Khan, A. Majid, M. R. Akhtar, and N. I. Hashmi. 1986. *Increasing wheat in the context of Pakistan's irrigated cropping sustems: A view from the farmer's field.* Islamabad: Pakistan Agricultural Research Council

(PARC)/Centro Internacional de Mejoramiento de Maiz y Trigo (CIMMYT), Collaborative Program.

Byerlee, D., and M. K. Maredia. 1999. Measures of technical efficiency of national and international wheat research systems. In *The global wheat improvement system: Prospects for enhancing efficiency in the presence of spillovers,* ed. M. K. Maredia and D. Byerlee. Research Report No. 5. Mexico City: Centro Internacional de Mejoramiento de Maiz y Trigo (CIMMYT).

Byerlee, D., and P. Moya. 1993. *Impacts of international wheat breeding research in the developing world, 1966–90.* Mexico City: Centro Internacional de Mejoramiento de Maiz y Trigo (CIMMYT).

Byerlee, D., and P. L. Pingali. 1994. *Agricultural research in Asia: Fulfillments and frustrations:* Proceedings of the Twenty-Second Conference of the International Association of Agricultural Economists, Harare, August 22–29.

———. 1995. Agricultural research in Asia: Fulfillments and frustrations. In *Agricultural competitiveness, market forces and policy choices,* ed. D. Headley and G. H. Peters. Gower, U.K.: Aldershot.

Byerlee, D., and P. L. Siddiq. 1994. Has the Green Revolution been sustained?: The quantitative impact of the seed fertilizer technology in Pakistan revisited. *World Development* 22 (9):1345–1361.

Byerlee, D., and G. Traxler. 1995. National and international wheat improvement research in the Post–Green Revolution period: Evolution and impacts. *Journal of Agricultural Economics* 77 (2):268–278.

Caballero, R. J., and A. B. Jaffe. 1993. How high are the giant's shoulders? In *Macroeconomics annual 1993.* Cambridge, Mass.: National Bureau of Economic Research.

Capalbo, S. M. 1988. Measuring the components of aggregate productivity growth. *Western Journal of Agricultural Economics* 13:53–62.

Capalbo, S. M., and T. T. Vo. 1988. A review of the evidence on agricultural productivity and aggregate technology. In *Agricultural productivity: Measurement and explanation.* Washington, D.C.: Resources for the Future.

Cassman, S., and P. L. Pingali. 1993. Extrapolating trends from long-term experiments to farmers' fields: The case of irrigated rice systems in Asia. In *Proceedings of the Working Conference on Measuring Sustainability Using Long-Term Experiments.* Rothamsted Experimental Station, April 28–30, funded by the Rockefeller Foundation, Agricultural Science Division.

———. 1995. Extrapolating trends from long-term experiments to farmers' fields: The case of irrigated rice systems in Asia. In *Agricultural sustainability: Economic, environmental and statistical considerations.* New York: John Wiley & Sons.

Chamberlain, G. 1984. Panel data. In *Handbook of econometrics.* Amsterdam: North-Holland.

Chang, C. C. 1984. Conservation of rice genetic resources: Luxury or necessity? *Science* 224:251–256.

Chang, T. T. 1989. The case for a large collection. In *The uses of plant genetic resources,* ed. A. H. D. Brown, D. Frankel, D. R. Marshall, and J. T. Williams. Cambridge: Cambridge University Press.

———. 1992. Availability of plant germplasm for use in crop improvement. In *Plant breeding in the 1990s,* ed. H. T. Stalker and J. P. Murphy. Wallingford, U.K.: CAB International.

Chapman, S. C., and H. J. Barreto. 1994. Using simulation models and spatial databases to improve the efficiency of plant breeding programs. Paper presented to the GxE Workshop sponsored by the International Crops Research Institute for the Semi-Arid Tropics, Hyderabad, India, November 28–December 2.

Chen, Y. 1987. China, Republic of. In Asian Productivity Organization (APO), *Productivity measurement and analysis: Asian agriculture,* 133–193. Tokyo: Asian Productivity Organization.

China, Chung Yang ti chih tiao ch'a so. 1930–44. *T'u jang chuun pao (Soil bulletin).* 1 (1936)–24 (1944).

China, Office of the National Soil Survey. 1996. *Zhonggao turang pu cha Shu jiu.* Beijing: China Agricultural Department Publishers.

China, State Statistical Bureau. 1996. *China Statistical Yearbook 1996.* Beijing: China Statistical Publishing House.

Chopra, V. L. 1994. ICAR director general calls for strong NARS-CGIAR partnerships. *ISNAR Newsletter* (August). The Hague: International Service for National Agricultural Research (ISNAR).

Clark, C. 1976. *Mathematical bioeconomics: The optimal management of renewable resources.* New York: John Wiley & Sons.

Cohen, W. M., and R. C. Levin. 1989. Innovation and market structure. In *Handbook of industrial organization,* ed. R. Schmalensee and R. D. Willig. Amsterdam: Elsevier.

Committee on Natural Resources, United Nations Economic and Social Council. 1996. *Minerals and Agenda 21: Key issues.* New York: United Nations.

Constantine, J. H., J. M. Alston, and V. H. Smith. 1994. Economic impacts of the California one-variety cotton law. *Journal of Political Economy* 102 (5): 951–974.

Contracting Parties to the General Agreement of Tariffs and Trade, Uruguay Round. 1994. *World Trade Agreement* (establishing the WTO and including GATT 1994). Marrakesh.

Cox, T., J. Mullen, and W. Hu. 1996. Nonparametric measures of the impacts of public research and extension on Australian broadacre agriculture: Preliminary results. Paper contributed to the conference Global Agricultural Science Policy for the 21st Century. Melbourne, Australia, August 26–28.

Cox, T. S., J. P. Murphy, and M. M. Goodman. 1988. The Contribution of exotic germplasm to American agriculture. In *Seeds and sovereignty: The use and control of plant genetic resources,* ed. J. R. Kloppenburg Jr. Durham, N.C.: Duke University.

Craig, B., and P. G. Pardey. 1990. *Multidimensional output indices.* Department of Agricultural and Applied Economics Staff Paper. St. Paul: University of Minnesota.

———. 1996a. *Agricultural capital services.* Davis: University of California.

———. 1996b. *Productivity measurement in the presence of quality change.* Washington, D.C.: Resources for the Future.

Craig, B. J., P. G. Pardey, and J. Roseboom. 1997. International productivity patterns: Accounting for input quality, infrastructure, and research. *American Journal of Agricultural Economics* 79 (4):1064–1076.

Crosson, P. 1985. National costs of erosion effects on productivity. In *Erosion and Soil Productivity,* Proceedings of the National Symposium on Erosion and Soil Productivity, New Orleans.

―――. 1995. *Soil erosion and its on-farm productivity consequences: What do we know?* Discussion Paper 95-29. Washington, D.C.: Resources for the Future.

Crosson, P., and A. Stout. 1983. *Productivity effects of cropland erosion in the United States.* Washington, D.C.: Resources for the Future.

Dalrymple, D. G., and J. P. Srivastava. 1994. Transfer of plant cultivars: Seeds, sectors and society. In *Agricultural technology: Policy issues for the international community,* ed. J. R. Anderson. Wallingford, U.K.: CAB International.

Daly, H. 1995. On Wilfred Beckerman's critique of sustainable development. *Environmental Values* 4:49–56.

Darrah, L. L., and M. S. Zuber. 1986. 1985 United States farm maize germplasm base and commercial breeding strategies. *Crop Science* 26:1109–1113.

Dasgupta, P. A., and K-G Mäler. 1990. The environment and emerging development issues. In *Proceedings of the World Bank Annual Conference on Development Economics.* Washington, D.C.: World Bank.

David, C., and K. Otsuka. 1994. *Modern rice technology and income distribution in Asia.* Los Baños, the Philippines: International Rice Research Institute.

David, C. D., and R. E. Evenson. 1993. Rice technology and structural change. In *Technology and developing country agriculture,* ed. C. Brenner. Paris: OECD.

Davis, C. E., B. M. Rifkind, H. Gordon, and D. J. Gordon. 1990. A single cholesterol measurement underestimates the risk of coronary heart disease: An empirical example from the Lipid Research Clinics Mortality Follow-up Study. *Journal of the American Medical Association* 264:3044–3046.

Davis, J. S., P. A. Oram, and J. G. Ryan. 1987. *Assessment of agricultural research priorities: An international perspective.* Canberra: Australian Centre for International Agricultural Research (ACIAR).

Deininger, K. W. 1993. Technical change, human capital, and spillovers in U.S. agriculture, 1949–85. Ph.D. diss., University of Minnesota.

Department of the Environment and Government Statistical Service. 1996. *Indicators of sustainable development for the United Kingdom.* London: Her Majesty's Stationery Office (HMSO).

Dey, M. M., and R. E. Evenson. 1991. *The economic impact of rice research in Bangladesh.*Gazipur, Bangladesh; Los Baños, Laguna, Philippines; and Dhaka, Banglesh: Bangladesh Rice Research Institute, International Rice Research Institute, and Bangladesh Agricultural Research Council. Mimeo.

Dholakia, R. H., and B. H. Dholakia. 1993. Growth of total factor productivity in Indian agriculture. *Indian Economic Review* 28 (1):25–40.

Diemont, W. H., A. C. Smiet, and Nurdin. 1991. Re-thinking erosion on Java. *Netherlands Journal of Agricultural Science* 39:213–224.

Diewert, W. E. 1976. Extract and superlative index numbers. *Journal of Econometrics* 115–145.

Dixit, A., and V. Norman. 1978. Advertising and welfare. *Bell Journal of Economics* 1:1–17.

Doran, J. W., D. C. Coleman, D. F. Bexdicek, and B. A. Stewart. 1994. *Defining soil quality for a sustainable environment.* Madison, Wisc.: Soil Science Society of America and American Society of Agronomy.

Dorfman, R., and P. O. Steiner. 1954. Optimal advertising and optimal quality. *American Economic Review* 826–836.

Downey, K., and G. Robbelen. 1989. Brassica species. In *Oilcrops of the world,* ed. G. Robbelen, K. Downey, and A. Ashri. New York: McGraw-Hill.

Drechler, L. 1973. Weighting of index numbers in multilateral international comparisons. *Review of Income and Wealth* 17–35.

Dregne, H. E. 1982. *Impact of land degradation on future world food production.* Washington, D.C.: U.S. Department of Agriculture, Economic Research Service, International Economics Division.

Dupont, J., P. J. White, K. M. Johnston, H. A. Heggteit, B. E. McDonald, S. M. Grudy, and A. Bonarome. 1989. Food safety and health effects of canola oil. *Journal of the American College of Nutrition* 8:360–375.

Duvick, D. N. 1984. Genetic diversity in major farm crops on the farm and in reserve. *Economic Botany* 38:161–178.

———. 1996. *What is yield?* Summary poster workshop. Johnson, Iowa: Centro Internacional de Mejoramiento de Maiz y Trigo (CIMMYT).

Dwidjono, H. D. 1993. Rice varietal improvements and productivity growth in Indonesia. Ph.D. diss., University of the Philippines, Los Baños.

Dyson, T. 1994. Population growth and food production: Recent global and regional trends. *Population and Development Review* 20 (2): 397–411.

———. 1995. World food demand and supply prospects. Paper presented to the International Fertilizer Society, December, Cambridge, U.K.

Eckholm, E. P. 1976. *Losing ground: Environmental stress and world food prospects.* New York: W. W. Norton.

Ehrlich, P. 1968. *The population bomb.* New York: Sierra Club–Ballantine.

Englander, A. S. 1991. International technology transfer and agricultural productivity. In *Research and productivity in Asian agriculture,* ed. R. E. Evenson and C. E. Pray. Ithaca, N.Y.: Cornell University Press.

Epperson, J. E., D. Pachico, and C. L. Guevara. 1997. A cost analysis of maintaining cassava plant genetic resources. *Crop Science* 37:1641–1649.

Evenson, R. E. 1974. The Green Revolution in recent development experience. *American Journal of Agricultural Economics* 56:387–394.

———. 1978. The organization of research to improve crops and animals in low-income countries. In *Distortions of agricultural incentives,* ed. T. W. Schultz. Bloomington: Indiana University Press.

———. 1984. International invention: Implications for technology market analysis. In *R&D patents, and productivity.* Chicago: University of Chicago Press.

———. 1989. Spillover benefits of agricultural research: Evidence from the U.S. experience. *American Journal of Agricultural Economics* 71:447–452.

———. 1991. Genetic resources: Assessing economic value. Economic Growth Center, Yale University, New Haven, Conn. Mimeo.

———. 1994. Analyzing the transfer of agricultural technology. In *Agricultrual technology: Policy issues for the international community,* ed. J. R. Anderson. Wallingford, U.K.: CAB International.

———. 1998a. Crop-loss data and trait value estimates for rice in Indonesia. In *Agri-*

cultural values of plant genetic resources, ed. R. E. Evenson, D. Gollin, and V. Santaniello. Wallingford, U.K.: CAB International.

———. 1998b. Modern varieties, traits, commodity supply and factor demand in Indian agriculture. In *Agricultural values of plant genetic resources,* ed. R. E. Evenson, D. Gollin, and V. Santaniello. Wallingford, U.K.: CAB International.

———. 2000. Crop genetic improvement and agricultural development. Document No. SDR/TAC:IAR/00/17, CGIAR Mid-Term 2000 Meetings, Dresden, Germany, May 11–16.

Evenson, R. E., and H. P. Binswanger. 1978. Technology transfer and research resource allocation. In *Induced innovation: Technology, institutions, and development,* ed. H. P. Binswanger and V. W. Ruttan. Baltimore: Johns Hopkins University Press.

Evenson, R. E., and E. R. da Cruz. 1992. Economic impact of the PROCISUR programme: An international study. In *Issues in agricultural development: Sustainability and cooperation,* ed. M. Bellamy and B. Greenshields. IAAE Occasional Paper No. 6. London: Gower for the International Association of Agricultural Economists.

Evenson, R. E., and D. Gollin. 1997. Genetic resources, international organizations and rice varietal improvement. *Economic Development and Cultural Change* 45 (3):471–500.

Evenson, R. E., D. Gollin, and V. Santaniello. 1998. *Agricultural values of plant genetic resources.* Wallingford, U.K.: CAB International.

Evenson, R. E., R. W. Herdt, and M. Hossain. 1996. *Rice research in Asia: Progress and priorities.* Wallingford, U.K.: CAB International.

Evenson, R. E., and Y. Kislev. 1975. *Agricultural research and productivity.* New Haven: Yale University Press.

Evenson, R. E., D. Landau, and D. Ballou. 1987. Agricultural productivity measures for U.S. states, 1950–82. In *Evaluating agricultural research and productivity.* St. Paul: University of Minnesota.

Evenson, R. E., and J. W. McKinsey Jr. 1991. Research, extension, infrastructure, and productivity change in Indian agriculture. In *Research and productivity in Asian agriculture,* ed. R. E. Evenson and C. E. Pray. Ithaca, N.Y.: Cornell University Press.

Evenson, R. E., C. E. Pray, and M. W. Rosegrant. 1998. *Agricultural research and productivity in India.* Research Report 109. Washington, D.C.: IFPRI.

Evenson, R. E., and K. P. C. Rao. 1998. Varietal trait values for rice in India. In *Agricultural values of plant genetic resources.* Wallingford, U.K.: CABI.

Evenson, R. E., and M. Rosegrant. 1995. Productivity projections for commodity market modeling. Paper presented at workshop "Projections and Policy Implications of Medium and Long-Term Rice Supply and Demand," sponsored by the International Food Policy Research Institute, International Rice Research Institute, and China Center for Economic Research, Beijing, April 23–26.

Expert Panel on Detection, Evaluation and Treatment of High Blood Cholesterol in Adults. 1988. Summary report on the National Cholesterol Education Program Expert Panel on Detection, Evaluation and Treatment of High Blood Cholesterol in Adults. *Archives of Internal Medicine* 148 (January):36–39.

———. 1993. Summary of the Second Report on the National Cholesterol Education Program Expert Panel on Detection, Evaluation and Treatment of High Blood Cholesterol in Adults. *Journal of the American Medical Association* 3015–3023.

Eyzaguirre, P. 1996. *Agriculture and environmental research in small countries: Innovative approaches to strategic planning.* Chichester: John Wiley & Sons.

Fan, S. 1990. *Regional productivity growth in China's agriculture.* Boulder, Colo.: Westview Press.

———. 1991. Effects of technological change and institutional reform on production growth in Chinese agriculture. *American Journal of Agricultural Economics* 73 (2):266–275.

Fan, S., and P. Hazell. 1997. Technologies, infrastructure, productivity growth and poverty alleviation in rural india: Policy implications for government investments in less-favored Areas. Draft paper. International Food Policy Research Institute, Washington, D.C.

Faucheux, S., D. Pearce, and J. Proops, eds. 1996. *Models of sustainable development.* Cheltenham, U.K.: Edward Elgar.

Fernandez-Cornejo, J., and C. R. Shumway. 1997. Research and productivity in Mexican agriculture. *American Journal of Agricultural Economics* 79 (3):738–753.

Ferro-Luzzi, A., P. Strazzullo, C. Scaccini, A. Siani, S. Sette, M. A. Mariani, P. Mastranzo, R. M. Dougherty, J. M. Iacono, and M. Mancini. 1984. Changing the Mediterranean diet: Effects on blood lipids. *American Journal of Clinical Nutrition* 40:1027–1037.

Fowler, C. 1994. *Unnatural selection: Technology, politics, and plant evolution.* Yverdon, Switzerland: Gordon and Breach.

Fowler, C., and P. Mooney. 1990. *Shattering: Food politics and the loss of genetic diversity.* Tucson: University of Arizona Press.

Fox, P. N. 1995. *Impact of CIMMYT wheats in Australia: Evidence of international research spillovers.* Wagga Wagga: New South Wales Agriculture.

Frankfurt, H. 1997. Equality and respect. *Social Research* 64 (1).

Frye, W. W., and G. W. Thomas. 1991. Management of long-term experiments. *Agronomy Journal* 83 (1):38–43.

Gisselquist, D. 1994. *Import barriers for agricultural inputs.* UNDP–World Bank Trade Expansion Paper 10. Washington, D.C.: World Bank.

Gizlice, Z., T. E. Carter Jr., and J. W. Burton. 1994. Crop breeding, genetics, and cytology. *Crop Science* 34:1143–1151.

Gollin, D., and R. E. Evenson. 1996. The economic impact of the International Rice Germplasm Center (IRGC) and the International Network for the Genetic Evaluation of Rice (INGER). In *Economic development and cultural change.* Los Baños, the Philippines: International Rice Research Institute.

———. 1998a. An application of hedonic pricing methods to value rice genetic resources in India. In *Agricultural values of plant genetic resources,* ed. R. E. Evenson, D. Gollin, and V. Santaniello. Wallingford, U.K.: CAB International.

———. 1998b. Breeding values of rice genetic resources. In *Agricultural values of plant genetic resources,* ed. R. E. Evenson, D. Gollin, and V. Santaniello. Wallingford, U.K.: CAB International.

Goodin, R. 1983. Ethical principles for environmental protection. In *Environmental philosophy,* ed. R. Eliot and A. Garde. Brisbane, Australia: University of Queensland Press.

Goodman, M. M. 1990. Genetic and germ plasm stocks worth conserving. *Journal of Heredity* 81:11–16.

Gordon, H. S. 1954. Economic theory of a common property resource: The fishery. *Journal of Political Economy* 62:274–286.

Graves, S. B., and N. S. Langowitz. 1993. Innovative productivity and returns to scale in the pharmaceutical industry. *Strategic Management Journal* 14:593–605.

Greengrass, B. 1993. Non-U.S. protection procedures and practices: Implications for U.S. innovators? In *Intellectual property rights: Protection of plant materials,* ed. S. Baenziger, R. A. Kleese, and R. F. Barnes. CSSA Special Publication No. 21. Madison, Wisc.: Crop Science Society of America, American Society of Agronomy, and Soil Science Society of America.

Griliches, Z. 1958. Research cost and social returns: Hybrid corn and related innovations. *Journal of Political Economy* 66 (5):419–431.

———. 1964. Research expenditures, education, and the aggregate agricultural production function. *American Economic Review* 54 (6):961–974.

———. 1973. Research expenditures and growth accounting. In *Science and technology in economic growth,* ed. B. R. Williams. London: Macmillan.

———. 1979. Issues in assessing the contribution of R&D to productivity growth. *Bell Journal of Economics* 10 (1):92–116.

———. 1981. Market value, R&D, and patents. *Economics Letters* 7:183–187.

———. 1990. Patent statistics as economic indicators: A survey. *Journal of Economic Literature* 28 (4):1661–1707.

———. 1992. The search for R&D spillovers. *Scandanavian Journal of Economics* 94 (supplement):529–547

———. 1994. Productivity, R&D, and data constraint. *American Economic Review* 84 (1):1–23.

———. 1995. R&D and productivity: Econometric results and measurement issues. In *Handbook of the economics of innovation and technological change,* ed. P. Stoneman. Oxford: Basil Blackwell.

———. 1996. The discovery of the residual: A historical note. *Journal of Economic Literature* 34 (September):1324–1330.

Griliches, Z., and F. Lichtenberg. 1984. R&D and productivity growth at the industry level: Is there still a relationship? In *R&D, patents, and productivity,* ed. Z. Griliches. Chicago: University of Chicago Press.

Griliches, Z., and J. Mairesse. 1984. Productivity and R&D at the firm level. In *R&D, patents, and productivity,* ed. Z. Griliches. Chicago: University of Chicago Press.

———. 1995. *Production functions: The search for identification.* Cambridge, Mass.: National Bureau of Economic Research.

Griliches, Z., and H. Regev. 1995. Firm productivity in Israeli industry, 1979–88. *Journal of Econometrics* 65:175–203.

Grossman, G. M., and E. Helpman. 1991. *Innovation and growth in the global economy.* Cambridge: MIT Press.

Hall, B. H. 1993. Industrial research in the 1980s: Did the rate of return fall? *Brookings Papers on Economic Activity* 2:289–331.

———. 1996. The private and social returns to research and development. In *Technology, R&D, and the economy,* ed. B. Smith and C. Barfield. Washington, D.C.: Brookings Institution and American Enterprise Institute (AEI) Press.

Hall, B. H., and R. E. Hall. 1993. The value and performance of U.S. corporations. *Brookings Papers on Economic Activity* 1–50.

Hall, B. H., and F. Hayashi. 1989. *Research and development as an investment.* NBER Working Paper No. 2973. Cambridge, Mass.: National Bureau of Economic Research.

Halse, N. J. 1994. Lessons from attempts to transfer farming technologies from Mediterranean Australia to West Asia and North Africa. In *Agricultural technology: Policy issues for the international community,* ed. J. R. Anderson. Wallingford, U.K.: CAB International.

Hammond, K. 1996. The status of global farm animal genetic resources. Paper presented at the Symposium on the Economics of Valuation and Conservation of Genetic Resrouces for Agriculture, Centre for International Studies on Economic Growth, Tor Vergata University, Rome, May 13–15.

Hanson, J., J. T. Williams, and R. Freund. 1984. *Institutes conserving crop germplasm: The IBPGR global network of genebanks.* Rome: International Board for Plant Genetic Resources.

Hargrove, T. R., W. R. Coffman, and V. L. Cabanilla. 1990. Ancestry of improved cultivars of Asian rice. *Crop Science* 20:721–727.

Hausman, J., B. H. Hall, and Z. Griliches. 1984. Econometric models for count data with an application to the patents-R&D relationship. *Econometrica* 52:909–938.

Hayami, Y., and V. Ruttan. 1985. *Agricultural development:An international perspective.* Baltimore: Johns Hopkins University Press.

Heady, B. H., and J. Dillon. 1961. *Agricultural production functions.* Ames: Iowa State University Press.

Hegsted, D. M., R. B. McGandy, M. L. Myers, and F. J. Stare. 1965. Quantitative effects of dietary fat on serum cholesterol in man American. *Journal of Clinical Nutrition* 17:282–295.

Heisey, P. W., and M. Smale. 1995. *Maize technology in Malawi: A Green Revolution in the making?* CIMMYT Research Report No. 4. Mexico City: Centro Internacional de Mejoramiento de Maiz y Trigo (CIMMYT).

Henning, S. A., and B. R. Eddleman. 1986. Intra- and inter-state transferability of soybean variety research. *Southern Journal of Agricultural Economics* 18 (2):7–13.

Herdt, R. W. 1988. Increasing crop yields in developing countries. *Proceedings of the 1988 Meeting of the American Agricultural Economics Association,* July 30–August 3, Knoxville, Tenn.

Heston, A., R. Summers, D. A. Nuxoll, and B. Aten. 1995. *The Penn world tables mark 5.6 electronic dataset.* Philadelphia: University of Pennsylvania.

Higgins, G. M., A. H. Kassam, L. Naiken, G. Fischer, and M. M. Shah. 1982. *Potential population supporting capacities of lands in the developing world.* Rome: Food and Agriculture Organization (FAO), United Nation Fund for Population Activities, and International Institute for Applied Systems Analysis.

Hoch, I. 1955. Estimation of production function parameters and testing for efficiency. *Econometrica* 3:325–326.

Hodgkin, T. 1991. Improving utilization of plant genetic resources through core collections. In *Rice germplasm: Collecting, preservation, use.* Los Baños, the Philippines: International Rice Research Institute.

Homans, F. 1993. Modeling regulated open access resource use. Ph.D. diss., University of California, Davis, Department of Agricultural and Resource Economics.

Homans, F., and J. Wilen. 1997. A model of regulated open access resource use. *Journal of Environmental Economics and Management* 30 (1):1–21.

Howarth, R. B., and R. B. Norgaard. 1992. Environmental valuation under sustainable development. *American Economic Review* 82 (2):473–477.

Huang, J., and S. Rozelle. 1995. Environmental stress and grain yields in China. *American Journal of Agricultural Economics* 77 (4):853–864.

Huffman, W. E., and R. E. Evenson. 1993. *Science for agriculture: A long-term perspective.* Ames: Iowa State University Press.

Hulten, C. R. 1992. Growth accounting when technical change is embodied in capital. *American Economic Review* 2:964–980.

Industry Commission. 1995. *Research and development.* Report No. 44. Canberra: Australian Government Printing Office.

Jacobs, M. 1995. Sustainable development, capital substitution, and economic humility: A response to Beckerman. *Environmental Values* 4:57–68.

Jaffe, A. B., M. Trajtenberg, and R. Henderson. 1993. Geographic localization of knowledge spillovers as evidenced by patent citations. *Quarterly Journal of Economics* 10:577–598.

Jain, K. B. L, and D. Byerlee. 1999. Investment efficiency at the national level: Wheat improvement research in India. In *The global wheat improvement system: Prospects for enhancing efficiency in the presence of spillovers.* ed. M. K. Maredia and D. Byerlee. Research Report No. 5. Mexico City: Centro Internacional de Mejoramiento de Maiz y Trigo (CIMMYT).

Jensen, E. J. 1987. Research expenditures and the discovery of drugs. *Journal of Industrial Economics* 36:83–95.

Johnson, D. G. 1995. China's future food supply: Will China starve the world? University of Chicago. Mimeo.

Jones, C. I. 1995. R&D-based models of economic growth. *Journal of Political Economy* 4:759–784.

Jong, S. C., and J. M. Birmingham. 1996. Genetic resources of patented seeds available to the public worldwide. *Plant Genetic Resources* 106:35–38.

Jorgenson, D. W. 1973. The economic theory of replacement and depreciation. In *Econometrics and economic theory.* New York: Macmillan.

Jorgenson, D. W., and F. M. Gallop. 1992. Productivity growth in U.S. agriculture: A postwar perspective. *American Journal of Agricultural Economics* 3:745–750.

Jorgenson, D. W., and Z. Griliches. 1967. The explanation of productivity change. *Review of Economic Studies* 349–383.

Juma, C. 1989. *The gene hunters: Biotechnology and the scramble for seeds.* Princeton: Princeton University Press.

Kalirajan, K. P., M. B. Obwona, and S. Zhao. 1996. A decomposition of total factor productivity growth: The case of Chinese agricultural growth before and after reforms. *American Journal of Agricultural Economics* 78 (2):331–338.

Kamien, M. I., and N. L. Schwartz. 1982. *Market structure and innovation.* Cambridge: Cambridge University Press.

Kassam, A. 1991. Estimate of total arable land by AEZ by country, 1990. Technical Advisory Committee of the Consultative Group on International Agricultural Research, Rome. Mimeo.

Keys, A. 1970. Coronary heart disease in seven countries. *Circulation* 1–211.

Keys, A., J. T. Anderson, and F. Grande. 1965. Serum cholesterol response to changes in the diet: Iodine value of dietary fat versus 2S–P. *Metabolism* 114:747–758.

Khush, G. S. 1995. Modern varieties: Their real contribution to food supply and equity. *Geojournal* 35 (3):275–284.

Kikuchi, M., and Y. Hayami. 1978. Agricultural growth against a land resource constraint: A comparative history of Japan, Taiwan, Korea, and the Philippines. *Journal of Economic History* 38 (December).

Klette, T. J. 1994. *R&D, scope economies and company structure: A "not so fixed effect" model of plant performance.* Oslo: Statistics Norway. Mimeo.

Klette, T. J., and Z. Griliches with T. J. Klette. 1996. The inconsistency of common scale estimators when output prices are unobserved and endogenous. *Journal of Applied Econometrics* 343–361.

Kneen, B. 1992. *The rape of canola.* Toronto: NC Press.

Knudson, M. K., and V. Ruttan. 1988. Research and development of a biological innovation: Commercial hybrid wheat. *Food Research Institute Studies* 21 (1): 45–68.

Kovda, V. A. 1959. *Ocherki prirody i pochv Kitaia.* [Notes on nature and soils of China]. Moscow.

Kumar, P., and Mruthyunjaya. 1992. Measurement analysis of total factor productivity growth in wheat. *Indian Journal of Agricultural Economics* 47 (3):451–458.

Kumar, P., and M. W. Rosegrant. 1994. Productivity and sources of growth for rice in India. *Economic and Political Weekly* 29 (December 31):A183–188.

Lach, S. 1994. *Non-rivalry of knowledge and R&D's contribution to productivity.* Jerusalem: Hebrew University.

Lal, D. 1976. Agricultural growth, real wages, and the rural poor in India. *Economic and Political Weekly* 11 (26):A47–61.

Lal, R., G. F. Hall, and F. P. Miller. 1989. Soil degradation: I. Basic processes. *Land Degradation and Rehabilitation* 1:51–69.

Lau, L. J., and P. A. Yotopoulos. 1989. The meta-production function approach to technological change in world agriculture. *Journal of Development Economics* 31 (2):241–269.

Lemieux, C. M., and M. K. Wohlgenant. 1989. Ex ante evaluation of the economic impact of agricultural biotechnology: The case of porcine somatotropia. *American Journal of Agricultural Economics* 71:903–914.

Lin, J. Y. 1992. Rural reforms and agricultural growth in China. *American Economic Review* 82 (1):34–51.

Lindert, P. H. 1999. The bad earth?: China's soils and agricultural development since the 1930s. *Economic Development and Cultural Change* 47 (4):701–736.

———. 1997. *A half-century of soil change in Indonesia.* Davis: University of California.

Lindert, P. H., J. Lu, and W. Wu. 1995. *Soil trends in China since the 1930s.* Agricultural History Center Working Paper No. 79. Davis: University of California.

———. 1996a. Trends in the soil chemistry of North China since the 1930s. *Journal of Environmental Quality* 25 (4):1168–1178.

————. 1996b. Trends in the soil chemistry of South China since the 1930s. *Soil Science* 161 (5):329–342.

Lopez-Pereira, M. A., and M. L. Morris. 1994. *Impacts of international maize breeding research in the developing world, 1966–90.* Mexico City: Centro Internacional de Mejoramiento de Maiz y Trigo (CIMMYT).

Mairesse, J., and Z. Griliches. 1990. Heterogeneity in panel data: Are there stable production functions? In *Essays in honor of Edmond Malinvaud.* Cambridge: MIT Press.

Mairesse, J., and B. H. Hall. 1996. Estimating the productivity of research and development in French and U.S. manufacturing firms: An exploration of simultaneity issues with GMM methods. In *International productivity differences and their explanations.* London: Elsevier Science.

Mairesse, J., and P. Mohnen. 1995. R&D and productivity: A survey of the economic literature. Institut National de la Statistique et des Etudes Economiques (INSEE), Paris. Mimeo.

Mairesse, J., and M. Sassenou. 1991. *R&D and productivity: A survey of the econometric studies at the firm level.* Paris: OECD.

Malla, S. 1996. The distribution of the economic and health benefits from canola research. M.S. thesis, University of Saskatchewan, Department of Agricultural Economics.

Malla, S., R. S. Gray, and A. Stephen. 1995. *The health care cost of savings due to canola consumption in Canada.* Saskatoon: University of Saskatchewan.

Malthus goes east. 1995. *Economist,* August 12, 29.

Manski, C. F. 1991. Identification of endogenous social effects. *Review of economic studies* 3:531–542.

Maredia, M., and D. Byerlee. 1996. Efficiency of wheat improvement research: A comparative analysis of national and international research systems in developing countries. Paper presented at the conference Global Agricultural Science Policy for the 21st Century, August 25–28, Melbourne, Australia.

————. 1997. Determining the efficiency of research in the presence of international spillovers: Wheat research in developing countries. In *Efficiency of investment in national and international wheat improvement research,* ed. M. Maredia and D. Byerlee. Mexico City: Centro Internacional de Mejoramiento de Maiz y Trigo (CIMMYT).

————. 2000. Efficiency of research investments in the presence of international spillovers: Wheat research in developing countries. *Agricultural Economics* 22 (1):1–16.

Maredia, M., D. Byerlee, and R. Ward. 1996. Econometric estimation of a global spillover matrix for wheat varietal technology. *Agricultural Economics* 14 (3): 159–173.

Margalit, A. 1996. *The decent society.* Cambridge: Harvard University Press.

Marschak, J., and W. Andrews. 1944. Random simultaneous equations and the theory of production. *Econometrica* 143–205.

Mitchell, D. O., and M. D. Ingco. 1995. Global and regional food demand and supply prospects. In *Population and food in the early 21st century: Meeting the future demand of an increasing population,* ed. N. Islam. Washington, D.C.: International Food Policy Research Institute.

Moore, R., Y. Mao, J. Zhang, and K.Clark. 1996. Economic burden of illness in Canada, 1993. *Chronic Diseases in Canada.* Special Supplement (November).

Moore, S. 1992. So much for "scarce resources." *Public Interest* 106 (Winter):97–107.

Mujeeb-Kazi, A., and G. P. Hettel, eds. 1995. *Utilizing wild grass biodiversity in wheat improvement: 15 years of wide cross research at CIMMYT.* CIMMYT Research Report No. 2. Mexico City: Centro Internacional de Mejoramiento de Maiz y Trigo (CIMMYT).

Mundlak, Y. 1961. Empirical production function free of management bias. *Journal of Farm Economics* 44–56.

Murgai, R. 1997. Diversity in economic growth and technical change: A districtwise disaggregation of the Punjab and Haryana growth experience. Draft paper. World Bank, Washington, D.C.

Nadiri, M. I. 1993. *Innovations and technological spillovers.* Cambridge, Mass.: National Bureau of Economic Research.

Narayanan, S. 1996. Multi-factor productivity indexes for Canadian agriculture: Recent update, methodology, data, policy relevance, and growth comparisons (Canada, United States, European Union). Paper contributed to the conference Global Agricultural Science Policy for the 21st Century, August 26–28, Melbourne, Australia.

Narrod, C., and C. E. Pray. 2000. Technology, policies, and the global poultry revolution. Paper presented at the 24th International Conference of Agricultural Economists, August 13–19, Berlin.

National Research Council (NRC) Committee on Genetic Vulnerability of Major Crops. 1972. *Genetic vulnerability of major crops.* Washington, D.C.: National Academy of Sciences.

National Research Council (NRC) Committee on Managing Global Genetic Resources: Agricultural Imperatives. 1991. *Managing global genetic resources: The U.S. national plant system.* Washington, D.C.: National Academy Press.

———. 1993. *Agricultural crop issues and policies: Managing global genetic resources.* Washington, D.C.: National Academy Press.

Naylor, R. 1992. The rural labor market in Indonesia. In *Rice policy in Indonesia,* ed. S. S. Pearson. Ithaca, N.Y.: Cornell University Press.

Nerlove, M. 1958. *Distribution lags and demand analysis.* Washington, D.C.: United States Department of Agriculture.

Nguyen, D. 1979. On agricultural productivity differences among countries. *Journal of Agricultultural and Resource Economics* 61 (3):565–570.

Nordfeldt, S., N. Gellerstedt, and S. Falkmer. 1954. Studies with rapeseed oilmeal and its goitrogenic effect in pigs. *Acta Pathological et Microbiological Scandinavia* 35:217–236.

Norgaard, R. 1992. *Sustainability and the economics of assuring assets for future generations.* World Bank Policy Research Working Paper No. 832. Washington, D.C.: World Bank.

Nozick, R. 1989. *The examined life.* New York: Simon and Schuster.

Oils world annual. 1993. Hamburg: ISTA Mielke Gmbh.

Oldeman, L. R., R. T. A. Hakkeling, and W. G. Sombroek. 1991. *World map of the status of human-induced soil degradation: An explanatory note.* Rev. 2d ed. Wageningen, the Netherlands: United Nations Environment Programme (UNEP), International Soil Reference and Information Center.

Olley, S., and A. Pakes. 1996. The dynamics of productivity in the telecommunications equipment industry. *Econometrica* 6:1263–1297.

Orleans, L. A. 1992. Loss and misuse of China's cultivated land. In *China's economic dilemmas in the 1990s: The problems of reforms, modernization, and independence,* ed. U.S. Congress, Joint Economic Committee. Armonk, N.Y.: M. E. Sharpe.

Orton, T. J. 1988. New technologies and the enhancement of crop germplasm diversity. In *Seeds and sovereignty: The use and control of plant genetic resources,* ed. J. R. Kloppenburg Jr. Durham, N.C.: Duke University Press.

Oster, G., and A. M. Epstein. 1986. Primary prevention and coronary heart disease: The economic benefits of lowering serum cholesterol. *American Journal of Public Health* 78:647–656.

Oster, G., and D. Thompson. 1996. Estimated effects of reducing dietary saturated fat intake on the incidence and costs of coronary heart disease in the United States. *American Journal of Public Health* 96:127–131.

Ostrom, E. 1990. *Governing the commons: The evolution of institutions for collective action.* Cambridge: Cambridge University Press.

Ostrom, E., R. Gardner, and J. Walker. 1994. *Rules, games, and common-pool resources.* Ann Arbor: University of Michigan Press.

Pakes, A. 1985. On patents, R&D and the stock market rate of return. *Journal of Political Economy* 2:390–409.

Pardey, P. G., J. M. Alston, J. E. Christian, and S. Fan. 1996. *A productive partnership: The benefits from U.S. participation in the CGIAR.* Washington, D.C.: Consultative Group on International Agricultural Research.

Pardey, P. G., B. Craig, and K. W. Deninger. 1994. A new look at state-level productivity growth in U.S. agriculture. In *Evaluating research and productivity in an era of resource scarcity.* St. Paul: University of Minnesota.

Pardey, P. G., R. Lindner, E. Abdurachman, S. Wood, S. Fan, W. M. Eveleens, B. Zhang, and J. M. Alston. 1992. The economic returns to Indonesian rice and soybean research. Draft paper. Agency for Agricultural Research and Development (AARD) and International Service for National Agricultural Research, Jakarta and the Hague.

Pardey, P. G., J. Roseboom, and J. R. Anderson. 1991. Topical perspectives on national agricultural research. In *Agricultural research policy: International quantitative perspectives,* ed. P. G. Pardey, J. Roseboom, and J. R. Anderson. Cambridge: Cambridge University Press.

Pardey, P. G., J. Roseboom, and B. Craig. 1992. A yardstick for international comparisons: An application to national agricultural research expenditures. *Economic Development and Cultural Change* 40 (2):333–350.

———. 1999. Agricultural R&D investments and impacts. In *Paying for Agricultural Productivity,* ed. J. M. Alston, P. G. Pardey, and V. H. Smith. Baltimore: Johns Hopkins University Press for the International Food Policy Research Institute.

Pardey, P. G., and S. Wood. 1994. Targeting research by agricultural environments. In *Agricultural technology: Policy issues for the international community,* ed. J. R. Anderson. Wallingford, U.K.: CAB International.

Pasek, J. 1992. Obligations to future generations: A philosophical note. *World Development* 29:513–521.

Peters, L. H. 1995. The Canadian canola industry in the context of world oilseeds complex. M.Sc. thesis, University of Manitoba.

Peterson, W. 1986. Land quality and prices. *American Journal of Agricultural Economics* 68 (4):812–819.

Pezzey, J. 1992. *Sustainable development concepts: An economic analysis.* World Bank Environment Paper No. 2. Washington, D.C.: World Bank.

Pierce, F. J., W. E. Larson, R. H. Dowdy, and W. A. P. Graham. 1983. Productivity of soils: Assessing long-term changes due to erosion. *Journal of Soil and Water Conservation* 38 (1):39–44.

Pingali, P. L. 1992. Diversifying Asian rice farming systems: A deterministic paradigm. In *Trends in agricultural diversification: Regional perspectives,* ed. S. Barghouti, L. Garbux, and D. Umali.. Washington, D.C.: World Bank.

Pingali, P. L., Y. Bigot, and H. P. Binswanger. 1987. *Agricultural mechanization and the evolution of farming systems in Sub-Saharan Africa.* Baltimore: Johns Hopkins University Press.

Pingali, P. L., and H. P. Binswanger. 1987. Population density and agricultural intensification: A study of the evolution of technologies in tropical agriculture. In *Population growth and economic development: Issues and evidence,* ed. D. G. Johnson and R. D. Lee. London: University of Wisconsin.

Pingali, P. L., M. Hossain, and R. Gerpacio. 1997. *Rice bowls of Asia: The returning crisis?* Wallingford, U.K.: International Rice Research Institute and CAB International.

Pingali, P. L., P. Moya, and L. E. Velasco. 1990. *The post–Green Revolution blues in Asian rice production: The diminished gap between experiment station and farmer yields.* Social Science Division Paper No. 90-01. Manila: International Rice Research Institute.

Pingali, P. L., and M. Rosegrant. 1993. Confronting the environmental consequences of the Green Revolution in Asia. In *Proceedings of the 1993 American Agricultural Economist Association International Pre-Conference on Post Green Revolution Agricultural Development Strategies in the Third World: What Next.*

Pingali, P. L., and G. Traxler. 1997. International linkages in wheat varietal improvement: Will incentives for cooperation persist in the 21st century? Paper presented at the 41st Annual Conference of the Australian Agricultural and Resource Economics Society, January 20–25, Gold Coast, Queensland.

Pingali, P. L., and V. T. Xuan. 1992. Vietnam: Decollectivization and rice productivity growth. *Economic Development and Cultural Change* 40 (4):697–718.

Pioneer Hi-Bred International, Inc. 1993. *Annual report.* Des Moines, Iowa: Pioneer Hi-Bred International.

Plucknett, D. L., J. H. Smith, J. T. Williams, and N. M. Anishetty. 1987. *Gene banks and the world's food.* Princeton: Princeton University Press.

Prairie Pools, Inc. Various years. *Prairies grain variety survey.*

Ramsey, F. 1928. A mathematical theory of saving. *Economic Journal* 38:543–559.

Rao, D. S. P., K. C. Sharma, and W. F. Shepherd. 1991. On the aggregation problem in international comparisons of agricultural production aggregates. *Journal of Development Economics* 35:197–204.

Rao, K. P. C., and R. E. Evenson. 1998. Varietal trait values for rice in India. In

Agricultural values of plant genetic resources, ed. R. E. Evenson, D. Gollin, and V. Santaniello. Wallingford, U.K.: CAB International.

Rapeseed Association of Canada. 1970. *Proceedings of the International Conference on the Science, Technology and Marketing of Rapeseed and Rapeseed Products.* Conference held in Sainte Adele, Quebec, 1970. Ottawa: Rapeseed Association of Canada in cooperation with the Department of Industry, Trade, and Commerce.

Rawls, J. 1972. *A theory of justice.* Oxford: Clarendon Press.

Raz, J. 1986. *The morality of freedom.* Oxford: Oxford University Press.

Reeder, B. A., A. Chockalingam, G. R. Dagenais, D. MacLean, Y. Mao, C. Nair, A. Petrasovits, A. Shuaib, A. T. Wielgosz, and E. Wilson. 1995. *Cardiovascular diseases in Canada, 1995.* Ottawa: Heart and Stroke Foundation of Canada.

Reiser, R., J. L. Probstfield, A. Silvers, L. W. Scott, M. L. Shorney, R. D. Wood, B. C. O'Brien, A. M. Gotto, D. Phil, and W. Insull. 1985. Plasma lipid and lipoprotein response of humans to beef fat, coconut oil and safflower oil. *American Journal of Clinical Nutrition* 42:190–197.

Rejesus, R. M., M. Smale, and M. van Ginkel. 1996. Wheat breeders' perspectives on genetic diversity and germplasm use: Findings from an international survey. *Plant Varieties and Seeds* 9 (3):129–147.

Reynolds, M., S. Rajaram, and A. McNab, eds. 1996. *Increasing the yield potential in wheat: Breaking the barriers.* Mexico City: Centro Internacional de Mejoramiento de Maiz y Trigo (CIMMYT).

Richter, M. K. 1966. Invariance axioms and economic indexes. *Econometrica* 739–755.

Rijsbergen, F. R., and M. G. Wolman, eds. 1984. *Quantification of the effect of erosion on soil productivity in an international context.* Delft, the Netherlands: Delft Hydraulics Laboratory.

Romer, P. M. 1990. Endogenous technological change. *Journal of Political Economy* 5:S71–S102

Rosegrant, M., and R. E. Evenson. 1993. Agricultural productivity growth in Pakistan and India: A comparative analysis. *Pakistan Development Review* 32 (4):433–451.

———. 1995. *Total factor productivity and sources for long-term growth in Indian agriculture.* EPTD Discussion Paper No. 7. Washington, D.C.: International Food Policy Research Institute (IFPRI).

Rosegrant, M., and P. L. Pingali. 1994. Policy and technology for rice productivity growth in Asia. *Journal of International Development* 6 (6):665–688.

Rudel, R., J. L. Haines, and J. K. Sawer. 1990. Effects of plasma lipoproteins of monosaturated, saturated, and polyunsaturated fatty acids in the diet of African green monkeys. *Journal of Lipid Research* 31:1873–1882.

Rural Advancement Foundation International (RAFI). 1987. *A report on the security of the world's major gene banks.* New York: RAFI.

———. 1994. *Conserving indiginous knowledge.* New York: United Nations Development Programme (UNDP).

Ruttan, V. 1978. Comment on the organization of research to improve crops and animals in low-income countries. In *Distortions of agricultural incentives,* ed. T. W. Schultz. Bloomington: Indiana University Press.

———. 1982. *Agricultural research policy.* Minneapolis: University of Minnesota.

Salhuana, W., Q. Jones, and R. Sevilla. 1991. The Latin American maize project: Model for rescue and use of irreplaceable germplasm. *Diversity* 7:40–41.

Salhuana, W., L. Pollak, and D. Tiffany. N.d. Public/private collaboration proposed to. strengthen quality and production of U.S. corn through maize germplasm enhancement. *NGRP Network News.*

Salmon, E. E. 1970. Rapeseed oil in poultry diets. *Proceedings of the International Conference on the Science, Technology and Marketing of Rapeseed and Rapeseed Products.* Ottawa: Rapeseed Association of Canada in cooperation with the Department of Industry, Trade, and Commerce.

Sanders, J. H., B. I. Shapiro, and S. Ramaswamy. 1996. *The economics of agricultural technology in semi-arid Sub-Saharan Africa.* Baltimore: Johns Hopkins University Press.

Saskatchewan Agriculture and Food. Various years. *Varieties of rain crops for Saskatchewan.* Saskatoon: Saskatchewan Agriculture and Food.

Sauer, F. D., and J. K. G. Kramer. 1983. The problems associated with the feedings of high erucic rapeseed oils and some fish oils to experimental animals. In *High and low erucic acid rapeseed oils,* ed. J. K. G. Kramer, F. D. Sauer, and W. J. Pidgen. New York: Academic Press.

Sayre, K. D., S. Rajaram, and R. A. Fischer. 1997. Yield potential in short bread wheats in Northwest Mexico. *Crop Science* 7:36–42.

Schaefer, M. B. 1957. Some considerations of population dynamics and economics in relation to the management of marine fisheries. *Journal of the Fisheries Research Board of Canada* 14:669–681.

Scherer, F. M. 1984. *Innovation and growth: Schumpeterian perspectives.* Cambridge: MIT Press.

Schultz, T. W. 1953. *The economic organization of agriculture.* New York: McGraw-Hill.

———. 1956. Reflections on agricultural production, output and supply. *Journal of Farm Economics* 3:748–762.

Schweikhardt, D. B., and J. T. Bonnen. 1992. Financing agricultural research in the presence of international benefit spillovers: The need for international cooperation and innovation. In *Sustainable agricultural development: The role of international cooperation,* ed. G. H. Peters and B. F. Stanton. London: Gower Publications.

Seay, N. J. 1993. Intellectual property rights. In *Intellectual property rights: Protection of plant materials,* ed. S. Baenziger, R. A. Kleese, and R. F. Barnes. CSSA Special Publication No. 21. Madison, Wisc: Crop Science Society of America, American Society of Agronomy, and Soil Science Society of America.

Sen, A. 1994. Population: Delusion and reality. *New York Review of Books,* September 22.

Shane, M., T. Roe, and M. Gopinath. 1998. *U.S. agricultural growth and productivity: An economywide perspective.* Agricultural Economic Report No. 758. Washington, D.C.: United States Department of Agriculture, Economic Research Service, Market and Trade Economics Division.

Sidhu, D. S., and D. Byerlee. 1992. *Technical change and wheat productivity in the Indian Punjab in the post–Green Revolution period.* CIMMYT Economics Working Paper 92-02. Mexico City: Centro Internacional de Mejoramiento de Maiz y Trigo (CIMMYT).

Silbernagel, M. J., and R. M. Hannan. 1992. Use of plant introductions to develop U.S. bean cultivars. In *Use of plant introductions in cultivar development,* Part 2, ed. H. L. Shands and L. E. Weisner. CSSA Special Publication No. 20. Madison, Wisc.: Crop Science Society of America.

Simon, J. L. 1996. *The ultimate resource 2.* Princeton: Princeton University Press.

Simpson, R. D., and R. A. Sedjo. 1996. The value of genetic resources for use in agricultural improvement. Paper presented at the Symposium on the Economics of Valuation and Conservation of Genetic Resources for Agriculture, Centre for International Studies on Economic Growth, Tor Vergatta University, Rome, May 13–15.

Smil, V. 1984. *The bad earth: Environmental degradation in China.* Armonk, N.Y.: M. E. Sharpe.

Smith, J. S. C. 1988. Diversity of United States hybrid maize germplasm: Isozymic and chromatographic evidence. *Crop Science* 28:63–69.

Smith, V. 1968. Economics of production from natural resources. *American Economic Review* 58:409–431.

Snape, J. W. 1996. The contribution of new biotechnologies to wheat breeding. Paper presented at the International Symposium on Raising Yield Potential in Wheat: Breaking the Barriers. Ciudad Obregon, Mexico, March 28–30.

Solow, R. M. 1957. Technical change and the aggregate production function. *Review of Economics and Statistics* 312–320.

———. 1970. *Growth theory: An exposition.* Oxford: Oxford University Press.

Sperling, L., M. Loevinsohn, and B. Ntambovura. 1993. Rethinking the farmers' role in plant breeding: Local bean experts and on-station selection in Rwanda. *Experimental Agriculture* 29:509–519.

Sprecht, J. E., and J. H. Williams. 1984. Contribution of genetic technology to soybean productivity: Retrospect and prospect. In *Genetic contributions to yield gains of five major crop plants,* ed. W. H. Fehr. Madison, Wisc.: Crop Science Society of America.

Star, S. 1974. Accounting for the growth of output. *American Economic Review* 1:123–135.

Statistics Canada. Various issues. *Cereal and oilseed review.* Ottawa: Statistics Canada.

———. 1994. *Direct CANSIM time series: CPI and all goods for Canada.* Ottawa: Statistics Canada.

Stefansson, B. R. 1990. Canola, its historical development and adoption. In *Proceedings: International Canola Conference.*

Stone, B. 1986. Chinese fertilizer application the 1980s and 1990s: Issues of growth, balance, allocation, efficiency and response. In *China's economy looks toward the year 2000,* U.S. Congress, Joint Economic Committee, Vol. 1. Washington, D.C.: U.S. Government Printing Office.

———. 1988. Developments of agricultural technology. *China Quarterly* 116 (December):767–822.

Thirtle, C., J. Atkins, P. Bottomley, N. Gonese, J. Govereh, and Y. Khatri. 1993. Agricultural productivity in Zimbabwe, 1970–1990. *Economic Journal* 103 (March):474–480.

Thirtle, C., V. E. Ball, J. C. Bureau, and R. Townsend. 1995. Accounting for efficiency differences in European agriculture: Cointegration, multilateral productivity indices and R&D spillovers. In *Agricultural competitiveness, market forces, and policy choices,* ed. D. Headley and G. H. Peters. Gower, U.K.: Aldershot.

Thirtle C., D. Hadley, and R. Townsend. 1995. Policy-induced innovation in Sub-Saharan African agriculture. *Development Policy Review* 13 (4):323–348.

Thirtle, S. von Bach, and J. van Zyl. 1993. Total factor productivity in South African agriculture, 1947–91. *Development Southern Africa* 10 (3):301–318.

Thompson, A. E., D. A. Dierig, and G. A. White. 1992. Use of plant introductions to develop new industrial crop cultivars. In *Use of plant introductions in cultivar development,* Part 2, ed. H. L. Shands and L. E. Weisner. CSSA Special Publication No. 20. Madison, Wisc.: Crop Science Society of America.

Tintner, G. 1944. A note on the derivation of production functions from farm records. *Econometrica* 1:26–34.

Traxler, G., and D. Byerlee. 1992. Economic returns to crop management research in a post–Green Revolution setting. *American Journal of Agricultural Economics* 74:573–582.

———. 2000. Linking technical change to research effort: An examination of aggregation and spillover effects. Auburn University, Auburn, Ala. Mimeo.

Traxler, G., J. I. Falck-Zepeda, J. I. Ortiz-Monasterio, and K. D. Sayre. 1995. Production risk and the evolution of varietal technology. *American Journal of Agricultural Economics* 77 (1):1–7.

Trueblood, M. A. 1991. *Agricultural production functions estimated from aggregate inter-country observation: A selected survey.* Staff Report No. AGES 9132. Washington, D.C.: United States Department of Agriculture, Economic Research Service, Agriculture and Trade Analysis Division.

Ulrich, A., W. H. Furtan, and A. Schmitz. 1987. The cost of a licensing system regulation: An example from Canadian prairie agriculture. *Journal of Political Economy* 95:160–178.

United Nations Conference on Environment and Development. 1992. *Agenda 21: Programme of action for sustainable development.* New York: United Nations.

United States Department of Agriculture, Foreign Agriculture Service. 1994. *Production, supply, and disposition database.* Washington, D.C.: USDA, FAS.

United States Department of Agriculture, Economic Research Service. Various issues. *Agricultural Outlook.* Washington, D.C.: USDA, ERS.

United States Food and Drug Administration (FDA). 1985. *Direct food substances affirmed as generally recognized as safe: Low erucic acid rapeseed oil.* Federal Food and Cosmetic Act, 21 CFR Part 184, 1555 (c).Washington, D.C.: Department of Health and Human Services, Food and Drug Administration.

Unnevehr, L. J. 1986. Consumer demand for rice grain quality and returns to research for quality improvement in Southeast Asia. *American Journal of Agricultural Economics* 68:634–640.

van der Eng, P. 1996. *Agricultural growth in Indonesia since 1880: Productivity change and the impact of government policy.* Basingstoke: Macmillan.

Vellvé, R. 1992. *Saving the seed: Genetic diversity and European agriculture.* London: Earthscan.

Virmani, S. S., G. S. Khush, and P. L. Pingali. 1993. Hybrid rice for the Tropics: Potentials, research priorities, and policy issues. In *Hybrid research and development needs in major cereals in the Asia-Pacific region,* ed. R. S. Paroda and M.

Rai. Bangkok: Food and Agriculture Organization (FAO), Regional Office for Asia and the Pacific.

Voon, J. P. 1991. Measuring research benefits from a reduction of pale, soft and exudative pork in Australia. *Journal of Agricultural Economics* 43:180–184.

Voon, J. P., and G. W. Edwards. 1992. Research payoff from quality improvement: The case of protein in Australian wheat. *American Journal of Agricultural Economics* 74:564–572.

Waggoner, P. E. 1995. How much land can ten billion people spare for nature? Does technology make a difference? *Technology in Society* 17 (1):17–34.

Walker, B. L., S. P. Lall, S. J. Slinger, and H. S. Bayley. 1970. Nutritional aspects of rapeseed oil: Digestibility, processing and influence of erucic acid on tissue lipids. In *Proceedings of the International Conference on the Science, Technology and Marketing of Rapeseed and Rapeseed Products.* Ottawa: Rapeseed Association of Canada in cooperation with the Department of Industry, Trade, and Commerce.

Wardlaw, G. M., J. T. Lin, M. Snook, M. L. Puangco, and J. S. Kwon. 1992. Serum lipid and apoliprotein concentrations in healthy men on diets enriched in either canola oil or safflower oil. *American Journal of Clinical Nutrition* 54:104–110.

Waugh, F. V. 1929. *Quality determinant of vegetable prices.* New York: Columbia University Press.

Wen, Q. 1984. Utilization of organic materials in rice production in China. In *Organic matter and rice.* Los Baños, the Philippines: International Rice Research Institute (IRRI).

White, F. C., and J. Havlicek. 1981. *Interregional spillovers of agricultural research and intergovernmental finance.* Miscellaneous Pub. 8-1981. St. Paul: University of Minnesota Agricultural Experiment Station.

White, W. J. 1974. Production of rapeseed oil in Canada. In *The story of rapeseed in Western Canada.* Regina: Saskatchewan Wheat Pool.

Wilen, J. 1985. Towards a theory of the regulated fishery. *Marine Resource Economics* 1 (4):369–388.

Wilen, J., and F. Homans. 1994. Marketing losses in regulated open access fisheries. In *Fisheries economics and trade: Proceedings of the Sixth Conference,* ed. M. Antona, J. Catanzano, and J. Sutinen. Institute français de recherche pour l'exploitation de la mer (IFREMER-SEM).

Wilkes, G. 1992. *Strategies for sustaining crop germplasm preservation, enhancement, and use.* Issues in Agriculture 5.Washington, D.C.: Consultative Group on International Agricultural Research (CGIAR) Secretariat.

Winkelman, D. 1994. Quintessential internationalism in agricultural research. In *Agricultural technology: Policy issues for the international community,* ed. J. R. Anderson. Wallingford, U.K.: CAB International.

Winkelmann, R. 1994. *Count data models: Econometric theory and application to labor mobility.* Berlin: Springer-Verlag.

Witt, S. C. 1985. *Biotechnology and genetic diversity.* San Francisco: California Agricultural Lands Project.

World Bank. 1995. *World tables,* diskette version. Washington, D.C.: World Bank.

World Commission on Environment and Development. 1987. *Our common future.* Oxford: Oxford University Press.

Wright, B. D. 1996a. Agricultural genetic resource policy: Towards a research agenda. Revision of paper presented at Technical Consultation on Economic and Policy Research for Genetic Resource Conservation and Use, International Food Policy Research Institute, Washington, D.C., June 21–22, 1995.

————. 1996b. Intellectual property and farmers' rights. Paper presented at FAO symposium "The Economics of Conservation and Valuation of Genetic Resources for Agriculture, Tor Vergata University, Rome, May 13–15.

————. 1997. Crop genetic resource policy: The role of *ex situ* genebanks. *Australian Journal of Agriculture and Resource Economics* 41 (1):81–115.

Yen, S. T., and W. S. Chern. 1992. Flexible demand systems with serially correlated errors: Fat and oil consumption in the United States. *American Journal of Agricultural Economics* 74:689–697.

Youngs, C. G. 1974. Uses of rapeseed oil. In *The story of rapeseed in Western Canada.* Regina: Saskatchewan Wheat Pool.

Contributors

Julian M. Alston is a professor in the Department of Agricultural and Resource Economics, University of California–Davis, and associate director of the University of California Agricultural Issues Center. His main research interest is the economics of agriculture and policies that affect it. He is a coauthor of *Making Science Pay: The Economics of Agricultural R&D Policy* and *Science under Scarcity: Principles and Practice for Agricultural Research Evaluation and Priority Setting.*

Walter J. Armbruster is president of the Farm Foundation in Oak Brook, Illinois. His professional work focuses on food and agricultural marketing policy. Armbruster has devoted much effort to helping policymakers and academic administrators understand the importance of economics to the universe of agricultural research. He was cofounder and initial chairman of the Council of Food, Agricultural, and Resource Economics in the United States. He is a past president and a fellow of the American Agricultural Economics Association and is secretary-treasurer of the International Association of Agricultural Economists.

Peter J. Barry is a professor and holds the Distinguished Chair in Agricultural Finance at the University of Illinois. His professional work focuses on financial management, markets, and policies. He is a former editor of the *American Journal of Agricultural Economics,* as well as a past president and a fellow of the American Agricultural Economics Association.

Wilfred Beckerman is an emeritus fellow of Balliol College, University of Oxford, and was previously professor of political economy at University College London. He was a member of the Royal Commission on Environmental Pollution from 1970 to 1973 and chairman of the Department of the Environment's Academic Panel of Economists from 1990 to 1995. He has published numerous books and articles in the academic journals.

Derek Byerlee is lead economist in the Rural Development Department of the World Bank. His main area of interest is agricultural research policy and management, with specific reference to World Bank support to the bank's lending program in agricultural research. Previously he was director of the Economics Program at the International Maize and Wheat Improvement Center (CIMMYT), Mexico, where he undertook extensive research on the economics of agricultural research.

Barbara J. Craig is a professor in the Economics Department at Oberlin College. Her research interests include international economics, economic growth, and agricultural productivity.

Robert Evenson is a professor of economics and director of the Economic Growth Center at Yale University.

Richard Gray is a professor in the Department of Agricultural Economics and director of the Centre for Studies in Agriculture, Law, and the Environment at the University of Saskatchewan. Gray's research has addressed a broad range of policy issues relevant to western Canadian agriculture.

Zvi Griliches was the Paul M. Warburg Professor of Economics at Harvard University and director of the Productivity and Technical Change Program at the National Bureau of Economic Research. He was a member of the Statistics Canada Price Measurement Advisory Committee and a member of the U.S. Senate's Advisory Commission to Study the Consumer Price Index. Griliches died in 1999.

Paul W. Heisey is an economist with the Resource Economics Division, Economic Research Service, U.S. Department of Agriculture. From 1985 to 1998 he worked as an economist with CIMMYT (International Maize and Wheat Improvement Center) and was based at different times in Pakistan, Malawi, and Mexico. He is currently studying the economics of public-sector agricultural research in an era of rapid privatization. Past research and publications have focused on the economics of technical change in agriculture.

Frances Homans is an assistant professor in the Department of Applied Economics at the University of Minnesota. Her research has focused on the economics of renewable resource management. She has published her research in the *Journal of Environmental Economics and Management, Marine Resource Economics,* and *Land Economics.*

Peter Lindert is professor of economics and director of the Agricultural History Center at the University of California–Davis. His research interests are modern economic history, international economics, and agricultural history. He is the author of *Shifting Ground: The Changing Agricultural Soils of China* *and Indonesia,* as well as the textbook *International Economics,* currently being used in eight foreign languages.

Stavroula Malla is a Ph.D. candidate in the Department of Agricultural Economics at the University of Saskatchewan. Aside from the economics of research, Stavroula has been working on the economics of nutrition. In 2001 she will begin a two-year postdoctoral study awarded by the Social Sciences and Humanities Research Council of Canada to examine spillovers in agricultural research.

Philip G. Pardey is a senior research fellow at the International Food Policy Research Institute (IFPRI) and an adjunct professor at the University of Minnesota Department of Agricultural and Applied Economics. He leads IFPRI's science and technology policy program of research. Pardey is coeditor, along with Julian M. Alston and Vincent H. Smith, of *Paying for Agricultural Productivity.*

Prabhu L. Pingali is director of the Economics Program at the International Maize and Wheat Improvement Center (CIMMYT) in Mexico. Before joining CIMMYT in 1996, he worked at the International Rice Research Institute and the World Bank. Pingali is the author of five books and numerous journal articles and book chapters on technological change, productivity growth, and resource management issues in Asia as well as Africa. He is currently president-elect of the International Association of Agricultural Economics.

Ismail Serageldin served as chairman of the Consultative Group on International Agricultural Research (CGIAR) from 1994 to 2000 and the World Bank's vice president for special programs from 1998 to 2000. Serageldin is currently a special adviser to the World Bank, a distinguished visiting professor at the American University in Cairo, and an adviser to the Egyptian government on the Library of Alexandria. He also serves as chair and member of a number of advisory committees for academic, research, scientific, and international institutions and civil society efforts.

Michael J. Taylor is currently secretary of Australia's Department of Agriculture, Fisheries, and Forestry. Previously, he served as secretary to the Departments of Natural Resources and Environment; Agriculture, Energy, and Minerals; and Agriculture for the state of Victoria. Taylor has been extensively involved in preparing and negotiating commonwealth and state agreements and legislation and in advising state and commonwealth officials on a wide range of agricultural, food, forestry, fisheries, energy, minerals, water, environmental, and sustainable natural resource management issues.

Greg Traxler is professor of agricultural economics at Auburn University. He is also an affiliate scientist in the Economics Program of the International

Maize and Wheat Improvement Center (CIMMYT). His research focuses on the impacts of agricultural research, including the farm-level impacts of biotechnology and plant breeding; adoption of modern crop varieties; and the functioning of seed markets in Latin America.

James Wilen is a natural resource economist in the Department of Agricultural and Resource Economics at the University of California–Davis. Before joining the faculty at Davis, he was in the Economics Departments at the University of British Columbia and the University of Washington. Wilen's special interests are broadly in the area of renewable resource management. He has completed research on a wide range of fisheries issues, focusing mainly on the interrelationships between economic performance and institutional design. His most recent work examines the nature of regulations and the manner in which regulatory structures evolve in fisheries in response to economic and political forces.

Brian Wright's interest in agricultural economics dates from his early experiences on his family's sheep station in the Riverina district of New South Wales, Australia. He is now professor of agricultural and resource economics at the University of California, Berkeley, where he is also codirector of Environmental Science. His research interests include the economics of markets for storable commodities, including speculation and market stabilization, agricultural policy, the economics of research incentives, and the economics of conservation and innovation of genetic resources.

Index

Page numbers for entries occurring in figures are followed by an *f;* those for entries occurring in notes, by an *n;* and those for entries occurring in tables, by a *t.*

LIBRARY OF CONGRESS CATALOGING-IN-PUBLICATION DATA

Agricultural science policy: changing global agendas / edited by Julian M. Alston, Philip G.
  Pardey, and Michael J. Taylor
      p.   cm.
    Includes bibliographical references and index.
    ISBN 0-8018-6603-0 (alk. paper)   ISBN 0-8018-6604-9 (pbk.: alk. paper)
    1. Agriculture and state.   I. Alston, Julian M.   II. Pardey, Philip G.   III. Taylor, M. J.
  HD1415.A322   2001
  338.1'8—dc21

                                                            00-048130